IMAGES
*of America*

# THE JEWISH COMMUNITY OF SOUTH PHILADELPHIA

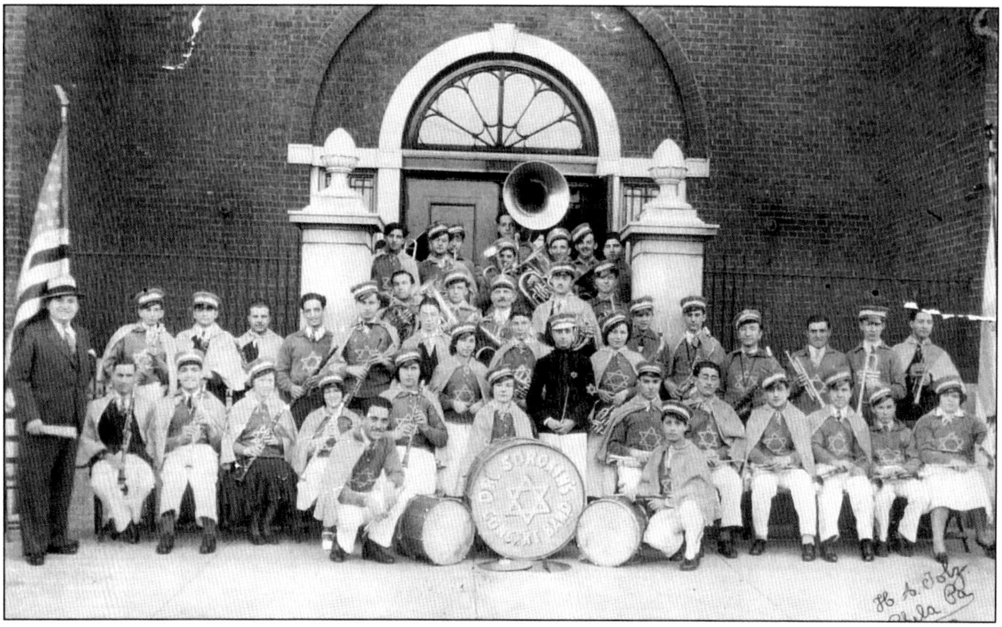

**STRIKE UP THE BAND, SOUTH PHILADELPHIA JEWISH STYLE!** Dr. Lewis Sorokin, a dentist by profession, organized 36 young men and women into a concert band in 1927. Dr. Sorokin gave freely of his time and resources to create a dignified group of young Jewish musicians for weddings, bar mitzvahs, Torah dedications, and Synagogue openings throughout South Philadelphia. The musicians are dressed up in their blues and whites with large Mogen David's or Jewish stars proudly displayed on their chests in front of the Settlement Music School on Queen near Fourth Street in this 1934 picture. (Courtesy of Hillard Sorokin.)

## ABOUT THE COVER

The Jewish community of South Philadelphia is best described as a tribute to traditions. Sol and Mollie Kuptsow lead their family through the row house community down Porter Street with several newly dedicated Torahs to Congregation Shaare Eli., in this early 1920s picture. Family members included Mollie's brother Louis and his son Izzy, holding up the canopy which symbolized the home. The little boy, Preston Kuptsow, who later became a doctor, represented the hope and future of the immigrant community transplanted from Europe that helped to create a new community called, America's Jews. (Courtesy of Dr. Aaron and Anita Kuptsow.)

IMAGES
*of America*

# THE JEWISH COMMUNITY OF SOUTH PHILADELPHIA

Allen Meyers

ARCADIA
PUBLISHING

ISBN 978-0-7385-4955-2

Published by Arcadia Publishing
Charleston, South Carolina

Printed in the United States of America

Library of Congress Catalog Card Number: 2006934174

For all general information contact Arcadia Publishing at:
Telephone 843-853-2070
Fax 843-853-0044
E-mail sales@arcadiapublishing.com
For customer service and orders:
Toll-Free 1-888-313-2665

Visit us on the Internet at www.arcadiapublishing.com

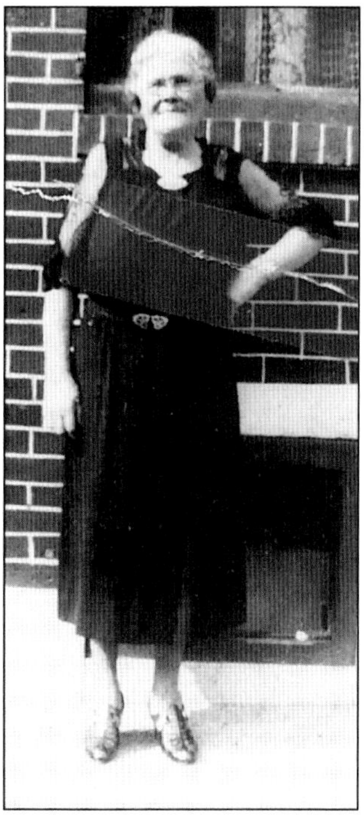

*This book is dedicated to my extended family:*

*To Anna Dubinsky and her husband, Anshel (who perished in the Flu Epidemic of 1918). Anna is the mother of Rose, Sam, Bernie, Revel, and Moishe, and my great-grandmother, for whom I'm named, Chaim-Zelig.*

*To my wife, Sandy (Manusov) Meyers, and my daughter Alisha, and to our families:*

*Esther and Leonard Meyers*
*Allen's parents*

*Rose and Louis Ponnock*
*Allen's maternal grandparents*

*Elsie and Alex Meyerowitz*
*Allen's paternal grandparents*

*Gloria and Robert Manusov*
*Sandy's parents*

*Anna and Sam Gendelman*
*Sandy's maternal grandparents*

*Ethel and Morris Manusov*
*Sandy's paternal grandparents*

# Contents

# Acknowledgments

Twenty years ago while I was a student at Gratz College, my maternal grandparents, Rose and Louis Ponnock who lived at 622 Mountain Street for 65 years, passed away one day apart in July 1978. The synagogue, Atereth Israel at Sixth and Morris Streets which served my grandparents and my great-grandparents in the early 20th century, shut its doors earlier that year. My mother's (Esther Ponnock) uncle, Sam Dubin of blessed memory, closed the shul in April 1978 and he donated the proceeds of its sale along with memorial plaques of the family to the oldest synagogue in South Philadelphia—B'nai Abraham at Sixth and Lombard Streets. In September 1978, I wrote a term paper for my Sociology class with Professor Rela Geffen about Jewish life in South Philadelphia that I recalled when growing up.

Little did I know that term paper would serve as the beginning of a life-long avocation—chronicling the history of Jewish life in Philadelphia. During the last 20 years, while managing McDonald's restaurants in the Delaware Valley, I gathered research information, wrote articles and books, gave slide lectures, assisted Ph.D. candidates at Penn and Temple Universities, conducted bus/walking tours of the region, and served many organizations as a history consultant.

I developed a large network of friends and associates who cherished the same ideals that drove me to spend great amounts of time, energy, and money to rescue stories, memorabilia, and artifacts of the various Jewish communities around the region. I would like to acknowledge Bettyanne Gray, Bob Weiss, Dr. Caroline Golub, Rabbi Fred Kazan, Dr. Murray Friedman, Steve Feldman, Leon Brown, Denise Scott, Mike Perloff, Lily Schwartz, Sue Popkin, Buddy Korn, Lee Levin, Bobby Block, Bobby and Henry Shaffner, Marjorie Whitelaw, Rhoda Netsky, Eva Cohen, Fran Miller, Sandy Wizov, Jerry Klein, and Frank Mamedov, who motivated me to complete this work.

The chore of collecting the photographs began in earnest after Thanksgiving Day 1997 and lasted one hundred days into the early spring of 1998. I believed that the history belonged to the community, and I received full cooperation in the community to compile this work. I personally was amazed at what I collected within a limited time period and then only realized that the lack of snow in Philadelphia due to the El Nino effect played a major role in this project. Determination and persistence was accompanied by my desire to follow through to acquire these photographs.

In addition, I wish to thank all the people who I met as complete strangers (nearly two thousand) to create this work and therefore too numerous to name—I am sincerely grateful!

Only recently I discovered, with the help of Edie Simon, that my drive to do this work was based on a love and appreciation of the larger extended family, whether or not blood related. Finally, I felt at home when invited into family, friends, and complete strangers homes to share their memories while flipping through old photograph albums. The process of sharing and being part of an extended family had come full circle for me.

Allen Meyers    Sewell, New Jersey
Sunday, May 31, 1998    Eruv Shavoth

# INTRODUCTION

One hundred and fifty years ago, about 50,000 Jews lived in the United States. Then, between the 1880s and the 1920s, approximately 2 million Jews came to our shores settling mainly in the port cities of New York, Boston, Baltimore, and Philadelphia. The arrival to this great and good city began at the immigration office located at the foot of Washington Avenue with a train running west from the Delaware River.

South Philadelphia became the neighborhood of choice for the new immigrants. They brought their families and their way of life. Here, synagogues, bathhouses, bakeries, fish and produce stands, butcher shops, home-style restaurants, delicatessens, stores, and push carts multiplied to serve the needs of each group of new arrivals. Landsmanschaften, or old world societies, were organized to help the new immigrants get settled in Philadelphia. A husband from Nezin lost his wife. He asked his landsmen to participate in a minyan and soon, the Neziner Synagogue was established. The Russische Shul welcomed middle-Russian Jews. Every schivitz or Russian bathhouse had its self-selected clientele from the old country.

Children of the immigrants grew up, lived through the Depression, and the young men served in the army in the Second World War. They returned, married, and moved to new neighborhoods in a time of full-employment and inexpensive housing, while South Philadelphia aged and changed.

Twenty years ago, I met Allen Meyers, a young man at Gratz College interested in an academic career in the field of local Jewish History. He was in love with South Philadelphia and the Jewish people who called it home. Allen questioned anyone he met to find out about their lives, their families, and their neighborhoods. Where were they raised? What was Jewish life like, especially in South Philadelphia?

Though decades apart in age, Allen Meyers and I grew up in South Philadelphia. We loved the place, and like anyone from South Philadelphia, "you can take us from South Philly, but you can never take South Philly out of us." This love became a passionate avocation for Allen. He amassed photographs and documents, collecting information about 450 synagogues, hundreds of businesses, family histories, and lists of Jewish cemeteries. He roamed the streets taking pictures. Many of the synagogues no longer exist. Today, there are empty lots where houses and synagogues once stood.

Allen and I share a love for Philadelphia—both of us are boosters and think this is the best place to live. In fact, we believe that other cities aspire to have what Philadelphia and its Jewish community already has.

From time to time, I lead bus tours (as Allen also has) of Jewish Philadelphia, explaining the history of various places. I end the tour at Dock Street where I speak of Haym Solomon and his commitment to America, being "uniform and loyal" to his new nation. A bus or walking tour is a must for those who want to soak up what it meant to live in South Philadelphia as an immigrant, or an immigrant's child or grandchild. The recent tour Allen conducted for Congregation Emanuel of Cherry Hill in April 1998 was a huge success, but this book of photographs is better. It can serve as a catalyst to make us more aware of whence we came.

Allen has rendered a great service to our community and to all who want to know what it was like to live in South Philadelphia.

This book is a great tribute to Allen Meyers's commitment to preserving Jewish life. We are the recipients of his ability to stay with a job and never falter. He interviewed hundreds of individuals and collected thousands of items of memorabilia which are now located at the Philadelphia Jewish Archive Center at the Balch Institute for Ethnic Studies. The material contained herein has been carefully selected. Here then is presented a series of pictures, which give the flavor of what life was like in South Philadelphia during the 20th century. All of us thank Allen for this wonderful work.

Rabbi Fred Kazan
Temple Adath Israel on the Main Line

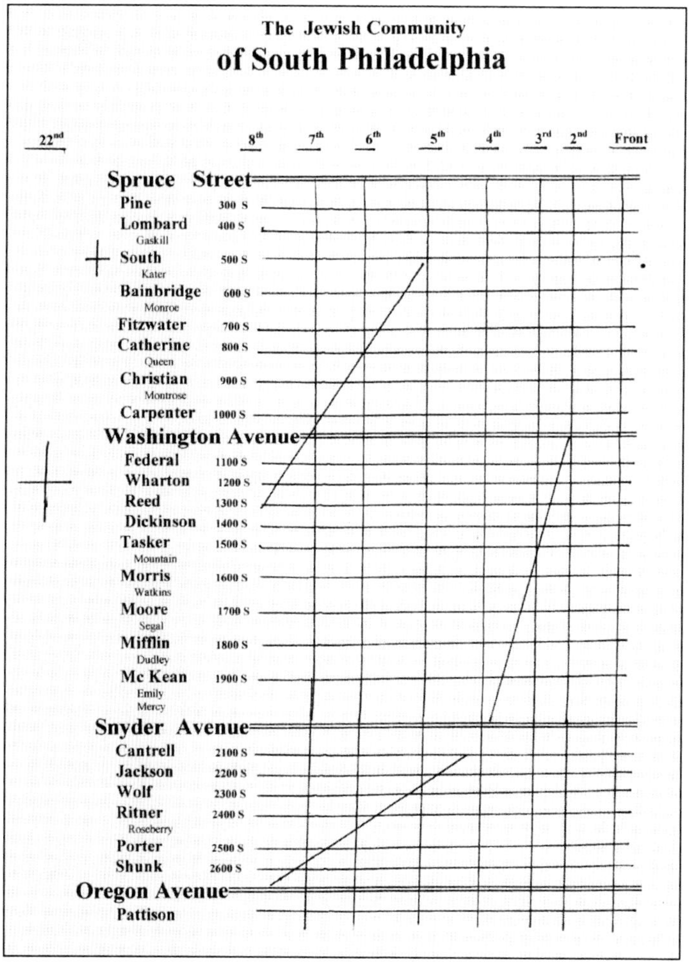

# *One*

# Destination: South Philadelphia

## East European Jews Transplant Themselves Via Voyages Across the Atlantic Ocean

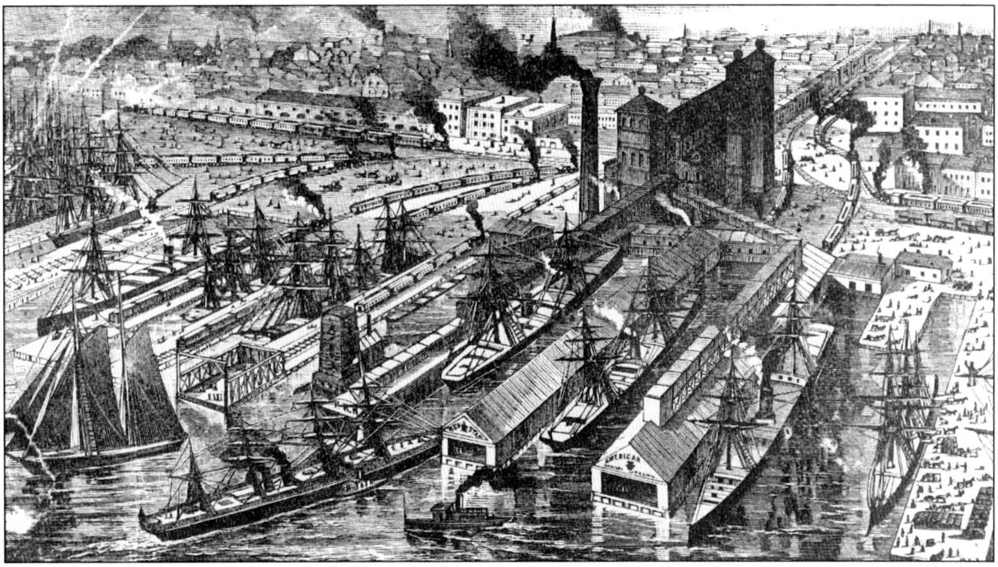

**European Steamships.** These ships came up the Delaware River and they stopped at several islands 2 miles south of Philadelphia for health inspections. Once cleared, the ships traveled up river to dock at the foot of Washington Avenue and the Philadelphia terminal of the Pennsylvania Railroad. While some immigrants had plans to travel west, most settled in the small side streets of South Philadelphia. (Courtesy of the Balch Institute for Ethnic Studies, Philadelphia Pennsylvania.)

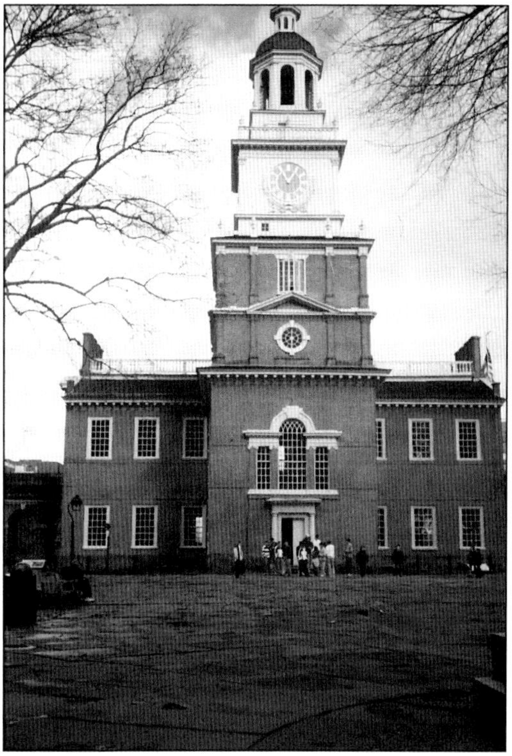

**INDEPENDENCE HALL.** Independence Hall on Chestnut between Fifth and Sixth Streets served as the northern gateway of the Jewish community of South Philadelphia. This historic building played a role in the lives of the Jewish immigrants who came to Philadelphia. The immigrants took their pledge of allegiance in Independence Hall to serve and protect the Constitution of the United States. (Courtesy of Allen Meyers.)

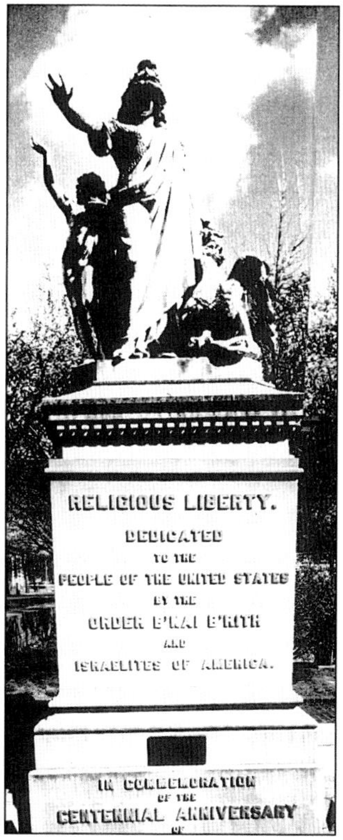


**THE RELIGIOUS LIBERTY STATUE.** The Religious Liberty Statue, carved from a single piece of marble, was created by Moses Jacob Ezekiel to commemorate the centennial anniversary of the nation. The statue arrived after the centennial on Thanksgiving 1876, and it was located in Fairmont Park at Belmont and Montgomery Avenues. The monument was relocated north on Fifth above Market Street, site of the new National Museum of American Jewish History and Philadelphia's first synagogue—Mikveh Israel, in 1985. (Courtesy of Allen Meyers.)

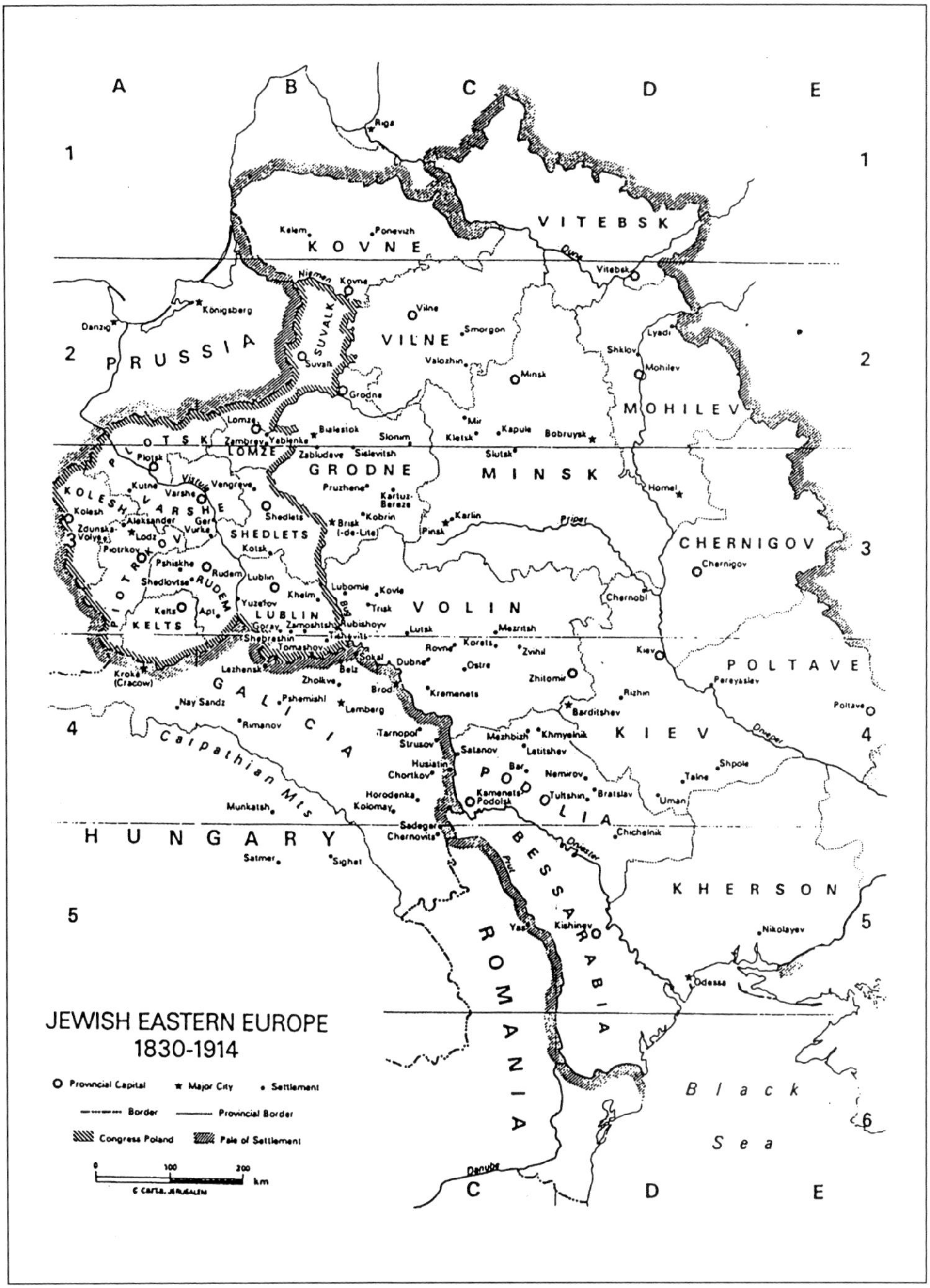


Pale of Settlement States and Large Towns. Four million Jews lived in the geographic area known as the Pale of Settlement from the 1700s until the late 19th century. The countryside between Central Europe and Moscow, Russia, included small towns or shtetls. Laws enacted by the Tsar government of Russia beginning in the 1880s led to mob attacks on Jews and ordered the Jewish population centers to vacate their shtetls for larger towns. This oppressive action led many Jews to migrate westward to America. (Courtesy of the Tuttleman Library Staff at Gratz College and Elaine Kolinsky.)

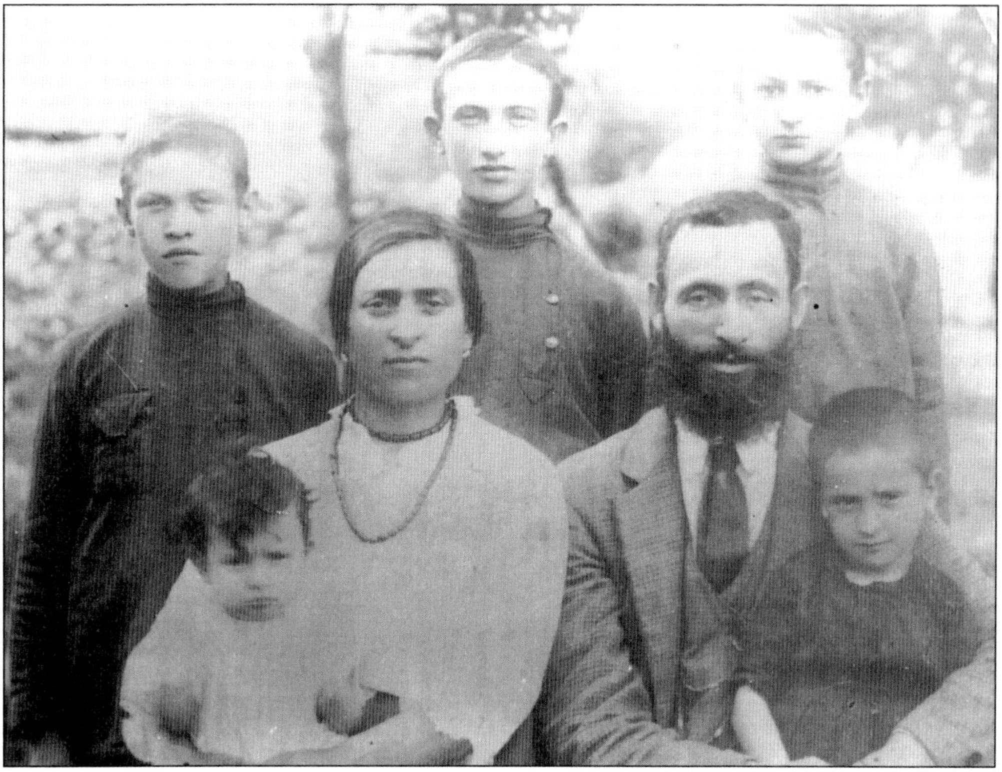

**ROMANIAN IMMIGRANT FAMILY.** Menachim Hasiuk's family lived in a small town, Neporotova in Romania, near Bucharest in the early 1910s, and he evaded conscription into the army by a self-inflicted eye injury. Abe Katz, a baker in South Philadelphia, and Menachim's half-brother sponsored the family's voyage to America. Pictured above on the top row from left to right are as follows: Abraham, Charlie, Sam, Rose (the baby), Minnie (Menachim's wife), Menachim, Sara, and Sol (not pictured), born here in Philadelphia a few days after they arrived on May 25th, 1921. (Courtesy of Sara Hasiuk Sadovnic.)

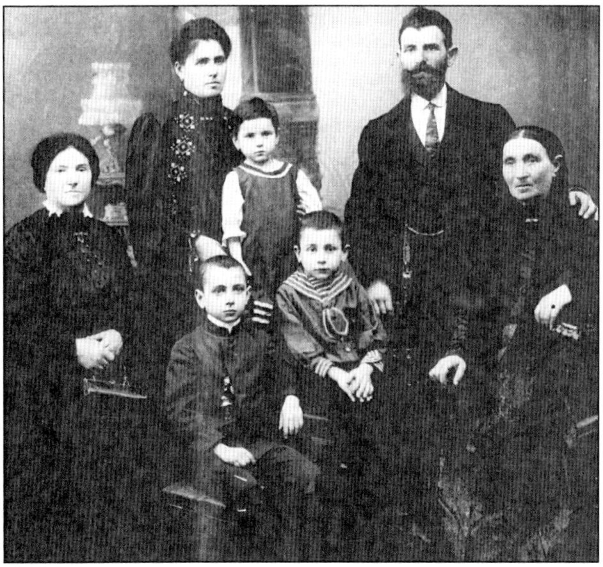

**RUSSIAN IMMIGRANT FAMILY.** Abraham and Ethel Sorokin were married in Russia, in 1893. Abraham served in the Tsar's army and returned home to Russia after its defeat in the Russo-Japanese War in 1905, only to experience pogroms in his shtetl. The Sorokin family migrated out of Russia in 1906, with official passports that allowed only temporary stays in various Gubernias or states. A family portrait was taken before leaving for America. Abraham stands with his mother, and his wife is to his right with their four children, Louis, Dave, Ida, and Ethel. (Courtesy of Hillard.Sorokin.)

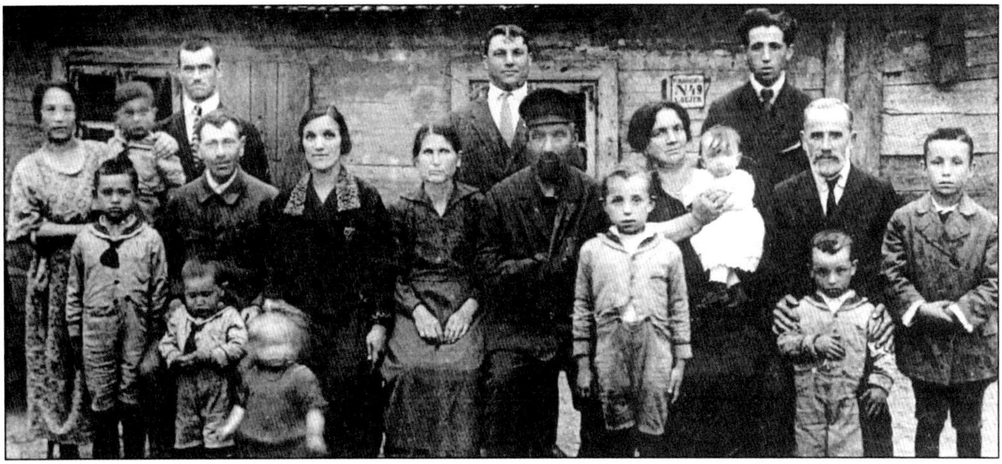

**POLISH IMMIGRANT FAMILY.** The rise of anti-Semitism in Poland led the Block family to seek freedom to make a living in America. It did not matter to the Block family if Poland or Russia dominated their small shtetl. The Block's large thatched-roof house was left behind as Sam Golden, the brother of Mollie Block, sponsored the whole family of Morris Block on their trip to South Philadelphia from Pruzana in 1923. (Courtesy of Bobby Block.)

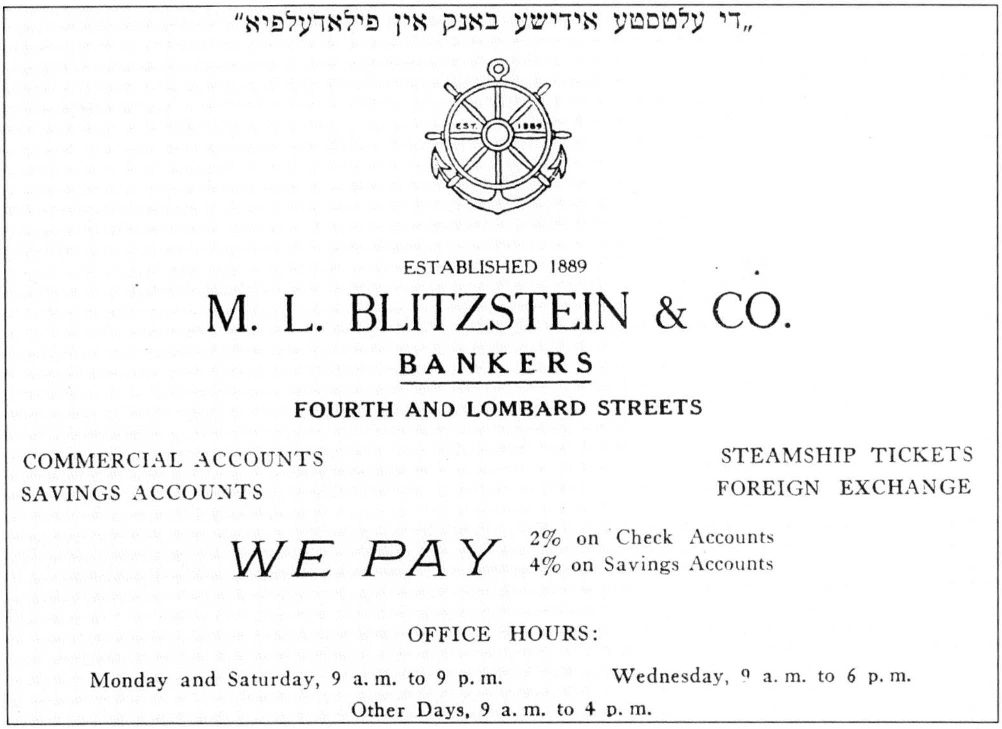


**JEWISH-OWNED BANKS.** From the outset of East European immigration to America in the early 1880s, small independent Jewish businessmen, usually grocers or saloon owners, provided access to the large shipping lines for tickets to America. Philadelphia had several ethnic banks, which included Blitzstein, Rosenbaum, Rosenbluth, and Lipshitz & Wertzell that sold steamship tickets for passage to America. The Jewish population increased as the men saved up the required amount at the same bank that sold the steamship tickets and then sent for their families. (Courtesy Allen Meyers Jewish History Collection.)

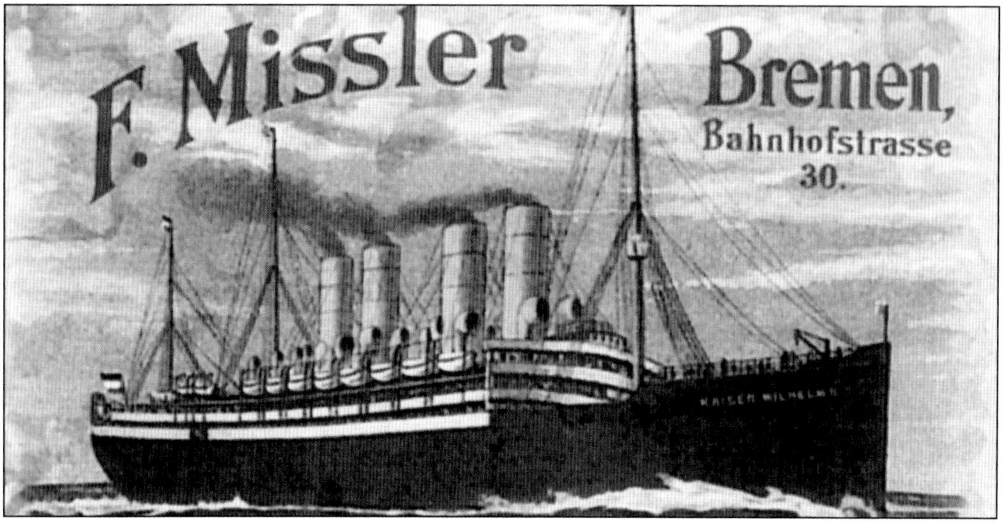


**EUROPEAN STEAMER.** Philadelphia's proximity to the Atlantic Ocean allowed steamships easy access to the Delaware River waterfront, where they docked. The Vine Street and Washington Avenue piers were busy places. This is where the Keystone, Hamberg American, and Red Star line docked. Immigrants made the voyage on many ships that left such ports as Bremen and Hamburg Germany, plus Liverpool Britain, which included, the *Illinois*, *Pennsylvania*, and the *Ohio*, in the early 1900s. The voyage to America lasted two weeks depending on weather conditions. (Courtesy of Hillard Sorokin.)

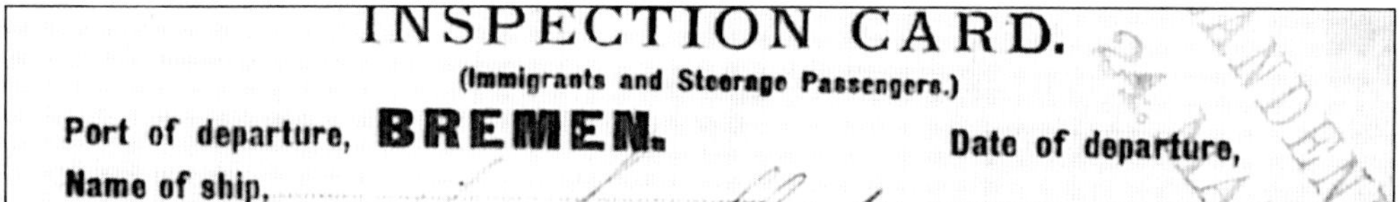
INSPECTION CARD.
(Immigrants and Steerage Passengers.)
Port of departure, BREMEN. Date of departure,
Name of ship,
Name of Immigrant,
Last residence, State,
Inspected and passed at
Passed at quarantine, port of U.S.
Passed by Immigration Bureau port of
(Date.) (Date.)
(The following to be filled in by ship's surgeon or agent prior to or after embarkation.)
Ship's list or manifest, No. on ship's list or manifest,
Berth No. Steamship inspection. 1st day

**STEAMSHIP TICKET AND INSPECTION CARD.** Tickets to cross the Atlantic Ocean on the way to America were available for sale in Europe and America. Regulation of the cards came under the jurisdiction of various United States Consulate offices in European seaport cities. Possession of these cards ensured a daily meal and a health inspection before disembarkment from the ship once in America. (Courtesy of Hillard Sorokin.)

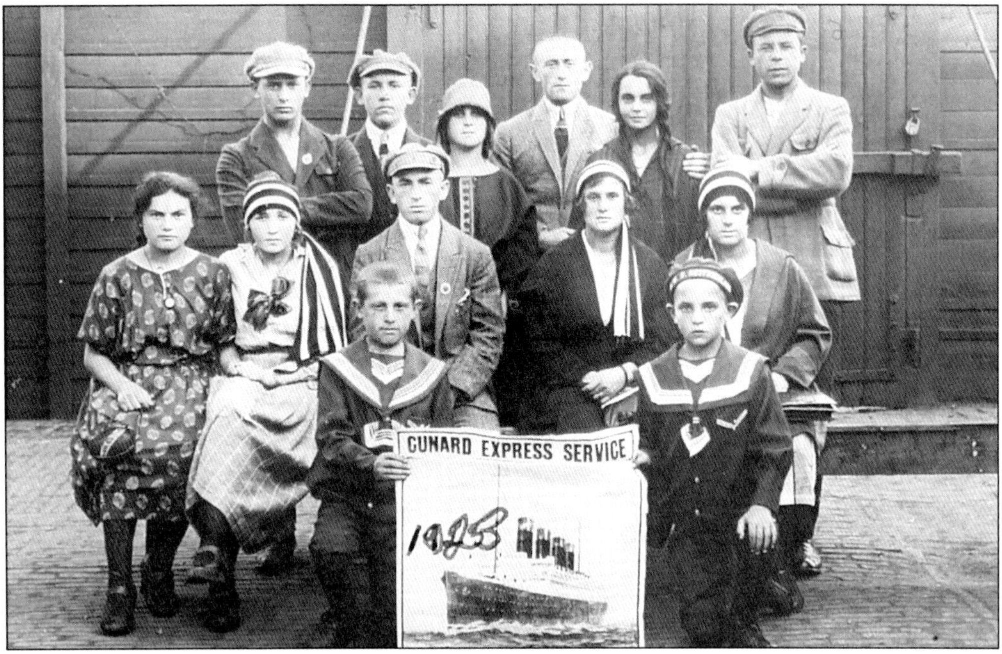


**Family Portrait Before Boarding Ship to America.** Large shipping lines transversed the Atlantic Ocean in state-of-the-art steamships similar to the *Titanic* in the 1910s. The Cunard line had an office and its own docking pier in Philadelphia. Tickets to cross the Atlantic Ocean were sold according to placement aboard the ship. Many immigrants traveled aboard the ships in cramped quarters best known as steerage. The Betoff family including Bertha and her brother, Martin, fled Ratchina, Russia, after a violent pogrom in 1923. (Courtesy of Zachary Kaplan.)

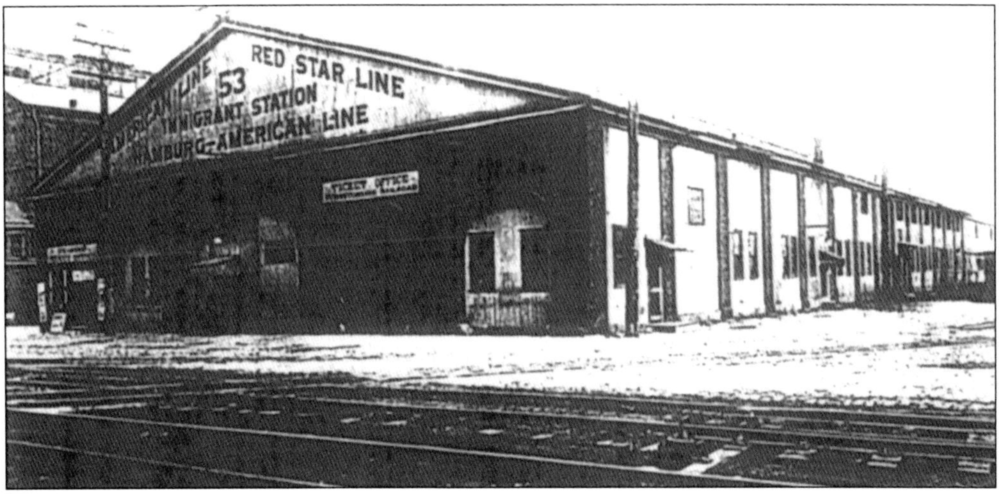


**Philadelphia Immigrant Station.** Philadelphia had its own immigrant station similar to Ellis Island located at the foot of Washington Avenue along the Delaware River. The American and Red Star shipping lines sponsored the new immigrant station at Pier 53, built in 1915, and designed by A. Stand. The immigrant station could process three thousand immigrants daily. (Courtesy of the Philadelphia City Archives.)

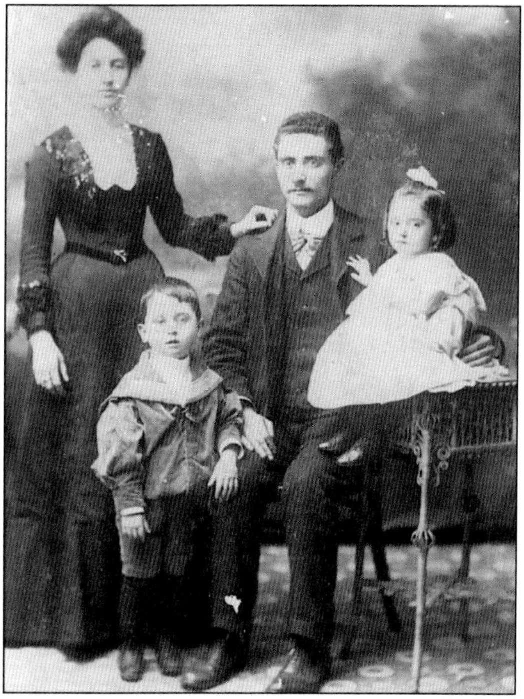

**FAMILY PORTRAIT.** Pictured above are Shaindel (Mary) and Shulem (Samuel) Rudolph with their two eldest of five children, Raphael and Irene. The outbreak of small pox in Philadelphia in 1903 forced many immigrant families to flee the city to escape the illness. The Rudolph family migrated to Rosenhayn outside of Bridgeton, New Jersey and were adopted by the Jewish farmers who made up the Garton Road Synagogue Community. (Courtesy of Natalie S. Rudolph.)

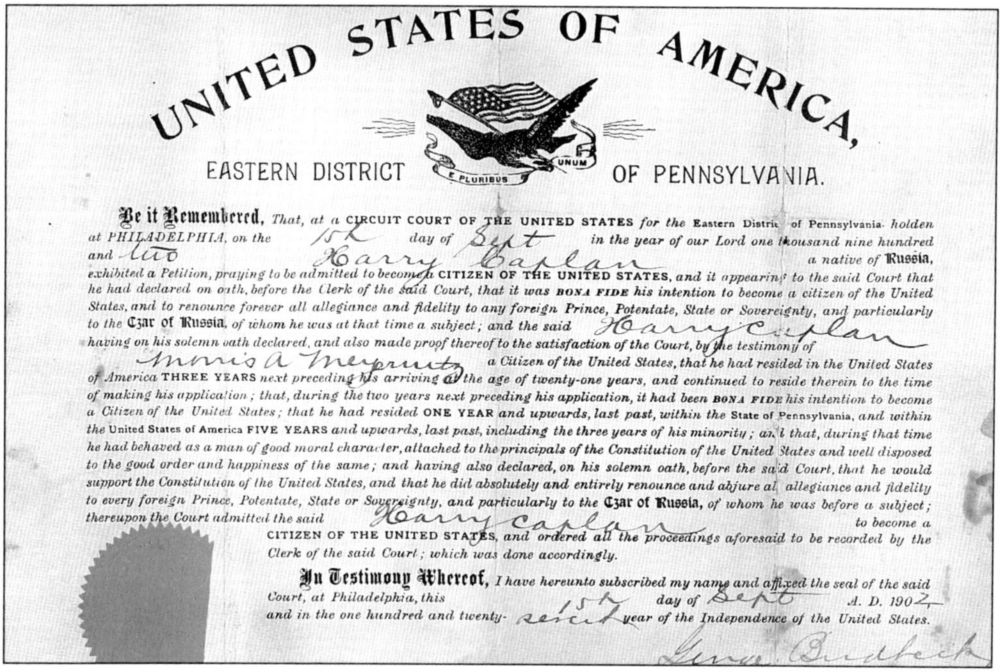

UNITED STATES OF AMERICA,

EASTERN DISTRICT OF PENNSYLVANIA.

Be it Remembered, That, at a CIRCUIT COURT OF THE UNITED STATES for the Eastern District of Pennsylvania holden at PHILADELPHIA, on the 15th day of Sept in the year of our Lord one thousand nine hundred and two Harry Caplan a native of Russia, exhibited a Petition, praying to be admitted to become a CITIZEN OF THE UNITED STATES, and it appearing to the said Court that he had declared on oath, before the Clerk of the said Court, that it was BONA FIDE his intention to become a citizen of the United States, and to renounce forever all allegiance and fidelity to any foreign Prince, Potentate, State or Sovereignty, and particularly to the Czar of Russia, of whom he was at that time a subject; and the said Harry Caplan having on his solemn oath declared, and also made proof thereof to the satisfaction of the Court, by the testimony of Morris A Meyerwitz a Citizen of the United States, that he had resided in the United States of America THREE YEARS next preceding his arriving at the age of twenty-one years, and continued to reside therein to the time of making his application; that, during the two years next preceding his application, it had been BONA FIDE his intention to become a Citizen of the United States; that he had resided ONE YEAR and upwards, last past, within the State of Pennsylvania, and within the United States of America FIVE YEARS and upwards, last past, including the three years of his minority; and that, during that time he had behaved as a man of good moral character, attached to the principals of the Constitution of the United States and well disposed to the good order and happiness of the same; and having also declared, on his solemn oath, before the said Court, that he would support the Constitution of the United States, and that he did absolutely and entirely renounce and abjure all allegiance and fidelity to every foreign Prince, Potentate, State or Sovereignty, and particularly to the Czar of Russia, of whom he was before a subject; thereupon the Court admitted the said Harry Caplan to become a CITIZEN OF THE UNITED STATES, and ordered all the proceedings aforesaid to be recorded by the Clerk of the said Court; which was done accordingly.

In Testimony Whereof, I have hereunto subscribed my name and affixed the seal of the said Court, at Philadelphia, this 15th day of Sept A. D. 1902 and in the one hundred and twenty-seventh year of the Independence of the United States.

**CITIZENSHIP PAPERS, 1902.** Harry Caplan came from Russia and settled at Second and Snyder Avenues in South Philadelphia where he earned an honest day's pay by peddling domestic goods along Broad Street and Route 611 all the way to Doylestown, Pennsylvania, with a horse and wagon in the late 1890s. In 1902, before the Jewish holidays, Harry received his citizenship with Morris A. Meyerowitz as a witness. The official document included a denouncement of loyalty to the czar of Russia. (Courtesy of Bobbie Caplan Shaffner.)

**RECOLLECTIONS OF SOUTH PHILADELPHIA BY AN IMMIGRANT.** The immigrant experience in Philadelphia left a lifetime of many memorable moments. A few hearty people learned to read, write, and communicate in English immediately after their arrival. Many immigrants delayed learning English for decades. Finally, as older adults, immigrants wrote their stories, which included their feelings and experiences. (Courtesy of Helen Appell Oxman.)

**Recollection**

Before my seventy-five-year-old sister died
She recalled her childhood at the
turn of the 20th century
My mother and father, sister and oldest brother
(I wasn't born yet)
Chose this part of Philadelphia—
Fourth and South Streets—to make
their home among other immigrant Jews
Who fled the pograms in Poland, Rumania and Russia.
They found freedom but also hardship;
They transported their religious beliefs,
customs, modes of dress, language and a
zealousness for achieving success in
their "adopted" country.
Sometimes, conditions were such that
only a few family members could cross
the Atlantic and start life anew.
All that they needed was there—at
Fourth and South
The synagogue, the kosher butcher shop,
the delicatessen, the grocer, the
candy store, a dry goods store,
*The Jewish Daily Forward* with its
romantic stories, a doctor, a lawyer,
a tailor, the McCall School, bathhouses,
and pushcarts, laden with all kinds of wares.
As in days gone past
When the whistles blew from
the steamships on the Delaware,
South Street is alive and doing very well, thank you!

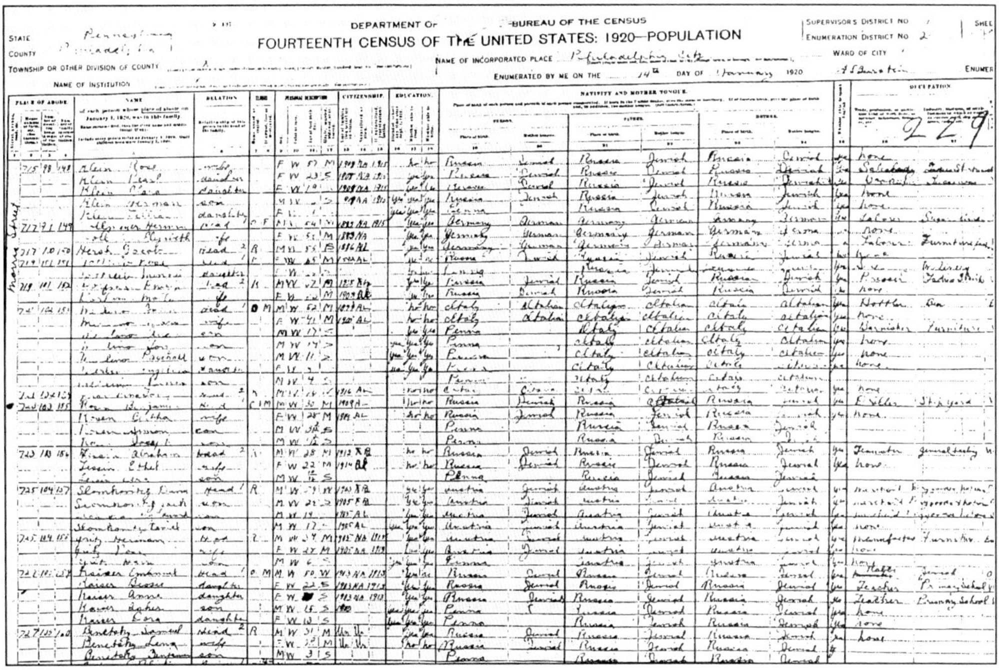


**CENSUS RECORDS.** The United States Census records of the 20th century are kept at the Mid-Atlantic branch of the National Archives located inside the post office building at Ninth and Market Streets in Philadelphia. Reverse address lists give information about the residents from 1890 every ten years until 1920. The document above listed the residents of the 700 block of Morris Street. Most were Jewish, came from Russia, and it lists their occupations. The Jewish population in South Philadelphia numbered 125,000 in its heyday during the 1920s, and the census included many boarders who lived in the multi-story row houses. (Courtesy of Gary Rosen.)

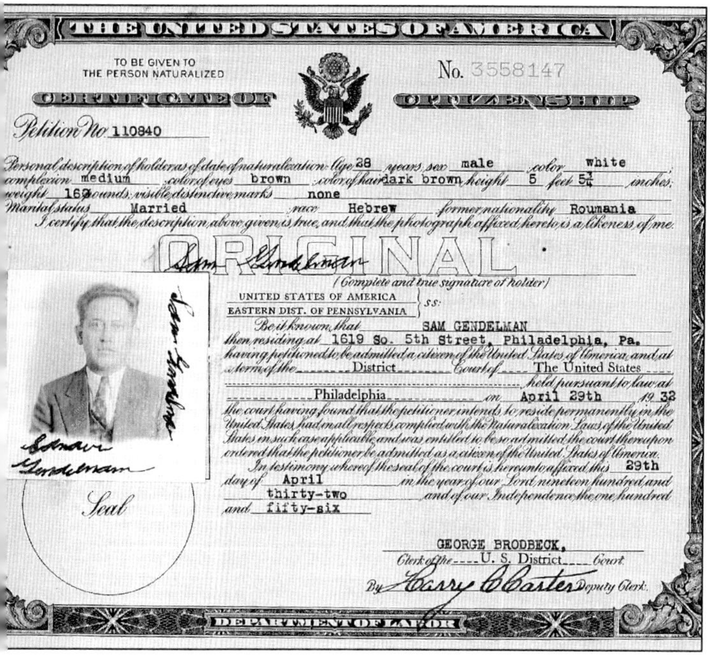

THE UNITED STATES OF AMERICA

TO BE GIVEN TO THE PERSON NATURALIZED

No. 3558147

CERTIFICATE OF CITIZENSHIP

Petition No. 110840

Personal description of holder as of date of naturalization: Age 28 years; sex male; color white; complexion medium; color of eyes brown; color of hair dark brown; height 5 feet 5¼ inches; weight 16? pounds; visible distinctive marks none

Marital status Married; race Hebrew; former nationality Roumania

I certify that the description above given is true, and that the photograph affixed hereto is a likeness of me.

ORIGINAL

Sam Gendelman

(Complete and true signature of holder)

UNITED STATES OF AMERICA
EASTERN DIST. OF PENNSYLVANIA } SS:

Be it known, that SAM GENDELMAN then residing at 1619 So. 5th Street, Philadelphia, Pa. having petitioned to be admitted a citizen of the United States of America, and at a term of the District Court of The United States held pursuant to law at Philadelphia on April 29th 1932 the court having found that the petitioner intends to reside permanently in the United States, had in all respects complied with the Naturalization Laws of the United States in such case applicable, and was entitled to be so admitted, the court thereupon ordered that the petitioner be admitted as a citizen of the United States of America.

In testimony whereof the seal of the court is hereunto affixed this 29th day of April in the year of our Lord nineteen hundred and thirty-two and of our Independence the one hundred and fifty-six

Seal

GEORGE BRODBECK,
Clerk of the U. S. District Court.
By Harry C. Carter Deputy Clerk.

DEPARTMENT OF LABOR

**CITIZENSHIP PAPERS OF SAM GENDELMAN.** Sam Gendelman, one of three children, arrived in Philadelphia as a teenager after World War I, with his parents, Mordechai and Gittel, from Belz, Bessarbia, near Romania. The Gendelman's lived near Fifth and Washington Avenues where Sam's father made a living as a shoemaker. Sam eloped with his sweetheart, Anna Aves, and settled in South Philadelphia at 1619 S. Fifth at Tasker Street. Sam worked for his brother, John, who became the president of After Six Formal Wear. Sam's citizenship papers were issued by the Department of Labor and listed his race as Hebrew in 1932. (Courtesy of Gloria Gendelman Manusov.)

**NATURALIZATION PAPERS OF ANNA GENDELMAN.** Anna Gendelman, one of four children, left Krementz, Poland, with her parents, Shaindel and Israel Aves, in the early 1920s. The family rented the second floor of a house on 2400 S. Sheridan Street and later moved to Third and Winton Streets. Anna worked at Bayuk's Cigar factory at Ninth and Columbia Avenue where she put the paper rings on the Phillies brand cigars until she married Sam Gendelman in the late 1920s. The couple lived at 2421 S. Marshall Street when she became a naturalized citizen in 1942. Anna's papers were issued by the Department of Justice. (Courtesy of Gloria Gendelman Manusov.)

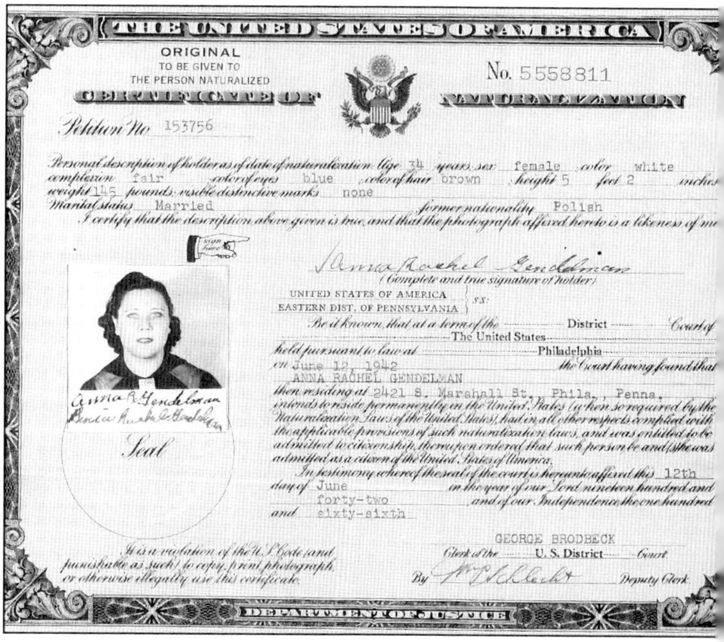

THE UNITED STATES OF AMERICA

ORIGINAL
TO BE GIVEN TO THE PERSON NATURALIZED

No. 5558811

CERTIFICATE OF NATURALIZATION

Petition No. 153756

Personal description of holder as of date of naturalization: Age 34 years; sex female; color white; complexion fair; color of eyes blue; color of hair brown; height 5 feet 2 inches; weight 145 pounds; visible distinctive marks none

Marital status Married; former nationality Polish

I certify that the description above given is true, and that the photograph affixed hereto is a likeness of me.

Anna Rachel Gendelman

(Complete and true signature of holder)

UNITED STATES OF AMERICA
EASTERN DIST. OF PENNSYLVANIA } SS:

Be it known, that at a term of the District Court of The United States held pursuant to law at Philadelphia on June 12, 1942 the Court having found that ANNA RACHEL GENDELMAN then residing at 2421 S. Marshall St., Phila., Penna. intends to reside permanently in the United States (when so required by the Naturalization Laws of the United States), had in all other respects complied with the applicable provisions of such naturalization laws, and was entitled to be admitted to citizenship, thereupon ordered that such person be and (s)he was admitted as a citizen of the United States of America.

In testimony whereof the seal of the court is hereunto affixed this 12th day of June in the year of our Lord nineteen hundred and forty-two and of our Independence the one hundred and sixty-sixth

Seal

It is a violation of the U.S. Code (and punishable as such) to copy, print, photograph, or otherwise illegally use this certificate.

GEORGE BRODBECK
Clerk of the U. S. District Court.
By W. F. Schlecht Deputy Clerk.

DEPARTMENT OF JUSTICE

# *Two*

# BENEFICIAL ASSOCIATIONS

## LANDSMANSCHAFTEN ORGANIZATIONS

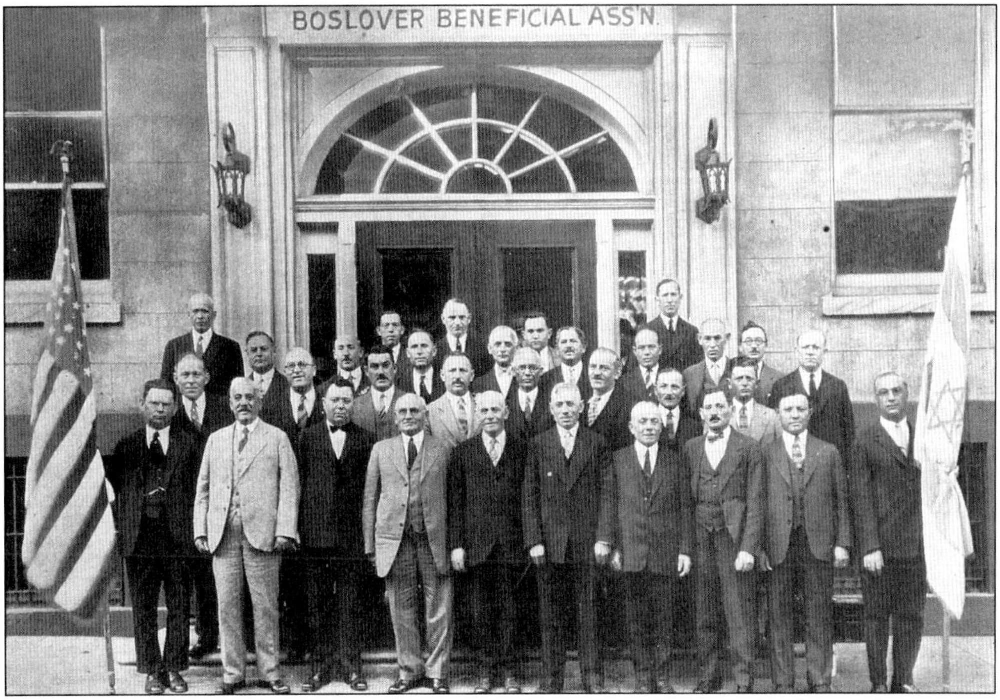


**GROUP PHOTOGRAPH OF THE BOSLOVER.** Immigrant societies known as landsmanschaften were formed from the 1880s until 1939 to aid the plight of human suffering and to provide a circle of brotherhood. Immigrants from the same town were called landsleit and they organized into groups to assist new members in finding other relatives, shelter, jobs, a place to pray according to Jewish law, and health and death benefits. The Boslover Beneficial Society was formed in 1903 by men from the town of Boguslov, Kiev. By popular demand, a ladies auxiliary was formed and acted as the fund-raising arm of the organization. Pictured above was the building committee that purchased its first facility on the northwest corner Seventh and Pine Streets in 1924. Today, Boslover is still in existence and meets in its own Boslover Hall at Bustleton and Unruh Avenues in Philadelphia. (Courtesy Lee Sherr, current secretary of Boslover.)

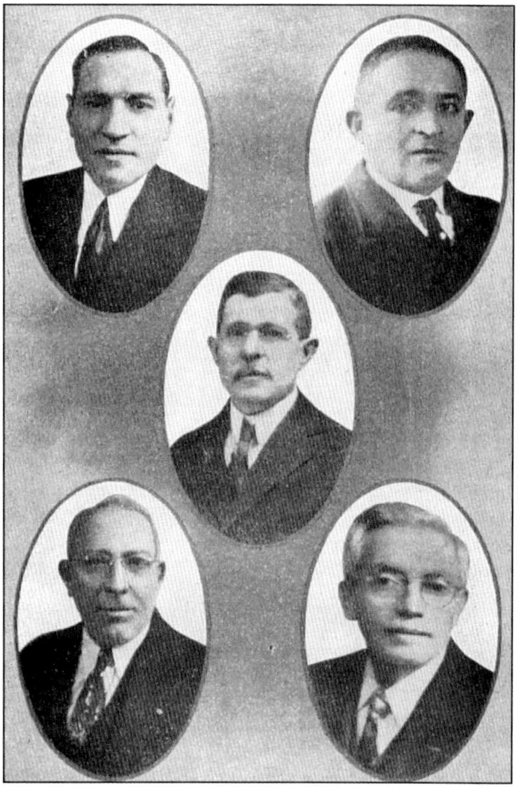

**Prushin-Shershow Officers.** Men from the town of Prushin, Russia (earlier occupied by Poland, Pruzana) organized a landsmanschaften at 240 Monroe Street shortly after the High Holidays in 1889. Many immigrants arrived by themselves with their loved ones left behind in the old country. The loneliness in a new country bonded familiar faces into one group that included A.P. Orleans, Max Korman, John Taxin, A. Pomeratz, and Harris Perilstein. Today, more than one hundred years later, the lodge accepts new members from the Philadelphia region and they meet monthly at the Boslover Hall in Northeast Philadelphia. (Courtesy of Bobby Block, current president.)

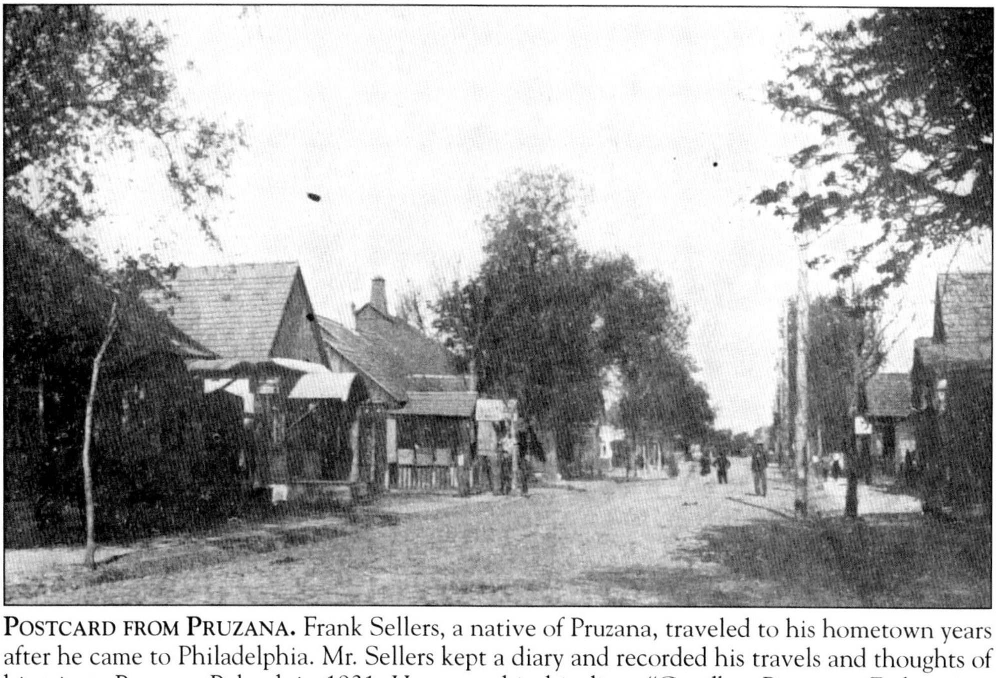

**Postcard from Pruzana.** Frank Sellers, a native of Pruzana, traveled to his hometown years after he came to Philadelphia. Mr. Sellers kept a diary and recorded his travels and thoughts of his trip to Pruzana, Poland, in 1931. He penned in his diary, "Goodbye Pruzana—Father time what will you bring in the days to come. . . " The town of Pruzana was eliminated as a Jewish center during the Holocaust only ten years later. (Courtesy Marlene Sellers.)

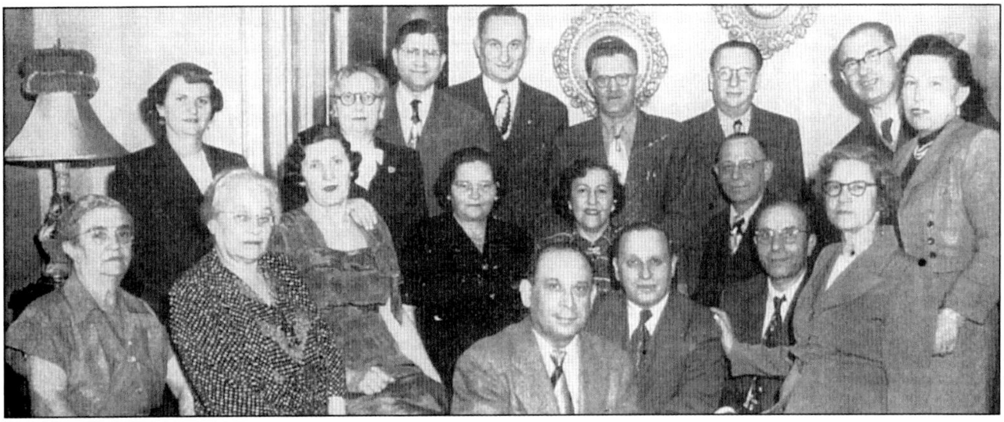

**PHILADELPHIA CHAPTER UNITED BESSARABIAN JEWS.** Large segments of the Bessarabian Jewish community in Eastern Romania arrived here after the Kishinev massacre and pogrom of 1903. Various Bessarabian Beneficial Associations in Philadelphia merged their resources and formed the Bessarabia Talmud Torah and Free Hebrew School and synagogue at 1627 S. Sixth and Mountain Streets. The organization led by Bertha Honikman, Ida Stein, Rose Goodheart, and others pictured above joined with the Zionist, Histadruth, to aid their fellow Jews in relief efforts around the world. (Courtesy of Gloria Manusov and Marty Stein (of blessed memory), son of Ida and David Stein.)

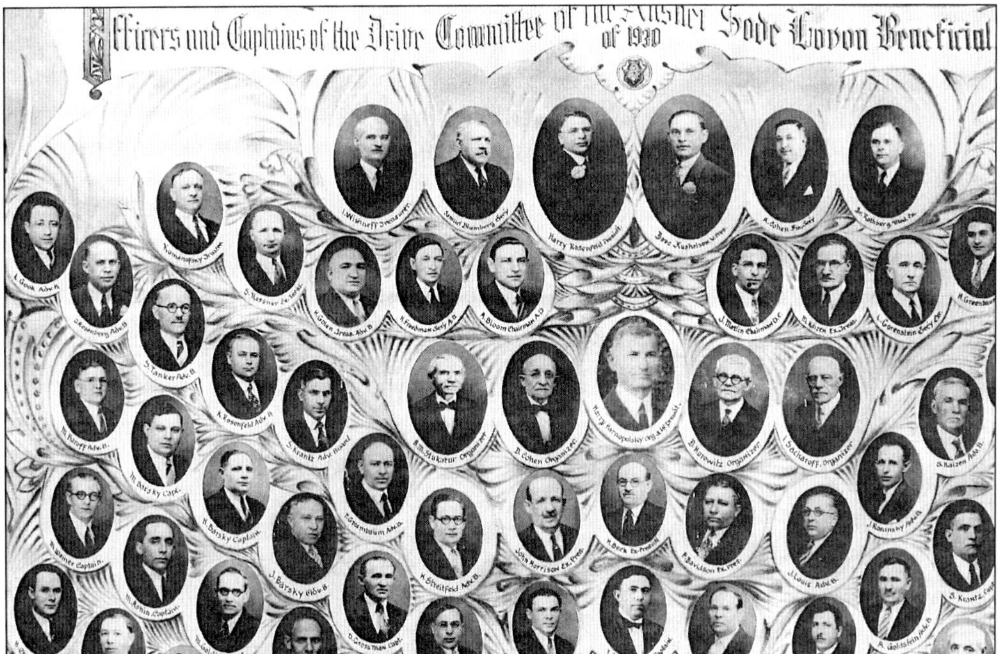

**GROUP PHOTOGRAPH ANSHE SODE LOVEN BENEFICIAL ASSOCIATION.** Beneficial associations organized and provided specific benefits for their members. The Anshei S'dai Loben, or men from the white fields of Russia, banded together in the 1910s to aid and comfort one another in locating missing relatives during WW I. A synagogue by the same name located at Fifth and Mercy Streets was a completely different and separate group of men from the same shtetl. The Dunoff family, who ran a shoe business on S. Seventh near Tasker Streets, still runs the organization today. (Courtesy Albert J. Mendel.)

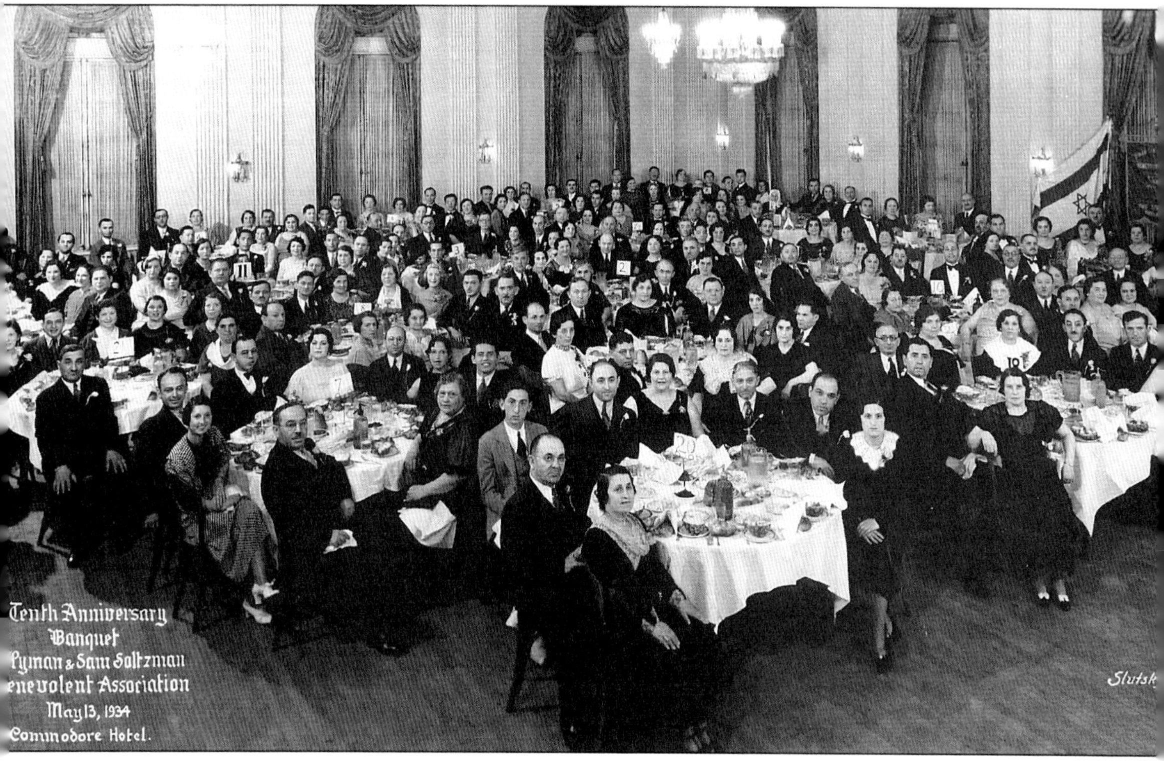


**HYMAN & SAM SOLTZMAN BENEVOLENT ASSOCIATION.** Two brothers, Hyman and Sam Soltzman, organized this landsmanschaften near their Butter & Egg business at Seventh and Tasker Street, in 1924. The men used the facilities of the Anshe Zitomer Shul located on Dickinson between Sixth and Seventh Streets for meetings. Rabbi Lebarsky from the shul opened meetings with a call to prayer. The purpose of this landsmanschaften was founded in its generosity to conduct a free loan society (with no interest), a ladies auxiliary, and a junior league for children. Pictured above is the tenth anniversary banquet held at the Commodore Hotel on South Broad Street. (Courtesy of Rifka S. Goldberg.)

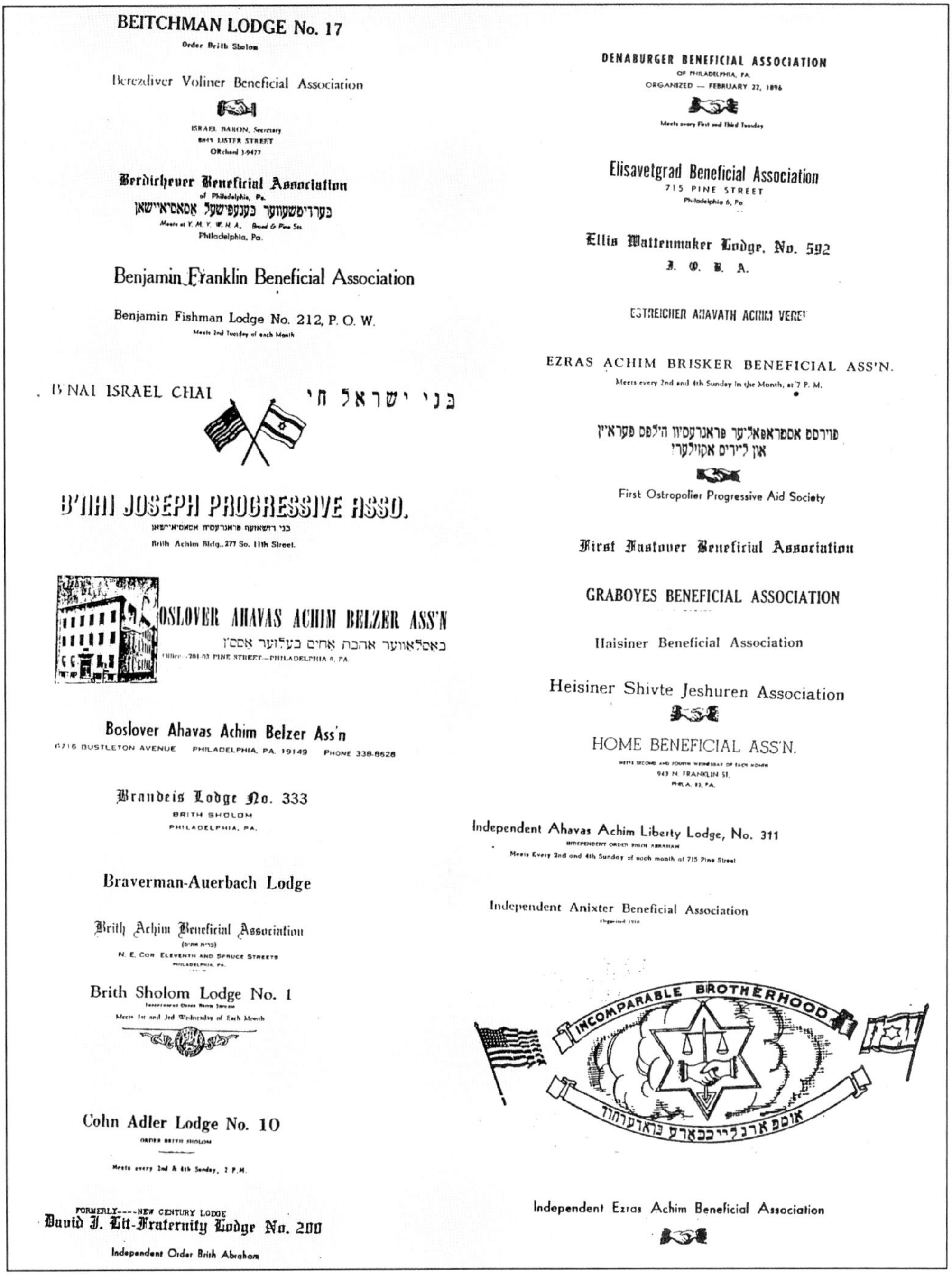


LETTERHEADS OF LANDSMANSCHAFTEN. In the early 1990s, I did research at the Jewish funeral homes on North Broad Street and spent time at four Jewish cemeteries to list the numerous landsmanschaften groups. Goldsteins's, with its central location at 6400 N. Broad, and the UJO (United Jewish Organization) became the repository of many defunct organizations. Unused ground of the many lodges was repurchased by the Jewish cemeteries. A directory of more than 475 landsmanschaften organizations resulted from my research through letters sent out for notices to its members. (Courtesy of Allen Meyers.)

Independent Krivözer Beneficial Ass'n.

Independent Proskurover Beneficial Ass'n

Independent Radiviller Voliner Beneficial Association

Independent Rovner Beneficial Association

Organized March 30th, 1914

Independent Ruziner Beneficial Association

Organized May 1915

Meets Every First and Third Sunday of Each Month
at 431 Pine Street

Independent Volkovinitzer Association

Independent Voliner Aid Society

אינדעפענדענט וואָלינער אונטערשטיצונג פאראיין

אינדיפּענדענט וויניצער לאדש 274, א.א.ב.א.

Independent Winitzer Lodge 274, I.O.B.A.

Independent Young Men's Beneficial Association

Dr. Jacob L. Heller Progressive Lodge No. 30

ORDER BRITH SHOLOM

Meets Every Second Sunday of the Month

Jewish Brotherhood

Judaic Fellowship

NATIONAL JEWISH CIVIL SERVICE EMPLOYEES INC.

Kaniver-Rezishtziver Beneficial Association

Meets every 2nd and 4th Sunday in each Month
at 1527 South Sixth Street

Kultser-Stanisther Beneficial Association

MEETS EVERY FOURTH SUNDAY OF THE MONTH

King Solomon Lodge No. 101

ORDER BRITH SHOLOM

קיפּעלער אונטערשטיצונג פעראיין

Kipiler Beneficial Association

SOL C. KRAUS LODGE No. 8

BRITH SHOLOM

Lechovitzer, Naisiner, Tripolier Beneficial Association

Rabbi Levinthal - Prof. Schechter Lodge No. 66

INDEPENDENT ORDER BRITH SHOLOM

Liberty United Southwark Ass'n.

PHILADELPHIA, PA.

Liberty Lodge No. 311

BRITH ABRAHAM

PHILADELPHIA, PA.

Lieber-Nussbaum Lodge

No. 233, P. O. W.

LOMZER MUTUAL BENEFICIAL ASSOCIATION

Maccabee Maharsho Lodge No. 26

I. O. B. S.

Max Bernstein Northern Free Loan Ass'n

Max E. Gordon Lodge, No. 169

Brith Sholom

MAX D. LIEBER LODGE No. 270

PROGRESSIVE ORDER OF THE WEST

Max Weinraub Lodge

Max B. Willig Lodge No. 4

Independent Order Brith Sholom

MAKAROVER BENEFICIAL ASSOCIATION

Organized January 1922

MENORAH LODGE

NO. 144

INDEPENDENT ORDER ODD FELLOWS

LETTERHEADS OF LANDSMANSCHAFTEN, RESEARCHED BY ALLEN MEYERS.

Mogilev Podolsk Fellowship
OF PHILADELPHIA

NEW KONSTANTINER BENEFICIAL ASSOCIATION
Organized [illegible]

New Pennsylvania Lodge, No. 71
I. O. B. S.

NEZINER TREEPOLER BENEFICIAL ASSOCIATION
MEETS EVERY FIRST AND THIRD SUNDAY OF THE MONTH

OBODOVKA INDEPENDENT FEREIN

Ochremaver-Socharhauer
Beneficial Ass'n.
MEETS EVERY 2nd & 4th SUNDAY OF EACH MONTH

Ochremaver - Zangwill Beneficial Association

OCHREMAVER-ZANGWILL BENEFICIAL ASS'N.

Odessa Indep. Beneficial Association
אדעסער אינדעפ. בענעפ. אססאן.
MEETS EVERY FIRST AND THIRD SUNDAY OF EACH MONTH

Old Friends' Society
Meets Every First Sunday of Each Month, 7.30 P. M. sharp at
YOUNG MEN'S AND YOUNG WOMEN'S
HEBREW ASSOCIATION
Broad and Pine Streets, 3rd Floor, Room 307
PHILADELPHIA 7, PA.

OSTRER MAHARSHO LODGE No. 160, I. O. B. S.
Meets Second Sunday of Each Month

Otic-Mohlev Ind. Beneficial Association

’alestine Don Abarbanel Lodge No. 273, I.O.B.A.

PALESTINE LODGE No. 273
INDEPENDENT ORDER BRITH ABRAHAM
Meets 2nd and 4th Sunday in the month
at 329 Pine St.

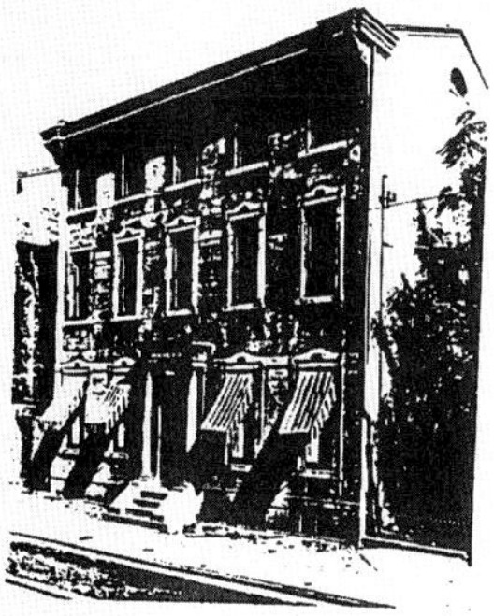

PANNONIA NEWS

VOL. 4 August 1, 1932 No. 8

This issue contains a Complete Copy of the By-Laws of Pannonia

Save it for future reference.

(The by-laws in the issue of July 7, 1930 are obsolete and should be destroyed.)

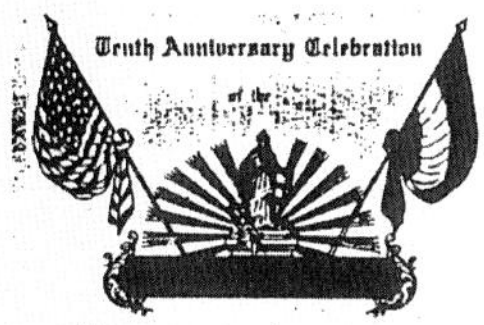


BENEFICIAL ASSOCIATION

Sunday, October 21, 1906

Gagg's Maennerchor Hall

PEREYASLOV PROGRESSIVE ASS'N

*Pereyaslov Progressive Beneficial Association*
Meets Every Second and Fourth Sundays
at Rooms 207 and 307, Y. M. H. A., Broad and Pine Streets

Pestchouker Progressive
Beneficial Association
PHILADELPHIA, PA.

LETTERHEADS OF LANDSMANSCHAFTEN, RESEARCHED BY ALLEN MEYERS.

**Progressive Beneficial Association**
פראגרעסיוו בענעפיט־פעריין

*Progressive Sons of Jacob Association of Philadelphia*
MEETS EVERY FIRST AND THIRD SUNDAY OF THE MONTH
AT 701 PINE STREET

**Parkside Prof. Shechter Lodge 66, O. B. S.**
Meets Every First and Third Sunday of the Month

**Rashkover - Tiraspolier Social Association**
AND LADIES AUXILIARY

**Roumanian American Oir Chudosh Benef. Ass'n**
*Meets every 1st and 3rd Sunday in the month 5 P. M. at 426 Spruce St.*

*Roumanian American Maimonides Beneficial Ass'n.*
*Meets Every Second Sunday of The Month*
301 PINE STREET

*Roumanian American Maimonides Beneficial Ass'n.*
*Meets Every Second Sunday of The Month*
1004 S. 6th. STREET

**Roumanian Hebrew Beneficial Association**
A. ROSENBERG, SECRETARY
4919 N. ELEVENTH STREET
PHILADELPHIA 41, PA.

**Louis Singer Beneficial Association**

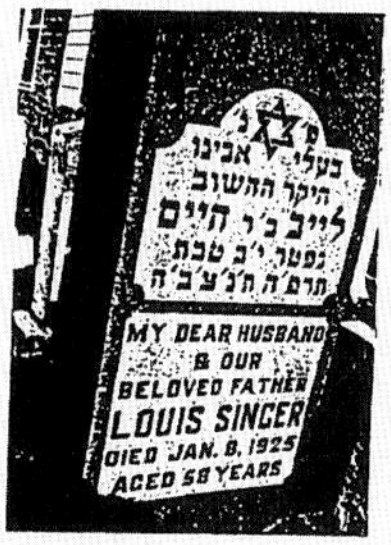


*Stashover Beneficial Association*
ORGANIZED FEBRUARY 9, 18[illegible] • PHILADELPHIA, PA.

סאטינאווער לאנדסמאנשאפט
און פילאדעלפיע
Satinover Landsmanschaft of Philadelphia

**Shivte Jeshurin Ind. Beneficial Association**
Meets every First and Third Sunday of the month

שלום עליכם
**Sholom Aleichem Pereyaslov Association**

**Sick Visitors Beneficial Association**
אינדעפענדענט לינת הצדק
MEETS SECOND AND FOURTH SUNDAY, 8 P. M.
AT 314 CATHARINE STREET
PHILADELPHIA 47, PA.

**Smiller Beneficial Association**

**Sokolifker Beneficial Ass'n**
סאקאליפקער בענעפישעל אסאסיאיישאן

**SONS OF ISRAEL ASSOCIATION**
סאנס אוו איזרעל אסאסיאיישאן
Organized · January 7, 1934 Chartered · July 2, 1934

*Soroker Teleneshter Bessarabia*
*Sick Beneficial Association*
Meets Every Second and Fourth Sunday in the Month, 8 P. M.
at 1036 North 32nd Street

Soroker Mohlev Lodge, No. 36, I. O. B. S.

*Stephen S. Wise Lodge No. One*
INDEPENDENT ORDER BRITH SHOLOM
*Meets First Sunday of Each Month*

Samuel Tepper Lodge
Meets every 2nd and 4th Sunday of the month

**THEODORE ROOSEVELT LODGE No. 15**

Dr. Theodore Herzl Lodge No. 183
BRITH ABRAHAM

**Tolner Dubner Brotherhood Ass'n**
MEETS EVERY FIRST AND THIRD SUNDAY

TULCHINER BENEFICIAL ASS'N
ORGANIZED IN 1907, IN EXISTENCE 50 YEARS
Meets every 2nd Sunday of the Month, at the "Y" Bldg., Broad & Pine Sts., Room 107

**Tulchiner Golden Chain Association**

LETTERHEADS OF LANDSMANSCHAFTEN, RESEARCHED BY ALLEN MEYERS.

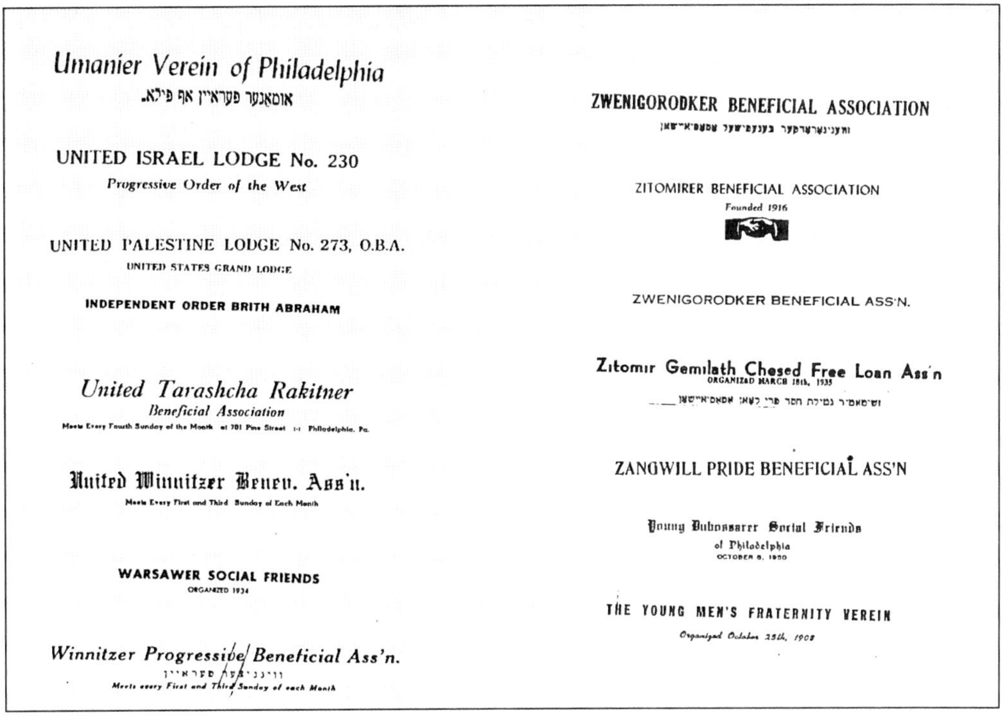


LETTERHEADS OF LANDSMANSCHAFTEN, RESEARCHED BY ALLEN MEYERS.

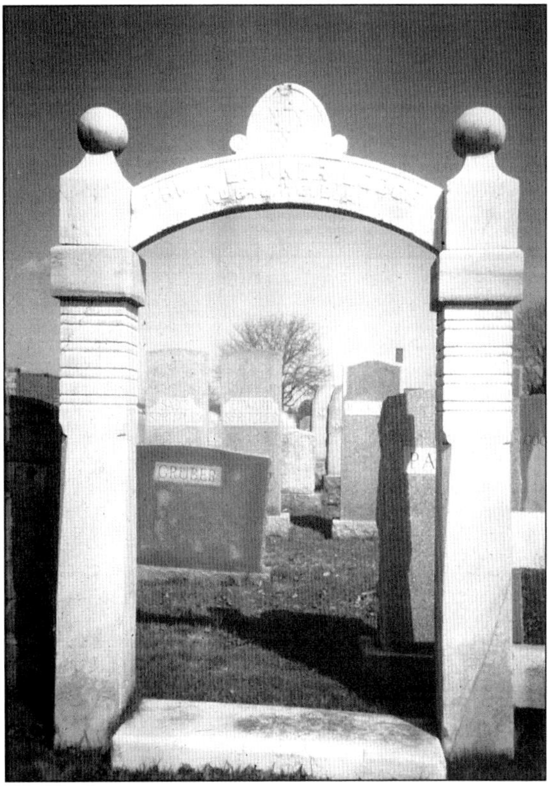

**STONE ARCH MEMORIAL BANNER LODGE AT HAR NEBO CEMETERY.** Many landsmanschaften organizations offered its members burial ground at their selected Jewish cemetery in exchange for weekly dues. Individual landsmanschaften lodges joined bigger organizations for recognition and leadership. Pictured above is the elaborate stone-arched memorial entrance to the Philadelphia Banner Lodge # 64 of Independent Order of Brith Achim on the Har Nebo Cemetery. (Courtesy of Allen Meyers.)

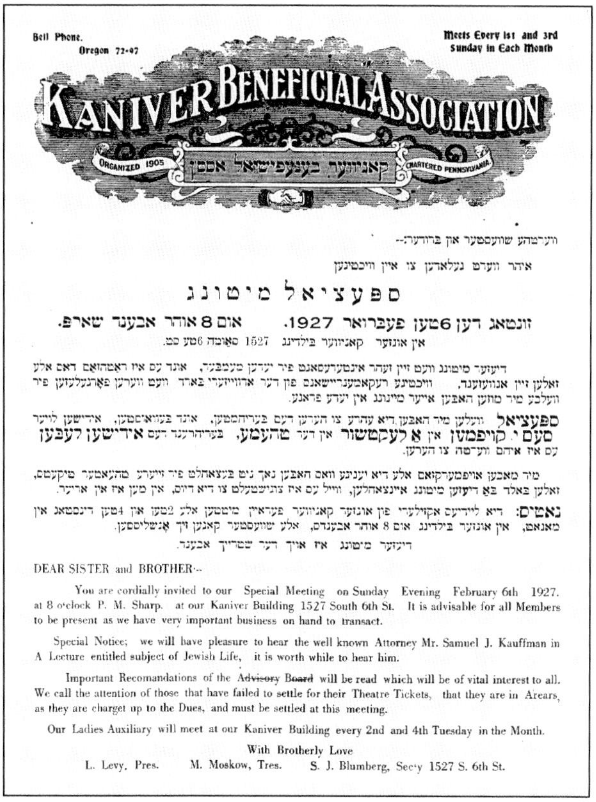

Bell Phone.
Oregon 72-97

Meets Every 1st and 3rd
Sunday in Each Month

KANIVER BENEFICIAL ASSOCIATION

ORGANIZED 1905 קאניוער בענעפישאל אסס׳ן CHARTERED PENNSYLVANIA

ווערטהע שוועסטער און ברודער:--

איהר ווערט געלאדען צו איין וויכטיגען

ספעציאל מיטונג

זונטאג דען 6טען פעברואר 1927. אום 8 אוהר אבענד שארפ.

אין אונזער קאניוער בילדינג 1527 סאוטה 6טע סט.

דיעזער מיטונג וועט זיין זעהר אינטערעסאנט פיר יעדען מעמבער, אונד עס איז ראטהזאם דאס אלע זאלען זיין אנוועזענד. וויכטיגע רעקאמענדיישאנס פון דער אדוויזערי באורד וועט ווערען פארגעלעזען פיר וועלכע מיר מוזען האבען אייער מיינונג אין יעדע פראגע.

ספעציאל וועלען מיר האבען די עהרע צו הערען דעם בעריהמטען, אונד בעוואוסטען, אידישען לויער סעם י. קויפמאן אין א לעקטשור אין דער טהעמע, בעריהרענד דעם אידישען לעבען עס איז איהם ווערטה צו הערען.

מיר מאכען אויפמערקזאם אלע דיא יעניגע וואס האבען נאך ניט בעצאהלט פיר זייערע טהעאטער טיקעטס, זאלען באלד באַ דיעזען מיטונג איינצאהלען, ווייל עס איז צוגעשטעלט צו דיא דיוס, און מען איז אין ארירס.

נאטיס: דיא לײדיעס אקזילערי פון אונזער קאניוער פעראיין מיטטען אלע 2טען און 4טען דינסטאג אין מאנאט, אין אונזער בילדינג אום 8 אוהר אבענדס, אלע שוועסטער קאנען זיך אנשליססען.

דיעזער מיטונג איז אויך דער שטריך אבענד.

DEAR SISTER and BROTHER--

You are cordially invited to our Special Meeting on Sunday Evening February 6th 1927. at 8 o'clock P. M. Sharp. at our Kaniver Building 1527 South 6th St. It is advisable for all Members to be present as we have very important business on hand to transact.

Special Notice; we will have pleasure to hear the well known Attorney Mr. Samuel J. Kauffman in A Lecture entitled subject of Jewish Life, it is worth while to hear him.

Important Recomandations of the ~~Advisory Board~~ will be read which will be of vital interest to all. We call the attention of those that have failed to settle for their Theatre Tickets, that they are in Arears, as they are charget up to the Dues, and must be settled at this meeting.

Our Ladies Auxiliary will meet at our Kaniver Building every 2nd and 4th Tuesday in the Month.

With Brotherly Love
L. Levy, Pres. M. Moskow, Tres. S. J. Blumberg, Sec'y 1527 S. 6th St.

**KANIVER BENEFICIAL ASSOCIATION.** Landsmanschaften lodges communicated upcoming activities through a variety of media including announcements in the Jewish press, and posters tacked to the many telephone poles on the streets of South Philadelphia. In addition, large cardboard posters were displayed in shopkeepers windows along Fourth, Seventh, South, and Ninth Streets. The Kaniver Beneficial Association offered a special program with a lecture by Attorney Samuel J. Kauffman on Jewish life located at their meeting hall, 1527 S. Sixth Street, on February 6, 1927. (Courtesy Philadelphia Jewish Archives Center at the Balch Institute.)

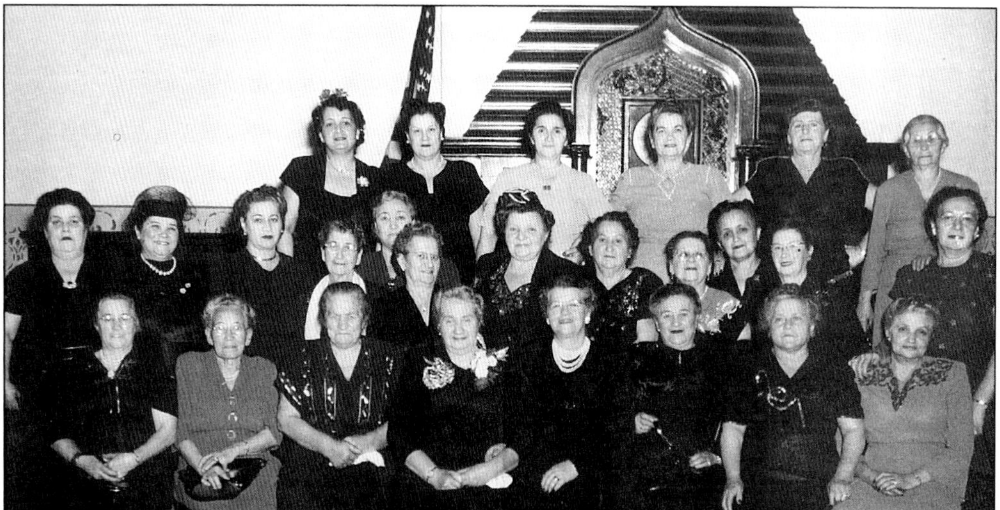

**TULCHINER LADIES AUXILIARY.** Landsmanschaften organizations originally were composed of only men when the East European immigrants began to arrive in Philadelphia, in the early 1900s. Families were split and the men came to prepare a life for their spouses and children free from the daily stress associated with finding a job, shelter, and final resting place. The nature of the organizations changed when the women finally did arrive. The Tulchiner Ladies Auxiliary met at the Boslover Hall at Seventh and Pine, in 1947, to raise funds for Hebrew Schools and synagogues in South Philadelphia. (Courtesy of Edith Weinstein.)

# *Three*

# FINAL RESTING PLACES

## JEWISH CEMETERIES AND FUNERAL HOMES

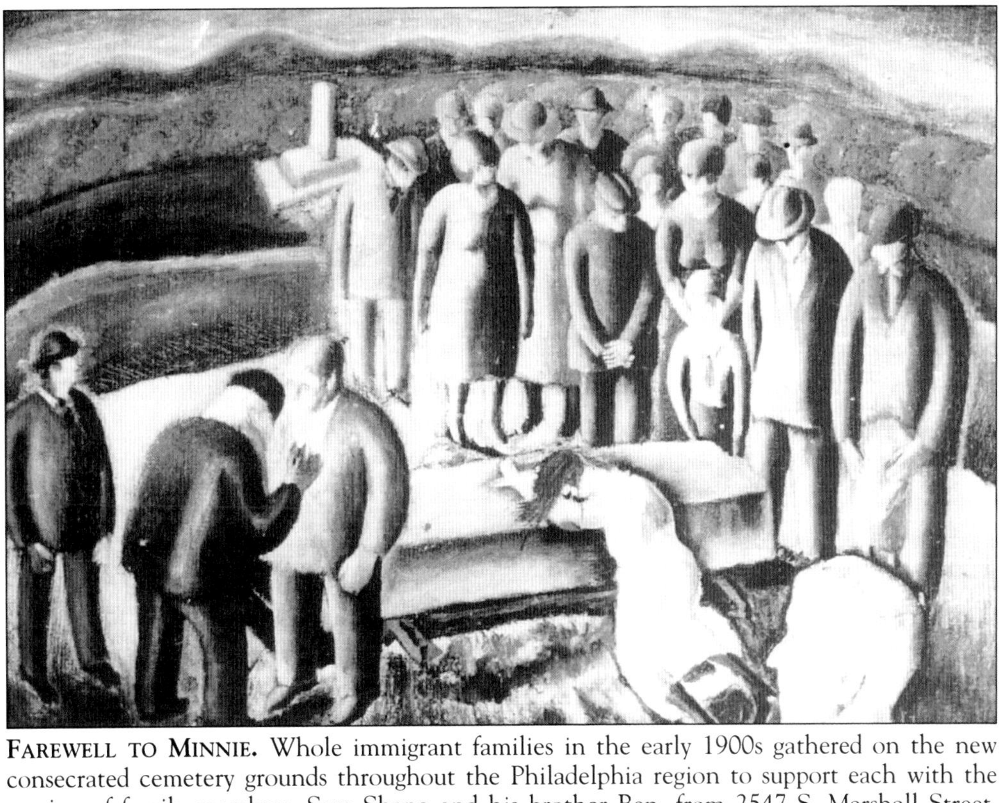

**FAREWELL TO MINNIE.** Whole immigrant families in the early 1900s gathered on the new consecrated cemetery grounds throughout the Philadelphia region to support each with the passing of family members. Sam Shane and his brother Ben, from 2547 S. Marshall Street, joined with extended family members to mourn the loss of a grandparent. Sam, a student of the Fleischer Graphic Sketch Club and Academy of Fine Arts, expressed his sorrow through his abstract realism etching of the funeral. Aunt Minne cried publicly over the casket of Liba overlooking a hilltop. (Courtesy of Paul Shane.)

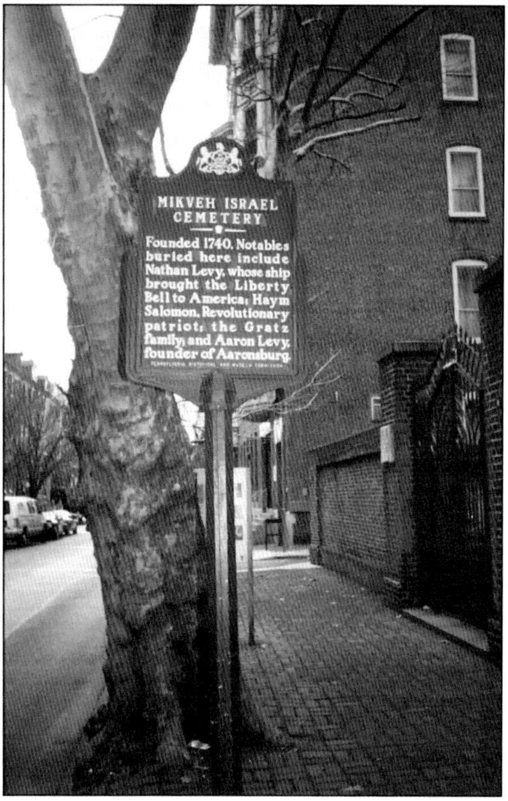


**MIKVEH ISRAEL CEMETERY.** Mikveh Israel, the first Jewish congregation in Philadelphia, started as a burial society in 1740. Nathan Levy, a prominent Jew, incorporated his family's burial ground into a communal institution. The consecrated ground at Ninth and Spruce Streets served as the southern boundary for the Colonial Jewish community. Where one community ended, a new community began. By the 1890s, 150 years later, a new community of Jewish East European immigrants settled below Spruce Street in South Philadelphia. (Courtesy of Allen Meyers.)

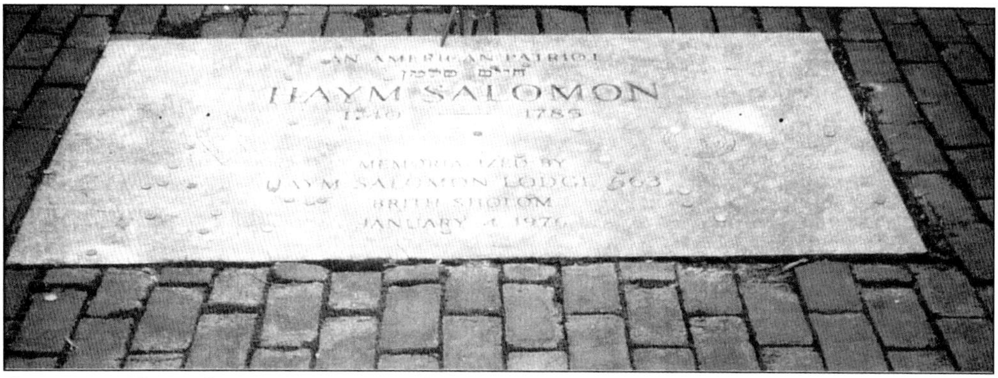


**GRAVE OF HAYM SALOMON.** Haym Salomon, an American patriot, provided funds for the United States of America during the Revolutionary War. In addition, Haym joined with Bernard Gratz, Joseph Simon, and Aaron Levy to compose the Jewish community in Philadelphia, and its extension westward to Lancaster, and northward to Easton, Pennsylvania, through commerce. (Courtesy of Allen Meyers.)

**Jewish Cemeteries**
**Philadelphia Region**
**1740 - 1964**

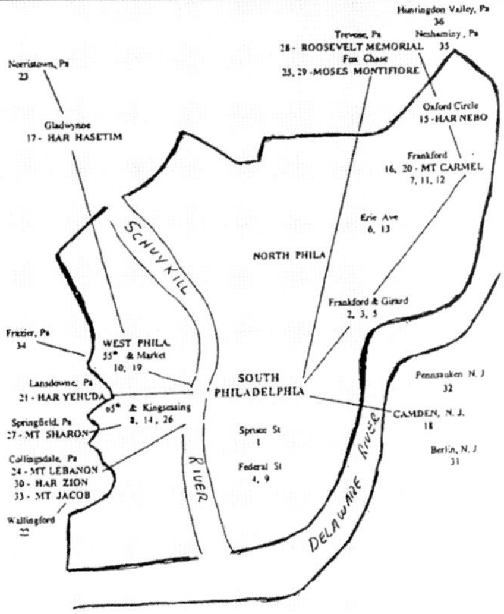


1740 1. **Mikveh Israel**
9th & Spruce

1801 2. **Rodeph Sholom** Thompson to Shackamaxon
near Frankford / Girard DB GGP 457, pg 244

1838 3. **Rodeph Sholom** Nice Street at Kerbaugh
North Liberties District DB WMG 191 pg. 127

1841 4. **Mikveh Israel** 11th & Federal
Deed Book GS 35 pg. 277

1847 5. **Keneseth Israel** Deed Book LRB Pg 107

1852 6. **Rodeph Sholom** K Street & Erie Ave
Deed Book 191 pg. 124

1853 7. **Mt. Sinai** Bridge & Jackson Streets

1857 8. **B'nai Israel** 65th & Kingsessing @ Cemetery Ln
Deed Book LW 8, pg. 18

1857 9. **Beth Israel** 6th & Federal
Deed Book 8, pg. 36

1857 10. **Beth El Emeth** 55th & Market
Deed Book RDW 133 pg. 289

1862 11. **Adath Jeshurun** Bridge & Jackson
Deed Book FTW 67 pg. 83

1873 12 **Chebrah Bikur Cholim** Bridge & Jackson
Deed Book FTW 67 pg 83

1877 13. **Belvue Cemetery** H Street & Venanago

1879 14. **Hebrew Mutual** ( Formerly B'nai Israel )

*1890 15. **Har Nebo** Deed Book JCC 9, pg 3

*1890 16. **Kra- Kauer Beth Elohim** Beneficial Association

*1893 17. **Har Hasetim** Gladwynne on Rt 23
Deed Book 384 pg. 482

1894 18. **Sons of Israel** Mt. Ephraim Ave & Ferry Avenue
Camden, N. J.

1895 19. **Mikveh Israel** 55th & Market
( formerly Beth El Emeth )

*1896 20. **Mt. Carmel** Frankford & Cheltenham
( Formely Kra-Kauer Beth Elohim )

*1899 21. **Har Yehuda** Lansdowne below West Chester Pike

1900 22. **Ohev Sholom** Cemetery, Wallingford, Pa

1900 23. **Norristown** Hebrew Cemetery
Ridge Pike, 4 miles west of Butler Pike

*1910 24. **Mt Lebanon** Oak Road above Mac Dade Blvd
Collingsdale, Pa

*1910 25. **Moses Montiefore** Church Rd off
Huntingdon Valley Pike

1920 26. **Jewish Cemetery Lane**
Cobbs Creek North of Chester Ave

* 1922 27. **Mt. Sharon** Springfield Road, below Rt 1
Springfield, Pa.

*1929 28. **Roosevelt Memorial Cemetery** Rt 1
off Street Road Trevose, Pa

1931 29. **Fischer Memorial Burial Park**
Moses Montifiore Cemetery

*1934 30. **Har Zion Memorial Cemetery** Mac Dade Blvd
at Oak Road Collingsdale, Pa

1939 31. **Crescent Burial Park** Rt 130, Pennsauken N. J.

* 1943 32. **Mt Jacob** Oak Road above Mac Dade Blvd
Collingsdale, Pa

1948 33. **Haym Solomon** Frazier, Pa

1953 34. **King David**, Neshaminy Valley
off Rt 1 and the Pa Turnpike

1959 35. **Shalom Memorial Park** Pine & Byberry Rds
Huntingdon Valley

Map by Allen Meyers
Research done at Philadelphia City Hall Deeds/ Records

* Jewish Cemeteries founded for East European Jews who resided in South Philadelphia ( 1890-1943 )

**JEWISH CEMETERIES IN THE PHILADELPHIA REGION.** The location of Jewish cemeteries in the late 19th and early 20th centuries aided in the future geo-demographic development of Jewish neighborhoods throughout Philadelphia. Ten new Jewish cemeteries situated on available farmland from 1890 until 1943 provided final places for thousands of Jewish immigrants who arrived in Philadelphia from Eastern Europe. Out-migration from South Philadelphia, the primary settlement district, spread out in two general directions, west and northward towards those cemeteries.

*Chevra Kadisho of Philadelphia*

חברה קדישא אף פילאדעלפיא

OFFICES: 228 SOUTH FOURTH STREET
PHILADELPHIA 6, PA.

# JEWISH FUNERAL GUIDE

Jewish law and tradition have endowed the funeral with profound religious significance. It should in every respect express the dignity, sanctity and modesty of a solemn religious service. To this end the following GUIDE is offered:

Any ostentation should be avoided, i.e., family and visitors should reflect in dress and deportment the solemnity of the occasion. Flowers and music have no place at the Jewish funeral service.

Embalming and viewing are contrary to Jewish law.

Interment should not be unduly delayed.

## JEWISH RELIGIOUS LAW PRESCRIBES:

### TAHARAH

The ritual washing and purification of the deceased by members of the Chevra Kadisha, "The Sacred Society," or, in its absence, by religiously and physically competent Jewish persons.

### SHMEERAH

The watching over the deceased by a pious Jew or Jewess until members of the family assemble for the funeral services, so that the deceased is not left unattended.

### TACHRICHIM

The traditional white burial shrouds symbolizing that all men are equal before their Creator.

### ORON

The wooden casket, in keeping with the Biblical dictum "And to dust thou shalt return."

### K'REEAH

The rending of the mourners' outer garments, a symbol of their anguish and grief.

### K'VURAH

The actual burial in the ground, filling in the grave with earth until a mound is formed. To participate in filling the grave is a religious privilege and duty. Kaddish cannot be recited at the open grave-side.

JEWISH BURIAL TRADITIONS. The East European Jews transplanted themselves in Philadelphia and carried their communal traditions with them. The Chevra Kadisha, or group of men and women, prepared the Jewish person's body for burial according to Jewish law with several groups in operation in South Philadelphia by the mid-1880s. The assimilation into American life included daily chores and the reliance upon Old World traditions to bond Jewish continuity throughout the ages. (Courtesy of Allen Meyers Jewish History Collection.)

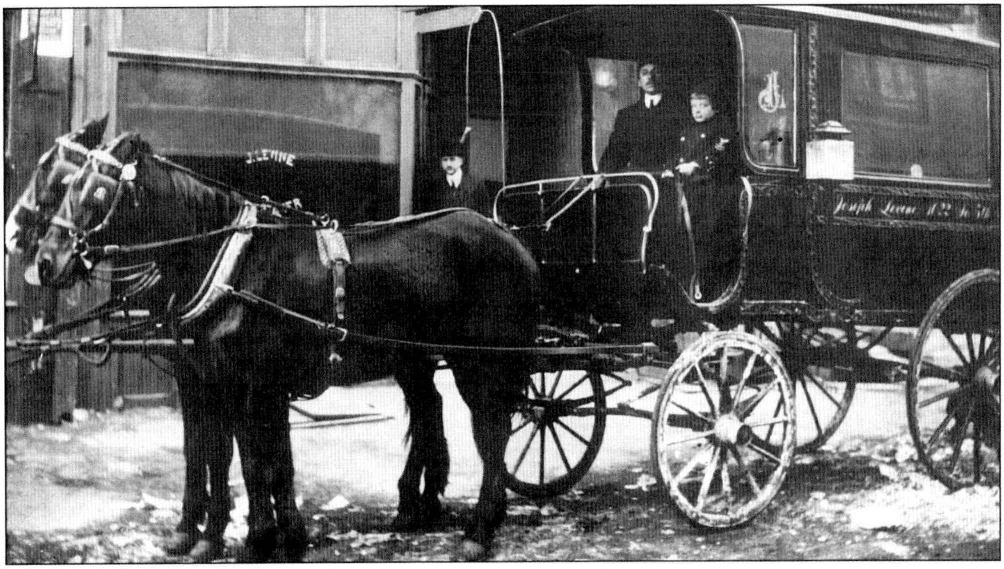

**LEVINE'S FUNERAL WAGON.** The Jewish undertaker in America started in a storefront and his business became well known. Jewish people for five generations have known the Levine family to provide the service of transportation of a deceased person to the cemetery with care and dignity, dating back to 1883. Pictured above is Joseph Levine, son of the founder, Louis, carefully watching his son Leonard take to the reins with the driver c. 1912 at 1022 S. Fifth Street. The sensitivity of the Levine family and its service to the community continues as Joseph H. Levine, fourth generation, prepares his children, Adam, Brian, and Lindsey, for involvement in the family business today. (Courtesy of Joseph H. Levine.)

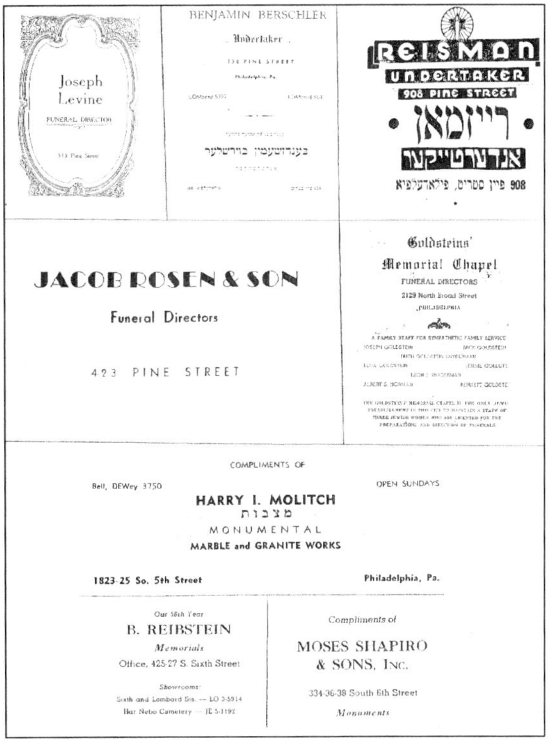


**JEWISH FUNERAL HOMES AND MEMORIAL DEALERS.** Pine Street, one block below Spruce in South Philadelphia, was once the home address for five Jewish undertakers, which included Levine, Berschler, Reisman, Rosen, and Kahn. The development of a Jewish undertaker expanding his business into a Jewish funeral parlor was an American-Jewish transformation that occurred in the early 1900s. The large funerals of East European Jews in South Philadelphia many times spilled into the small side streets. Thus, the need for one large facility to house all mourners with decorum and dignity was graciously approved by the community and situated on Pine Street where large homes prevailed. (Courtesy of Allen Meyers Jewish History Collection.)

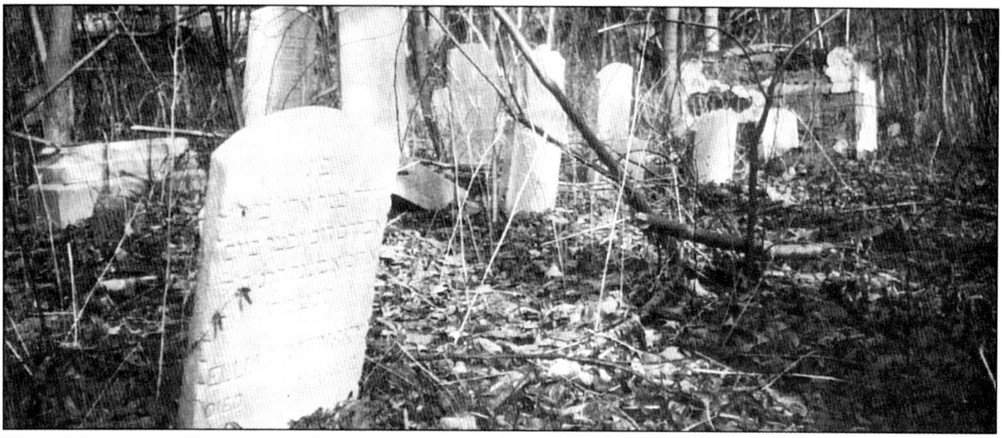

**HAR HAZAYSIM CEMETERY.** Har Hazaysim, or Mt. of Olives, became the first private Jewish cemetery established for East European Jews in the Philadelphia area. Jewish merchants from Norristown and members of several landsmanschaften jointly sponsored a burial ground along State Route # 23, Gladwyne, Pennsylvania, in Lower Merion Township in the early 1890s. The 19 acres of rocky terrain led families to create crude brick mausoleums aboveground, contrary to Jewish law. The Har Hazaysim burial association, according to local resident Judy Zalesne, dissolved over time and the grounds are in a shamble today with thick underbrush. (Courtesy of Allen Meyers.)

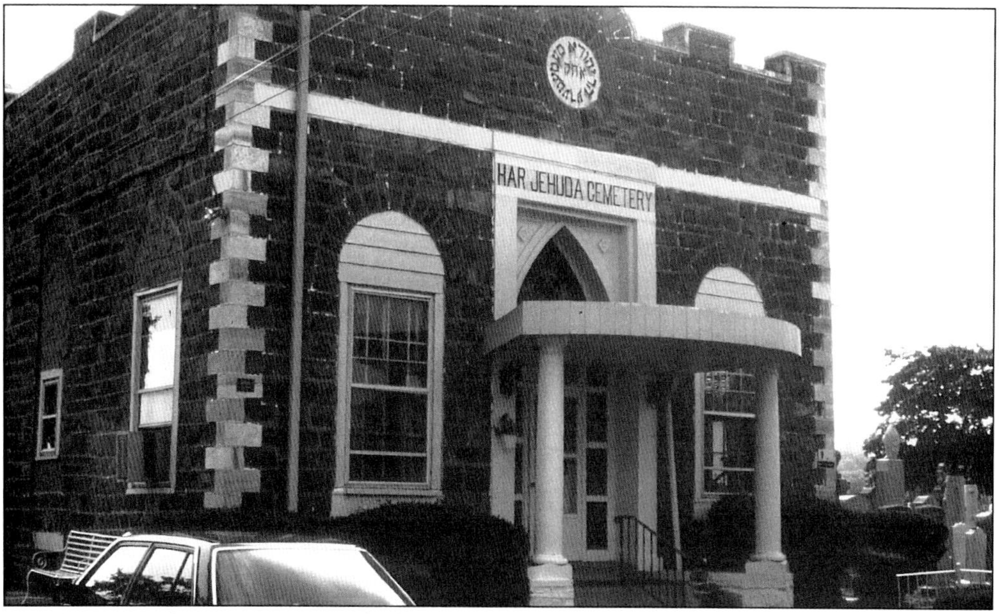


**HAR YEHUDA CEMETERY.** Har Yehuda Cemetery, situated on 27 acres and founded by Julius Moskowitz, represented the first Jewish cemetery to exist going west outside of Philadelphia. Julius Moskowitz, a Russian-Jew and president of the Independent Chevra Kadisha on 408 Christian Street in South Philadelphia, decided to create a burial ground for East European Jews without regard to country of origin in the mid-1890s. Har Yehuda cemetery along Lansdowne Avenue, one-half mile south of City Line Avenue, was accessible by inter-urban trolley car routes that connected Upper Darby and West Chester with Philadelphia. Har Yehuda was the first nonprofit cemetery established for the concentrated East European Jewish population in South Philadelphia. (Courtesy of Allen Meyers.)

**MT. CARMEL CEMETERY.** Mt. Carmel Cemetery evolved as a conglomeration of several burial grounds proposed by Michael Asch, formerly of congregation Mikveh Israel and founder of Kra-Kauer Beth Elohim Congregation at Fourth and Pine Streets. Michael Asch relied on Rev. Isaac Lesser's theory to provide a community service for all Jews. Only several blocks from the German-Jewish Cemeteries, in the Frankford section on Bridge Street, Mt. Carmel Cemetery included 20 acres of sloping land in the Wissinoming section of Northeast Philadelphia. Many Austro-Hungarian congregations acquired final resting places for their members at Mt. Carmel, which shared a location unique in American history, with the intersection of four different cemeteries, one on each corner at Frankford and Cheltenham Avenues. (Courtesy of Allen Meyers.)

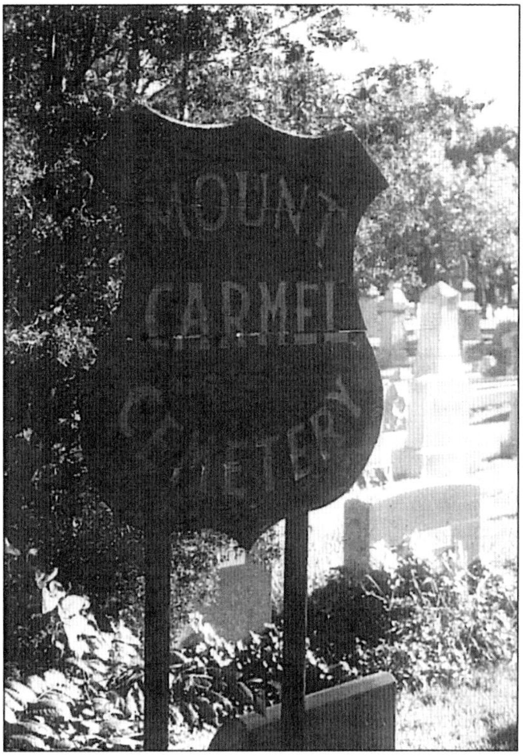


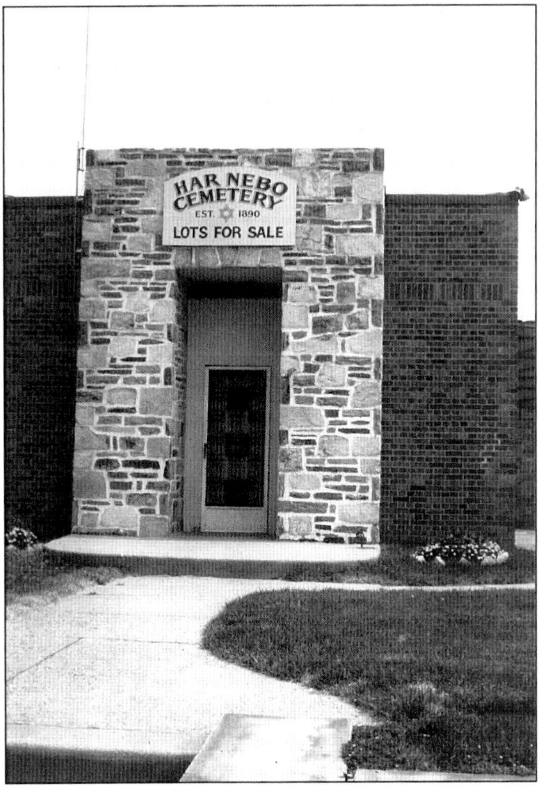


**HAR NEBO.** Isaac Levy founded Har Nebo Cemetery on the Oxford Pike northwest of the German-Jewish cemeteries near Bridge Street in the Frankford section of Northeast Philadelphia, in 1890. Horses and wagons were rented for the 2-mile journey into the countryside from the Frankford and Bridge Street trolley terminal that connected South Philadelphia, 12 miles away. In 1905, Har Nebo expanded its original cemetery of 10 acres with the addition of 6 acres due to the outbreak of small pox in Philadelphia. Jewish history and later migration of South Philadelphia Jews to the Oxford Circle during the mid-20th century could have been altered if Har Nebo had purchased an additional 125 acres that it declined in 1924. (Courtesy of Allen Meyers.)

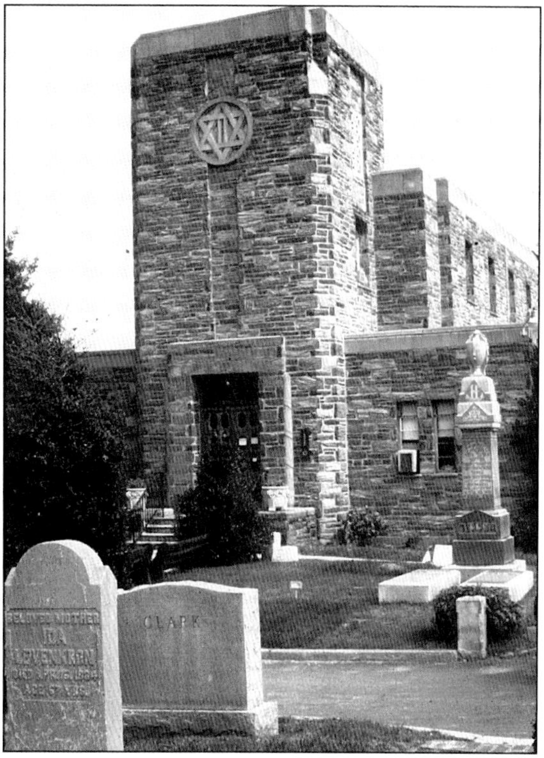


**MOSES MONTEFIORE CEMETERY.** Moses Montefiore, first organized as Lebanon Cemetery in 1910, changed its name to alleviate confusion with the Mt. Lebanon Cemetery that served the same South Philadelphia Jewish immigrant community. Jack Gutman and William Portner, community and B'nai Brith leaders, organized a corporation to sell individual graves, landsmanscaften, and synagogue burial plots. Located on 70 acres overlooking a hillside off Church Road in Rockledge, Pennsylvania, due north of Northeast Philadelphia's Fox Chase section, Montefiore was connected to South Philadelphia via the Route # 50 trolley car. The Shay family purchased the cemetery, which allowed the traditional burial method of sticks and straps to lower the casket into the ground, and included the Fischer Memorial section for indignant Jews. (Courtesy of Allen Meyers.)

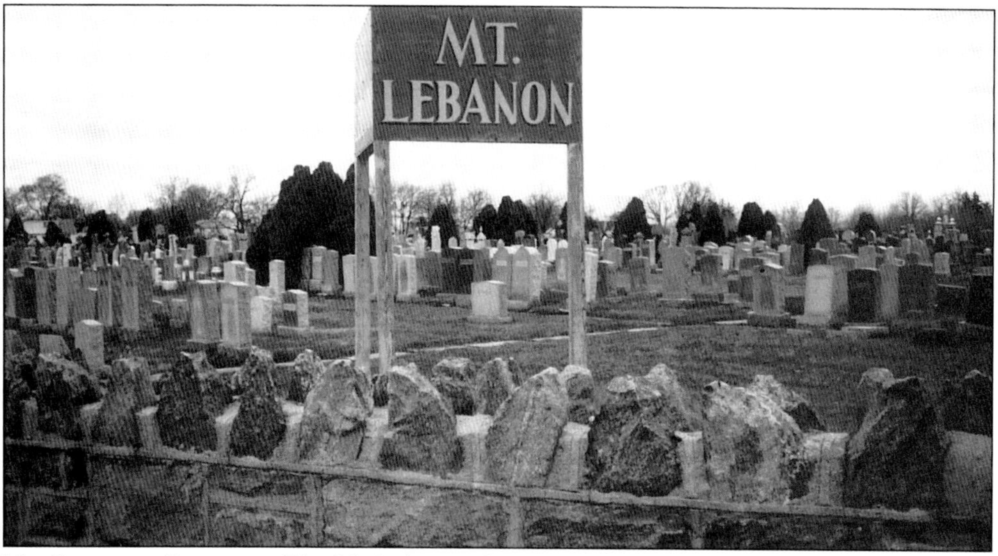


**MT. LEBANON CEMETERY.** The Mt. Lebanon Cemetery was founded by Morris Abrams and his brothers from White Russia. It was located on 55 acres of farmland in Collingdale, Pennsylvania, in 1910. Inter-urban trolley car service from Philadelphia to Chester provided access to Mt. Lebanon near Oak Road and McDade Boulevard. In the early 1900s, several South Philadelphia institutions, including the Mt. Sinai Hospital, the Jewish Maternity Hospital, the Jewish Consumptive Institute of Philadelphia, and the Deborah Sanitarium catered to the immigrant who developed Tuberculosis and enlisted the help of Mt. Lebanon Cemetery at the time of his death. (Courtesy of Allen Meyers.)

**ROOSEVELT MEMORIAL CEMETERY.** Roosevelt Memorial Cemetery developed on sprawling farmland in Trevose, Pennsylvania, beyond the city limits of Northeast Philadelphia in 1929. This cemetery represented a change in decorum with plain memorial markers. Access to the cemetery, by automobile, along the road to New York became popular. New Jewish neighborhoods opened on either side of U.S. Route 1. The second settlement area for South Philadelphia Jews migrated to new houses in Logan and Feltonville. (Courtesy of Allen Meyers.)

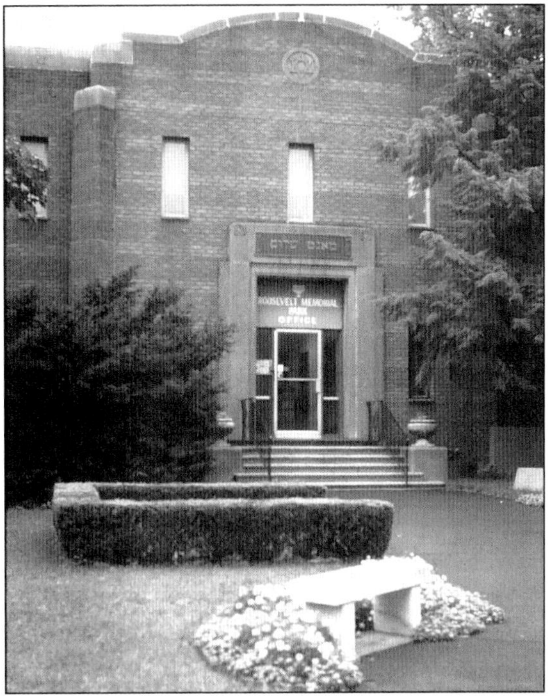

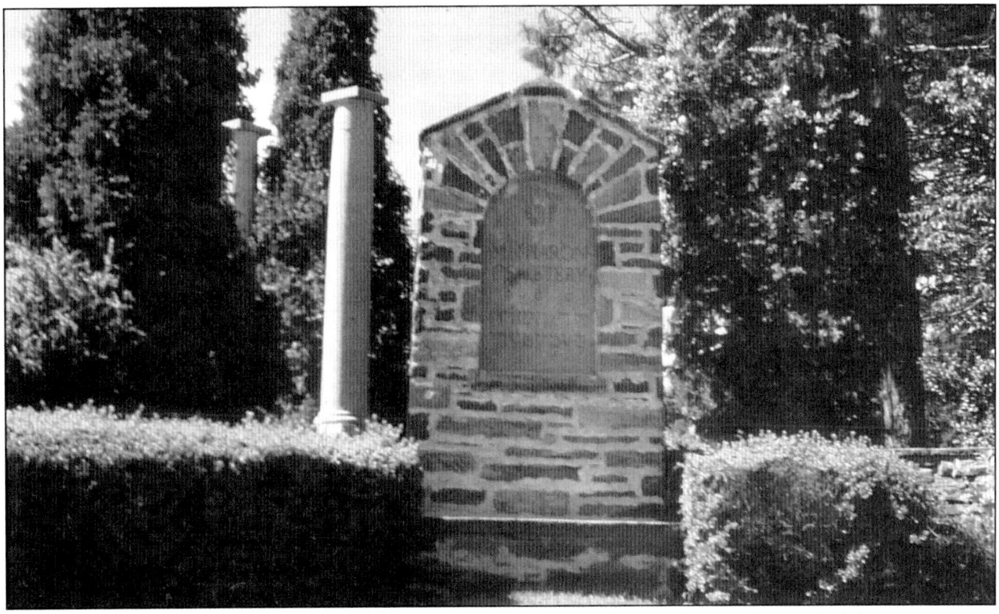

**MT. SHARON CEMETERY.** Mt. Sharon Cemetery is located on Springfield Avenue in Springfield, Pennsylvania. In 1922 there was easy access by the Sharon Hill and Media trolley car lines to the 69th Street Elevated terminal. The effects of the great flu epidemic of 1918 scared the Jewish community for some time when many families lost members throughout South Philadelphia and burial was strictly chronological. Jacob Rosen financially backed Mt. Sharon as an undertaker and he listened to people who wanted a return to burials according to gender on separate rows. Mt. Sharon provided a common resting place for the strictly orthodox. (Courtesy of Allen Meyers.)

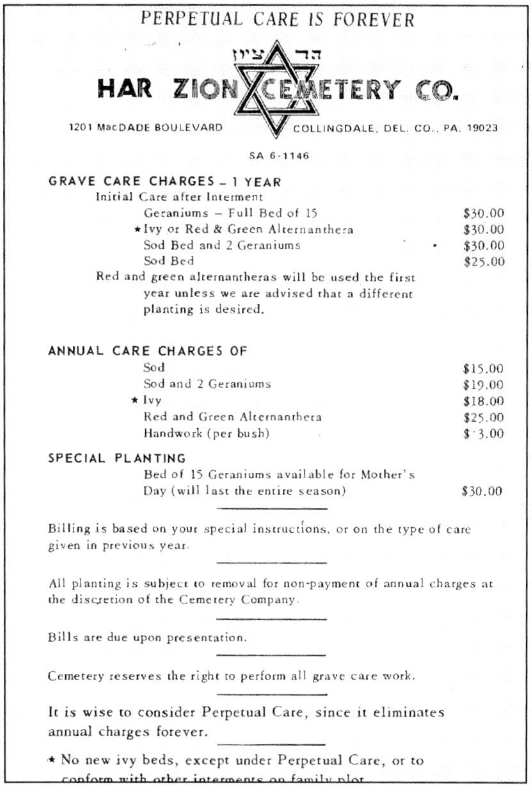

PERPETUAL CARE IS FOREVER

הר ציון

**HAR ZION CEMETERY CO.**

1201 MacDADE BOULEVARD COLLINGDALE, DEL. CO., PA. 19023

SA 6-1146

**GRAVE CARE CHARGES – 1 YEAR**

Initial Care after Interment

| | |
|---|---|
| Geraniums – Full Bed of 15 | $30.00 |
| ★Ivy or Red & Green Alternanthera | $30.00 |
| Sod Bed and 2 Geraniums | $30.00 |
| Sod Bed | $25.00 |

Red and green alternantheras will be used the first year unless we are advised that a different planting is desired.

**ANNUAL CARE CHARGES OF**

| | |
|---|---|
| Sod | $15.00 |
| Sod and 2 Geraniums | $19.00 |
| ★ Ivy | $18.00 |
| Red and Green Alternanthera | $25.00 |
| Handwork (per bush) | $ 3.00 |

**SPECIAL PLANTING**

| | |
|---|---|
| Bed of 15 Geraniums available for Mother's Day (will last the entire season) | $30.00 |

Billing is based on your special instructions, or on the type of care given in previous year.

All planting is subject to removal for non-payment of annual charges at the discretion of the Cemetery Company.

Bills are due upon presentation.

Cemetery reserves the right to perform all grave care work.

It is wise to consider Perpetual Care, since it eliminates annual charges forever.

★ No new ivy beds, except under Perpetual Care, or to conform with other interments on family plot

**HAR ZION CEMETERY.** Har Zion Cemetery started at the height of the Great Depression, in 1934. William B. Leaf, the editor of the *Yiddishe Velt or Jewish World* newspaper in Philadelphia, created Har Zion with the help of Jacob Babis and Jacob Hoffman on 30 acres of farmland south of Mt. Lebanon in Collingdale, Pennsylvania. Members of the Brith Achim, a Jewish fraternal organization, and the Hebrew Waiters Beneficial Association joined other groups to provide burial space for their members. Har Zion, under the supervision of Oscar Feldman, still provides landscaping today that includes ivy plants. (Courtesy of the Allen Meyers Jewish History Collection.)

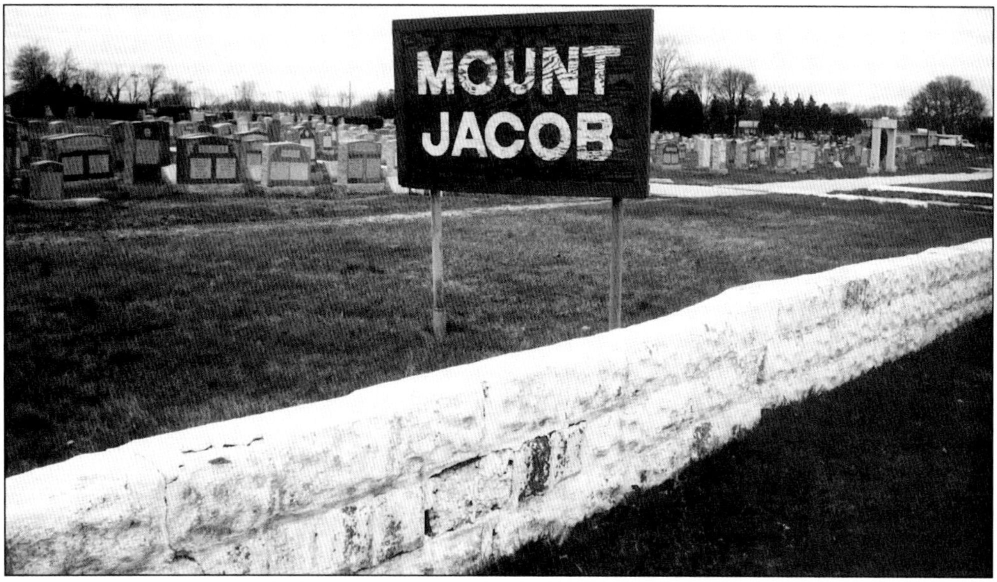


**MT. JACOB CEMETERY.** Mt. Jacob Cemetery, the fifth Jewish cemetery on the western fringe of Philadelphia, was opened by Jacob Babis, a real estate developer and builder, in 1943. Located across Oak Road from Mt. Lebanon Cemetery, in Glenolden, Pennsylvania, on 22 acres, Mt. Jacob became part of a sprawling 100-acre-three cemetery complex that offered a final resting place for many Jewish East European immigrants that originally settled in South Philadelphia in the late 19th and early 20th centuries. (Courtesy of Allen Meyers.)

# *Four*

# Trolley Car Metropolis

## Transportation Routes Originating in South Philadelphia and Radiating Out to All Sections of the City

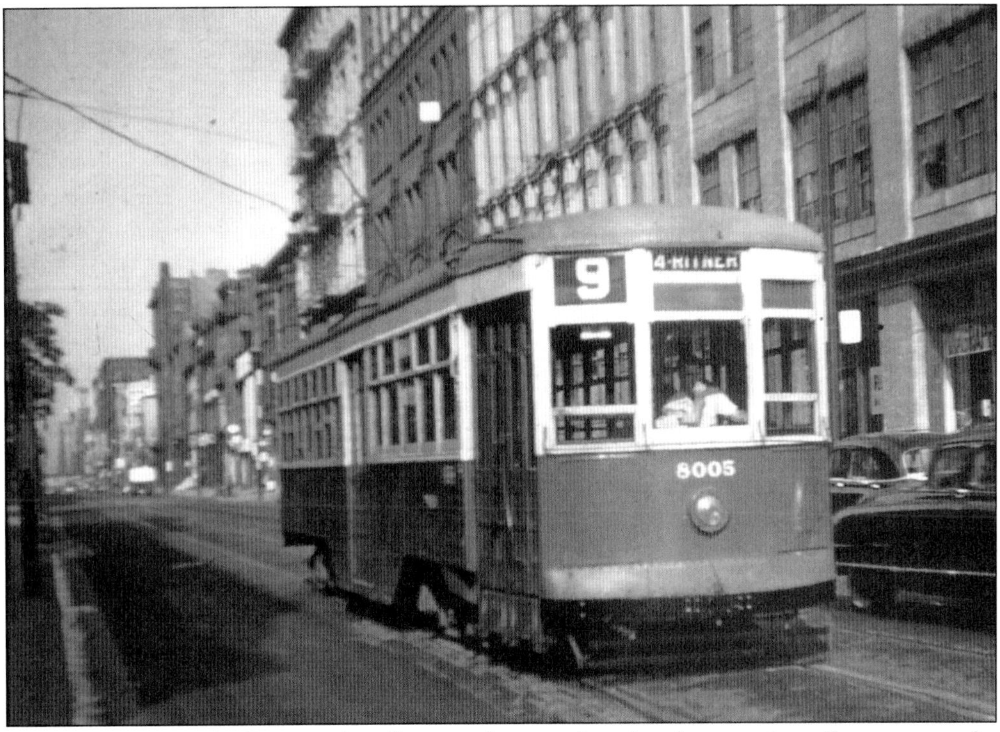


**The Route # 9.** The Route # 9 trolley car, the most loved and romantic trolley car route for the Jewish East European immigrants, connected South Philadelphia with its satellite urban suburb—Strawberry Mansion, in North Philadelphia, high on the banks of the Schuylkill River. The wooden-frame trolley car became an integral part of many Jewish people's lives from the 1920s until the 1950s. The trips on Sundays were filled with so many Jewish people visiting family and friends, it was often called the Hebrew Limited or the Jerusalem Express. (Courtesy of Joe Mannix.)

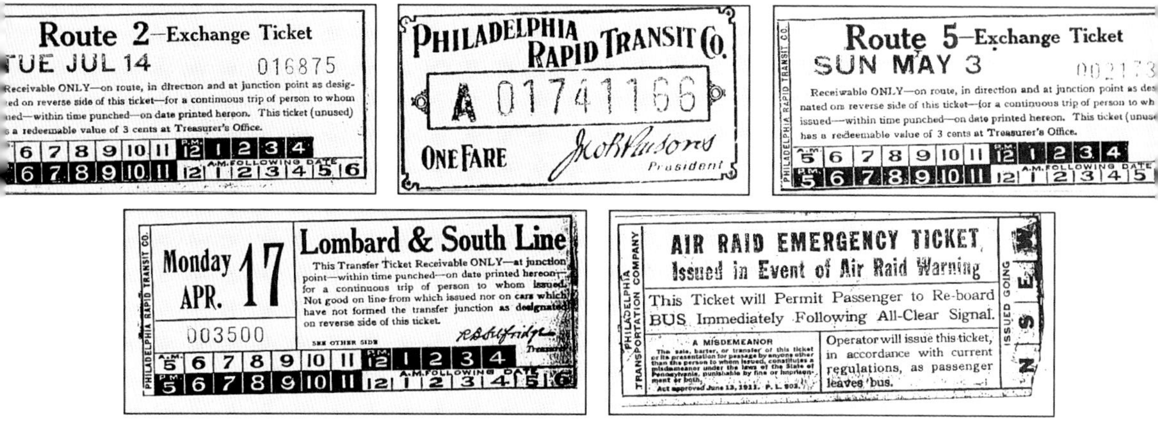


**A World of Transfers.** During the 1940s and 1950s, easy access to all parts of the city from South Philadelphia was only a trolley car ride away. Fares were two for 15¢ and transfers were free. The only worry people had in those days was the fear of a trolley car marked with a slash for a shortened run. Then, the wait for another trolley car was only ten minutes with more than 80 routes in Philadelphia that operated. You could wait at many corner trolley car stops and board different route cars that used the same tracks to drop you off within walking distance of your destination. (Courtesy of Joel Spivak.)

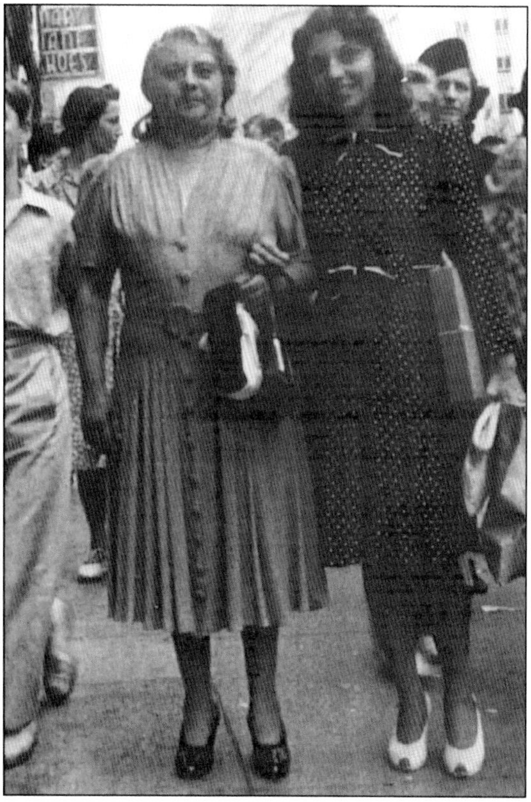

**A Trolley Car Story.** A trolley car chapter would not be complete without a story of romance. Loretta Bell lived with her parents at 1828 S. Seventh Street in the 1930s, and after graduating from Southern High School, she took a job at the Cooklyn Milk Company at 32nd and Dickinson. One day, Loretta boarded the Route # 29 trolley car on her way to work, and the driver, a nice Jewish man named Max, began to flirt with her, but he was too shy to ask her name. Then, Max asked his riders for the pretty girl's name, but they naturally refused to tell Max her name. So, Max finally made the connection and dated the young girl, who he married and lived with happily ever after at 2541 S. Darien Street in South Philadelphia. Minnie Bell and her daughter Loretta are pictured above as they walk down Market Street shopping for clothes. (Courtesy of Edie Goldberg Simon.)

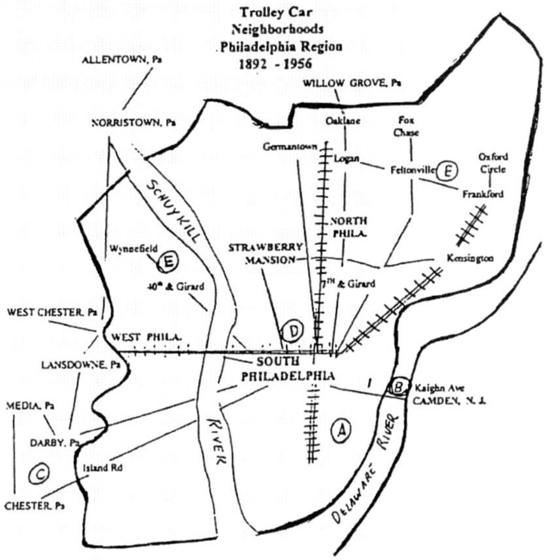


Excerpted from, " Philadelphia's Old Jewish Neighborhood Synagogues" by Allen Meyers --- Unpublished , ( Three Volumes - 1995). Funded through a Grant from the Pennsylvania Historic /Museum Commission in Harrisburg , sponsored thru Jewish Federation of Philadelphia and administrated by the Philadelphia Jewish Archives Center at the Balch Institute.

A. Twelve other Trolley Car Routes originated in South Philadelphia ( Route No. 17, 19, 20, 21, 26, 28, 32, 34, 36, 42, 49, 68 )

B. Ferry from Front and South Streets, across the Delaware River, with connection to Kaighn Avenue in New Jersey.

C. Inter-urban Trolley Car Routes include Rt 71 - Darby to Media ( 1900-1938 ), Rt. 76 - Darby to Chester ( 1900-1936 ), Rt. 77 - Chester - Media ( 1901-1936 ) Rt. 78 - Darby to Lansdowne ( 1902-1947 ), Rt 100 69th Street - Norristown and Allentown ( 1908 - 1935 ) Travel from South Philadelphia to Darby took less than one hour.

D. High Speed urban transportation via the Market Street Elevated Train ( 1907 ) and the connecting Frankford Elevated Train ( 1922 ). The Broad Street Subway ( 1928 )

E. Connector Trolley Car Lines to Second Settlement areas included Rt 70 to Wynnefield ( 1906 - 1955 ), Rt. 75 Logan to Feltonville and Frankford ( 1902-1948 ). Rt 59 Frankford to Oxford Circle Via Castor Avenue ( 1938- 1950 )

**TROLLEY CAR ROUTE MAP.** Jewish neighborhood development at the end of trolley car lines originated out of South Philadelphia. In the late 19th and early 20th centuries, the development of the electric power trolley added more routes to service all of Philadelphia. The extended service to the far reaches of Philadelphia and surrounding areas provided access to jobs and recreation. Jewish families migrated to newer neighborhoods radiating out from South Philadelphia due to upward mobility and an ever-increasing bulge in the immigrant population. (Courtesy of Allen Meyers.)

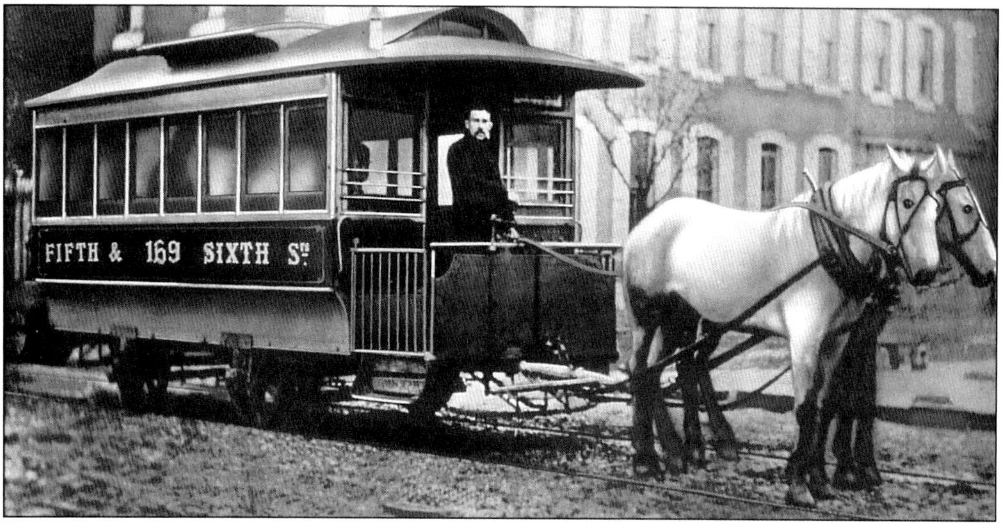


**THE FIFTH AND SIXTH LINES.** Street rail transportation between Port Richmond and Fifth and South Streets included horse-drawn streetcars. This northbound-southbound link began in the 1870s and connected the first Russian-Jewish settlement in Port Richmond at Lehigh and Aramingo Avenues with a similar colony near Fifth and South Streets. Family members who competed for jobs lived in both districts and supported the new B'nai Abraham congregation located at Sixth and Lombard. (Courtesy of Kurt Szabo.)

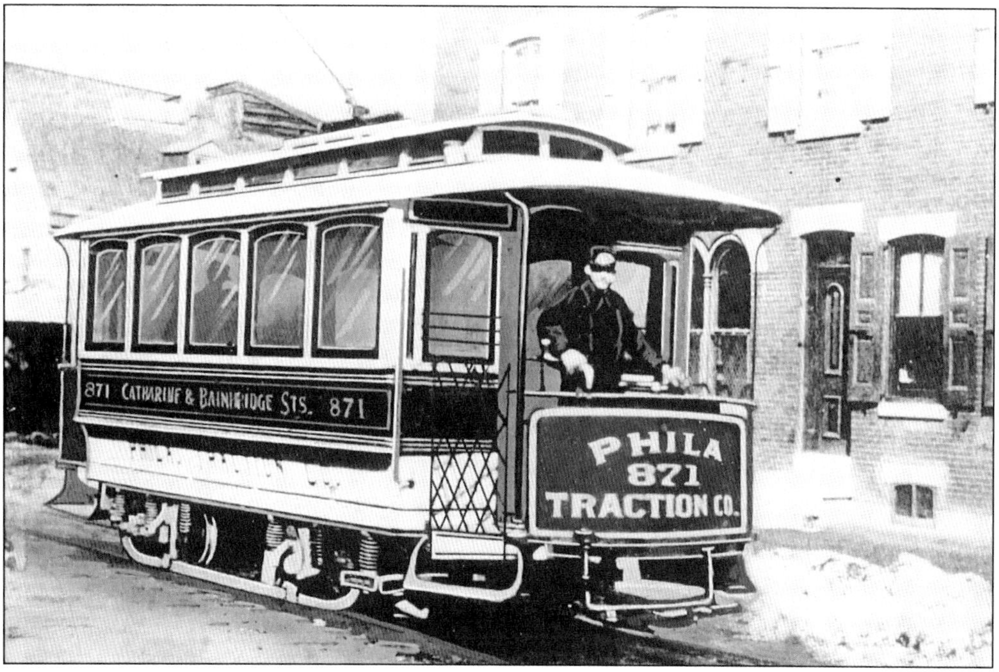


**THE CATHERINE-BAINBRIDGE LINE.** The Catherine-Bainbridge Street line served as an important westbound-eastbound line running through the Jewish East European immigrant community with service from the Delaware River to the Schuylkill River. The electrification of the line in 1892 added a dimension of modernity to the community. On Bainbridge, between Third and Fifth Streets, an open-air market attracted many ethnic groups with the excitement of a trolley car passing by for a gala 1890s atmosphere. (Courtesy of Joel Spivak.)

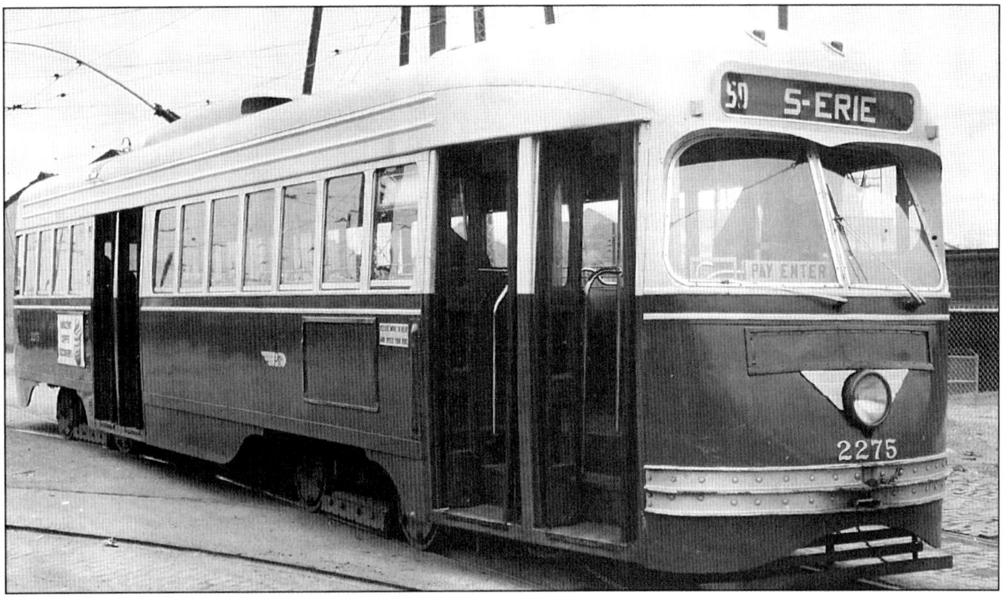


**THE ROUTE #50 LINE.** The Route #50 trolley line connected South Philadelphia to Fox Chase in the far reaches of the Northeast section of Philadelphia. The line started in 1896 and shuttled Jewish immigrants 1 mile south of Washington Avenue to Fourth and Ritner Streets. The #50 line connected Jewish families living in South Philadelphia with those living in North Philadelphia at Fifth and Girard, Fifth and Lehigh, Fifth and Allegheny, Fifth and Erie, and Feltonville. One of the longest trolley car lines in Philadelphia, the #50 provided many immigrants with access to the Moses Montefiore Cemetery above Fox Chase. (Courtesy of Andy Maginnis.)

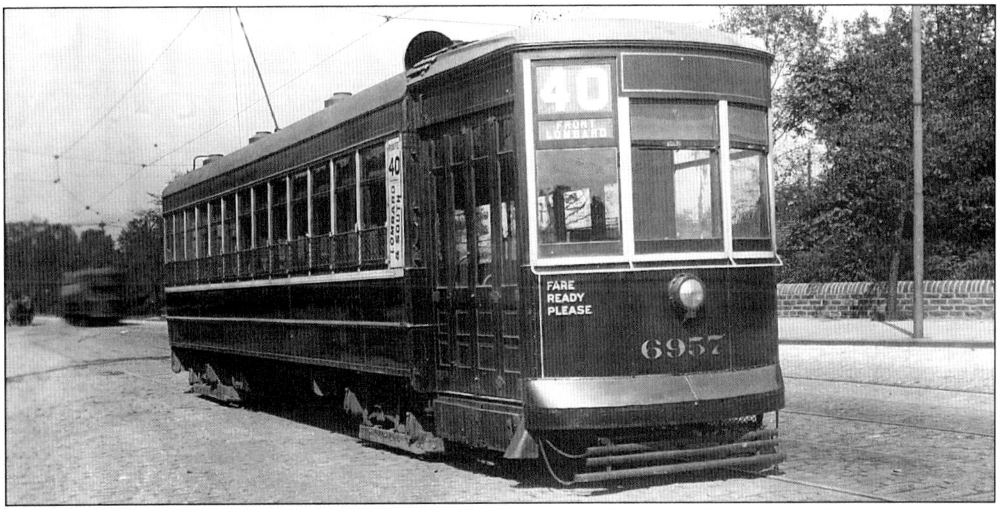


**THE ROUTE #40 LINE.** The Route #40 trolley car moved people from South Philadelphia out to West Philadelphia along the familiar Lombard-South Street corridor. Austro-Hungarian Jews migrated from South Philadelphia along the Route #40 line along 40th Street, which became electrified in1895. Jewish factory owners lived near 40th and Girard and commuted downtown in less than 45 minutes. Less congestion and a country atmosphere with wooden porches, front lawns, and wide streets made West Philadelphia an attractive place for the Jewish immigrants to live in their second settlement area. (Courtesy of Andy Maginnis.)

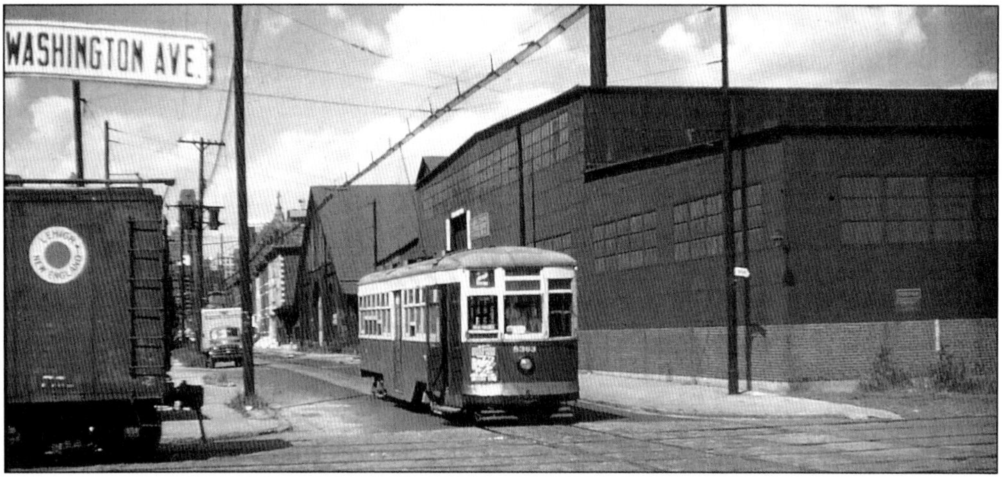


**THE ROUTE #2 LINE.** Philadelphia's urban trolley car service often connected two, three, or more Jewish enclaves of small stores clustered together originating from South Philadelphia. Most of the Jewish immigrant population settled east of Broad Street, and smaller settlements existed west of Broad in the early 1910s. The Route #2 ran down 15th and up 16th Streets connecting Jewish settlements at 17th and South with 17th and Venago in North Philadelphia. The Route #2 served as a direct line from Broad and Erie in North Philadelphia, to the Kuptsow Delicatessen near Pattison Avenue, and to the Navy Yard during WW II. (Courtesy of Joe Mannix Collection.)

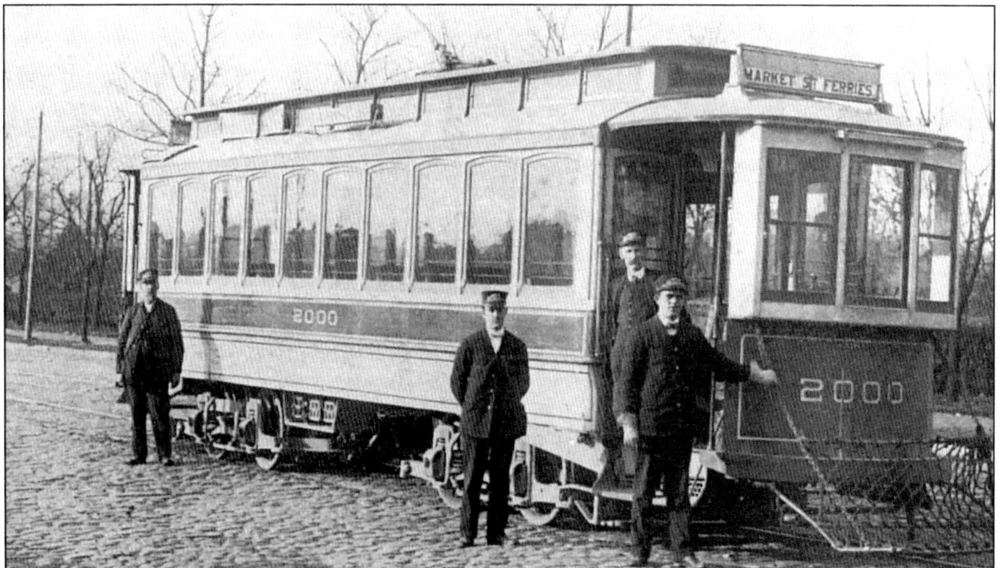


**THE MARKET STREET FERRIES.** Many lines ran from North, West, and South Philadelphia to the Front and Market Street loop. The Route #17 in South Philadelphia ran down 19th and up 20th Streets on its rendezvous with the ferries that crossed the Delaware River connecting Philadelphia with Camden, New Jersey. The Jewish community of Camden was founded in 1894 with merchants lined up and down Kaighn Avenue. Some ferries went as far south as Pennsgrove, New Jersey, which also had a Jewish merchant community with ties to South Philadelphia, especially through families who shopped for kosher provisions. (Courtesy of Andy Maginnis.)

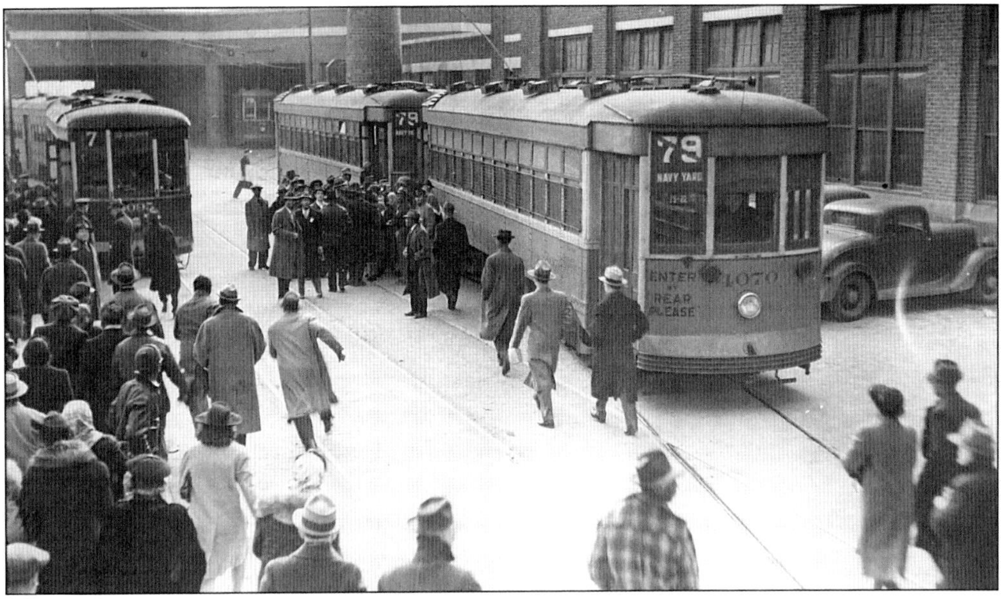


**THE ROUTE #79 LINE.** The Snyder Avenue trolley car, or the Route #79, served the community heading east to Front Street several blocks from the loading docks of great ocean-going cargo vessels. The westbound trolleys went to 29th and Snyder where many industries bordered Point Breeze Park near the Schuylkill River. During WW II, all southbound trolley cars let off huge crowds of people to transfer on the Route #79 that made a special loop to the Philadelphia Navy which employed thousands of people to prepare battle ships for combat in the Atlantic and Pacific Oceans. (Courtesy of Andy Maginnis.)

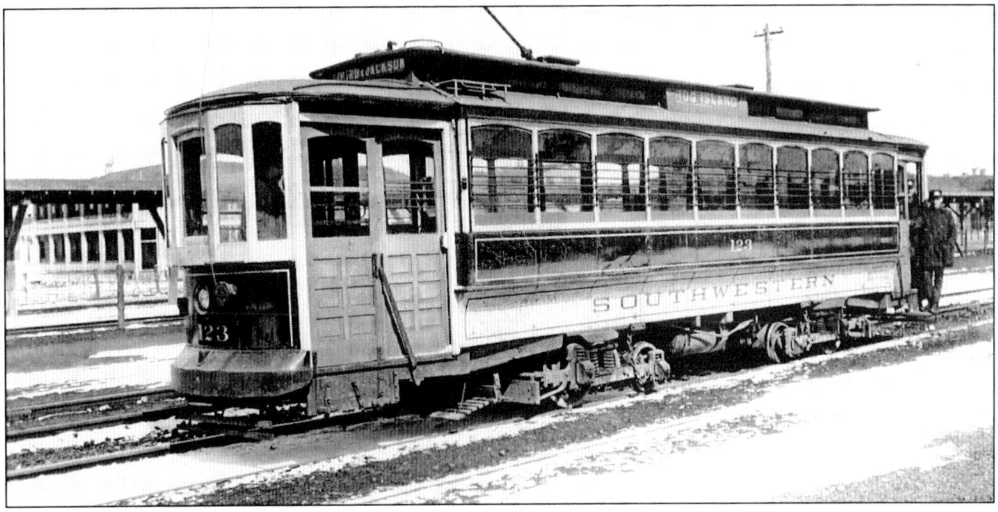


**THE SOUTHWESTERN LINE.** The Southwestern Line transported Jews from Third and Jackson Streets in South Philadelphia to the area referred to as the Meadows, or 84th and Eastwick Avenues, which served as the hub of a unique Jewish farmer colony in an urban metropolis. The Hebrew Immigrant Aid Society settled several hundred families who wanted a semi-rural atmosphere in the late 1890s. The Southwestern trolley continued through woods and swamps on its way to Chester, Pennsylvania, as a pioneer inter-urban service in the early 1900s. Trips to South Philadelphia were made especially to shop on South Seventh Street, the largest concentration of Jewish merchants assembled in Philadelphia. (Courtesy of Andy Maginnis.)

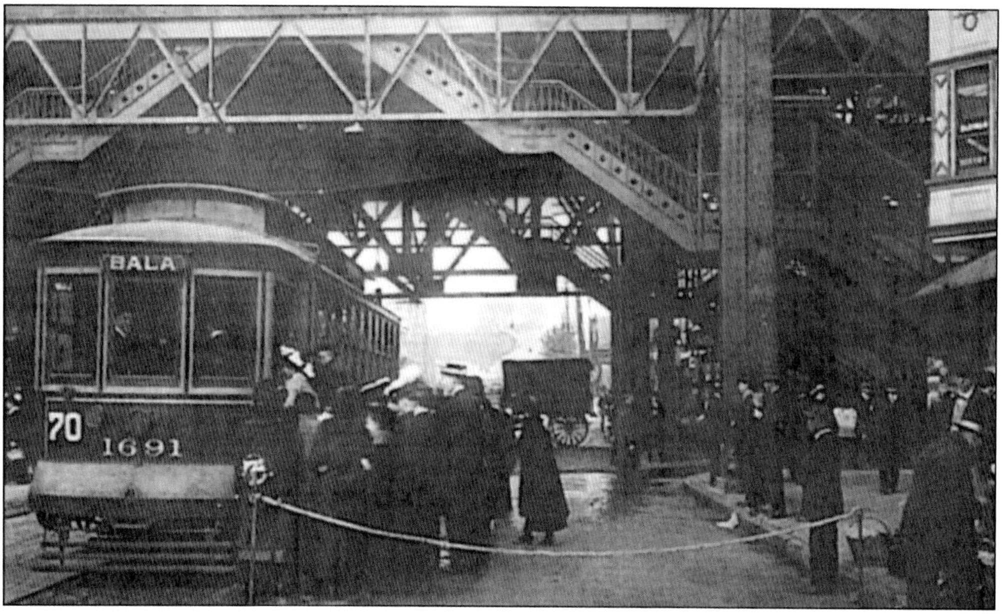


**THE BALA LINE.** By 1910, a high-speed overhead elevated train system running from downtown to the far reaches of West Philadelphia stimulated new housing and commerce development. Upward economic growth for the Jewish immigrants led to new second settlement areas at the end of trolley car lines that included, Wynnefield, Logan, Oaklane, and Feltonville. The Wynnefield section of Philadelphia became accessible via the Route #70 trolley car transfer at 52nd and Market Streets immediately before WW I, when a great exodus of Jews from South Philadelphia took place. (Courtesy of Andy Maginnis.)

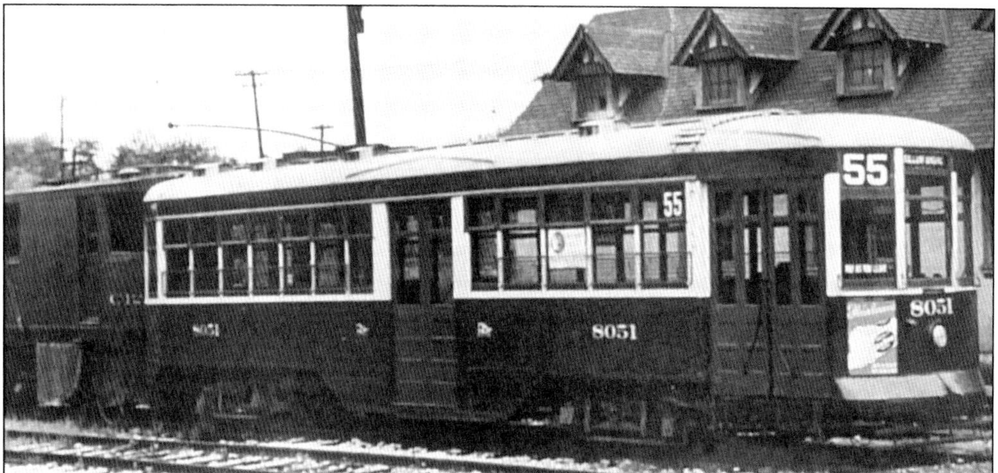


**THE ROUTE #55.** Inter-urban travel via high-speed trolley car lines provided Jewish continuity through uniting families even though they chose to live in villages, towns, and cities separated by 25 miles or more from Philadelphia. The Route #55 ran from Fourth and Pine to the Willow Grove Amusement Park from 1895 until 1952. Jewish farms were opened up as resort areas in the summertime for South Philadelphia Jews who were called pleasurniks. Phil Levicoff (of blessed memory) spent his life in the transportation field, and this chapter is dedicated to his vision and involvement in the planning of new routes and schedules for the Southeastern Public Transportation Authority (Septa). (Courtesy of Andy Maginnis.)

# *Five*

# Shopkeepers and Their Business Districts

## South Street, Fourth Street, Seventh Street, Ninth Street, Dock Street, and Point Breeze Avenue

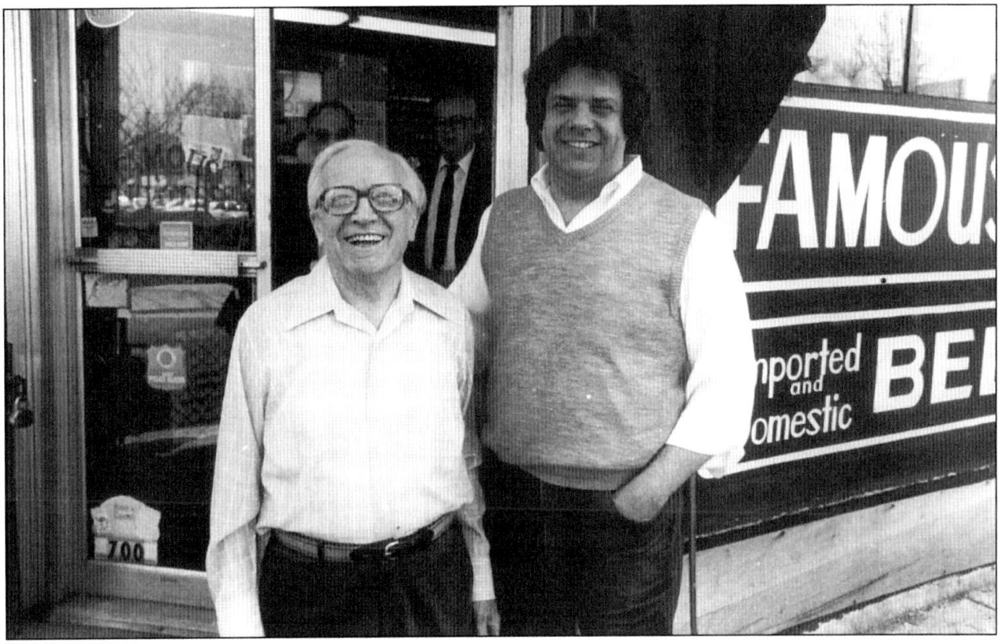


**Sam and David Auspitz.** The Auspitz family arrived in Philadelphia, from Poland, when immigration to America came to a halt, in 1923. Sam Auspitz established the Famous Delicatessen on the southwest corner of Fourth and Bainbridge Street in the South Philadelphia immigrant district. Additional family members created branches of the Famous Delicatessen in other Jewish neighborhoods, including Strawberry Mansion and Marshall & Girard. Also, in Camden, New Jersey, one could find a Famous Deli only a short ferry ride across the Delaware River, on Kaighn Avenue. The Famous Deli became a Philadelphia institution known for its thick corn beef sandwiches on rye. Father to son businesses represented a strong bond between the generations that is priceless to David, the current owner. (Courtesy of David Auspitz.)

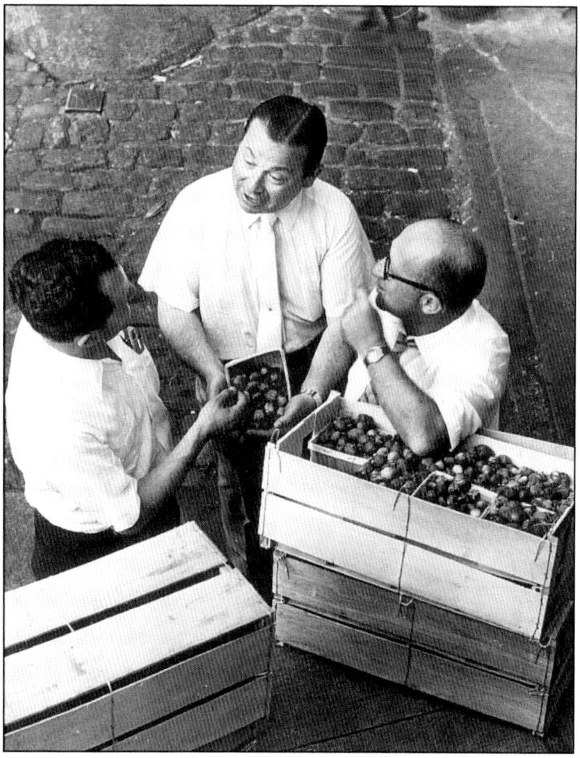

**JOHN TAXIN.** John Taxin, a successful businessman and the owner of Bookbinders Seafood Restaurant, sold fruit to the emerging supermarkets at the end of WW II, in the old world food center known as Dock Street. The market, with its cobble stone streets, surrounded an inlet harbor from the Delaware River that dated back to the 1850s. The center served as a hub of activity with trolley cars bringing thousands of people to the waterfront for passage on ferry boats to Camden, New Jersey, mingled with teamsters that drove horse and wagons to huckster fresh fruit, vegetables, and fish throughout South Philadelphia. Dock Street closed in the late 1950s with the opening of the Food Distribution Center on Pattison Avenue. (Courtesy of Urban Archives, Temple University, Philadelphia, Pennsylvania.)

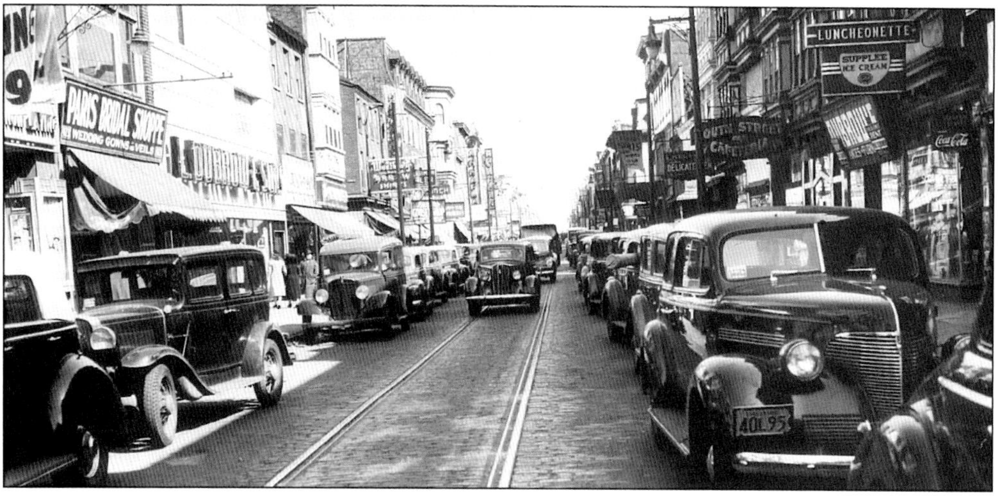


**SOUTH STREET SHOPPING DISTRICT.** The South Street shopping district distinctively known for its quality merchandise developed around the Jewish East European immigrant area focused at Fifth and South Streets. There was a mass arrival of Austro-Hungarian, Romanian, Polish, and Russian Jews in the late 19th century, and they turned to commerce for their livelihood. The merchants often started peddling with a hand basket, then a pushcart, and later acquired enough funds to rent a storefront with living quarters in the rear. The bustle of a city was found on South Street with trolley cars, automobiles, and a multitude of people on the sidewalks looking for a bargain or willing to haggle over the price of an item as was the custom, especially in Dubrow's Furniture Store pictured above in this late 1940s picture. (Courtesy of Urban Archives, Temple University, Philadelphia, Pennsylvania.)

## SOUTH STREET BUSINESS MEN'S ASSOCIATION

**Trimmings**
Fleischer
Sacks
Renitz
Braman
Anmuth

**Shoes**
Rival
Weinstein
Freloch
Belle
Goldstein

**Haberdashery - Men's Clothiers**
Lonker
Yuram
Harris
Berry
Wilk
Gordon
Diamond
Pure
Berman
Krass Bros.
Diamond
Leidner
Rossoff
Goldman
Gerson
Lippy's

**Dry Goods**
Brien
Weinstock
Prager
Tarnoff

**Bakeries**
Bogoslavsky's
Freidman's Matzoh
Teitelbaums
Moskowitz

**Boy's Wear**
Meyer's
Goldstein

**Gen. Merchandise**
Weintraub
Handle
Zeldin
Reiss

**Bridal Shops**
Silverman
Baum
Bluebird

**Floor Covering**
Klinghoffer
Shapiro
Kubert

**Meat Restaurants**
Uhr's
Himmelstein's
the Colonial

**Hat Stores**
Dietz
Rosenzweig
Felcowitz

**Furniture Stores**
Shubin
Dubrow
Carlsom
Krongold
Miller
Rubin
Fleishman

**Cafeteria's - Deli's**
Bain's
Kelem's
Cohen

**Women's Wear**
Berkowitz
Paramount
Wilf

**Dairy Restaurants**
the Ideal
the Royal
Bass

**Butter & Egg**
Saler's
Kaufmann

**Assorted Goods**
Goren's Fish
Kaplan's Lady Shop
Smith's hat cleaners
Cutler's Linen's
Sloppy Joe's Lamps
Green's Cut Rate
Frank Austin Pharmacy
New York Extract
Ward's neckties
Rosenbaum's Bank

**Jewish Newspapers**
The Jewish World
The Day
The Journal
The Jewish Forward
Freheit

**Toy Stores**
Weiss
Taub
Ponnock
Kostoff

**Furriers**
Gurak
Shusterman
Spigel
Klinghoffer
Sendler

**Barber's**
Carl Katz
Max Klein
Izzie Bennet

**Wall Paper Stores**
Shultz
Bonton

**Candy Stores**
Cornfeld
Stein

**Baby Furniture**
Paultin
Cramer

**Shoe Findings**
Abramson
Garber

SOUTH STREET BUSINESS MEN'S ASSOCIATION. The South Street Business Men's Association developed to unite the merchants on South Street and surrounding streets in an effort to regulate the type of business permitted in the area, in 1914. Store size, type of business, and regular dues to promote South Street became the main concerns of the association leaders who conducted business in the area. The definition of a businessman became synonymous with respect, integrity, and value, and Jack Yuram, long-time president of South Street who ran the Business Men's Association, portrayed those qualities for many years. (Courtesy of Mort and Bernie Uhr.)

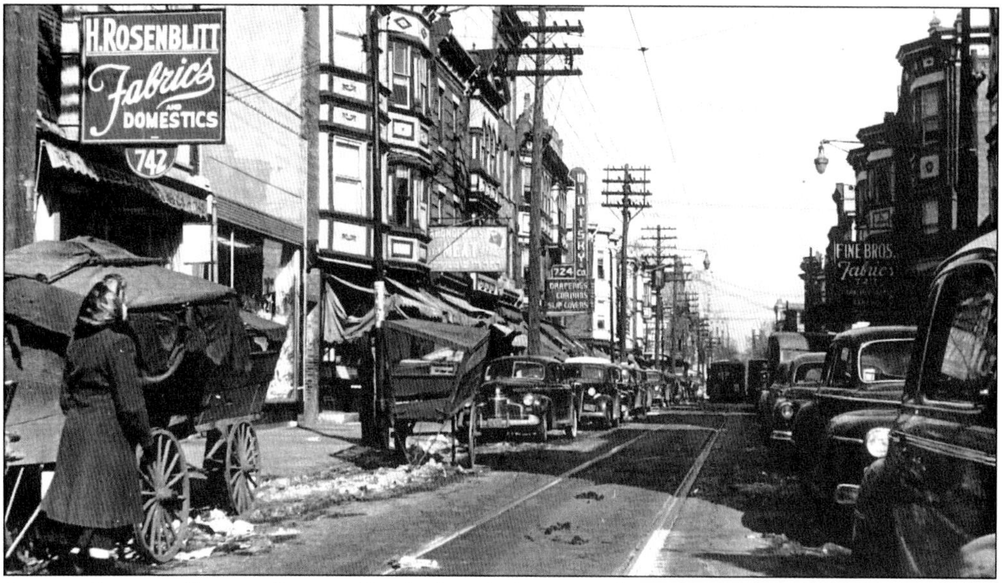


**SOUTH FOURTH STREET SCENE.** South Fourth Street, rich in American-Jewish history, once had metal awnings that hid the sunlight. During the 1920s, the Fourth Street Business Men's Association decided in conjunction with the city to remove the dangerous over hangs high above many store fronts. The well-known South Fourth shopping district included Louis Winitsky's Curtain Shop from 1923 until 1948. Many fabrics used for various end products were available from Catherine to Lombard Streets, and today the area is certified as Fabric Row, a status similar to that of Jeweler's Row which started in 1948 on Samson Street between Seventh and Eighth Streets. (Courtesy of the Atwater Kent Museum of History.)

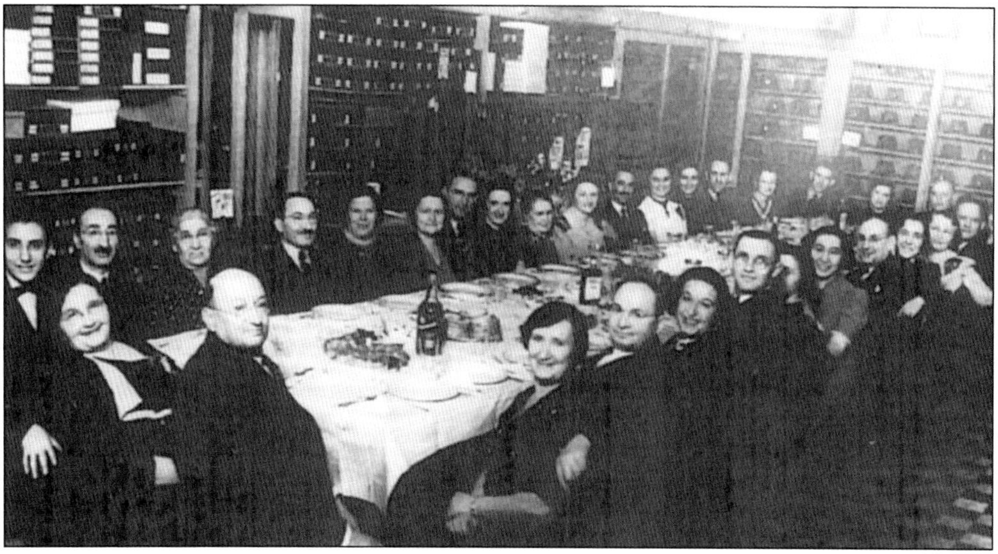

**THE ZUBROW'S STORE.** Business people took family celebrations very seriously. The long hours of retail merchandise required families such as the Zubrows who were in the silk business (762 S. Fourth) to hold simcha's (happy) life-cycle events in their own stores. The Zubrows held a family reunion in 1938, and Nathan, his wife, Sarah, and brother-in law Israel, moved all the merchandise to the side in order to fit three long tables end to end for the hamish (home-style) affair. (Courtesy of Dr. Sidney Zubrow.)

# SOUTH FOURTH STREET BUSINESS MEN'S ASSOCIATION

**Food Stores**

Goldstein Fish
Potamkin Fish
Nate's Fish
Guralick Deli
Famous Deli
Kramer Poultry
Reliable Poultry
Sam's Meats
Herb's Meats
Rutberg's Meats
Aronofsky Meats
Kagan Meats
Jack's Fruits/ Produce
Shupak Pickles

**Fabric Stores**

Zubrow silks
Rosenblitt's
Fine
Winitsky draperies
Dolgien furs
Myerson
Soltoff
Stapler
Rappoport
Paul's silks
Rubin's draperies
Weitzman
Katz

Porten Bros
Davidson
Brechers
Brookstein
Levitt
Rossman
Seltzer
Feldman
Libman
Abrams
Weinstein
Allenoff
Brood & Sons

**Today's Merchants**

Maggie's Drawers
Baldwin Tuxedo
Maxie's Daughter
Grossman's
Adler's Upholstery
Albert Zoll
Southwark Paint Co.
Kincus Fabrics
Goldberg's Fabrics
Silver Sity
Key Fabrics

**Dry Goods**

Giant Shoes
Royal Shoes
Mazis Corset
Klein's Hosiery
Mt. Carmel Wines
Margulis Wines
A. Gross Grocery
M. Schutzbank
Phil's Saloon
Berkowitz
Druker

Zipkin
Kravitz
Wilks
Cohen
Fishman
Epstein
Nager
Weiner
Balk
Dubin
Stuminkin
Marmelstein

THE SOUTH FOURTH STREET BUSINESS MEN'S ASSOCIATION. The South Fourth Street Business Men's Association represented a faction of merchants who broke away from the South Street Business Men's Association to form their own group in the 1940s. Issues of street sanitation, police security, hours of operations, and promotions due to the distinct differences of South Fourth stores aided in the application for membership into the city wide group of United Business Men's Associations. The South Fourth Street BMA met every month at Uhr's restaurant at Fifth and Gaskill Streets for a dinner. (Courtesy of Dan Sullivan, and old minutes of S. Fourth St. BMA.)

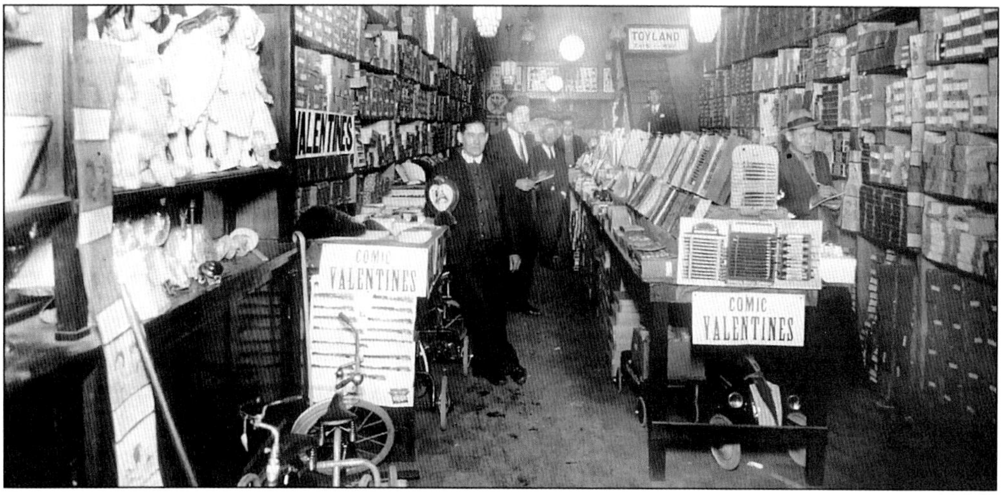


**PONNOCK'S TOY STORE.** The Ponnock's Toy empire, the largest wholesaler on the Eastern seaboard, began with Abe Ponnock selling toys from a pushcart as an immigrant from Russia, on South Street in 1910. The Ponnock's Abe, Louis, Esther, and all the children entered the business with operations in Philadelphia at Fifth and Market and in Camden, New Jersey. In-laws, such as Sam Dubin (brother of Rose Ponnock), entered the business after serving at the Navy Yard during WW I, and later, Sam formed General Novelty Toys. When South Philadelphia Jews became successful merchants, they established their business on Walnut, Chestnut, and Market Streets in the 1920s and 1930s. Pictured above are Sam and Bernie Dubin and Louis and Daniel Ponnock in this 1931 photograph. (Courtesy of Marvin and Irv Dubin.)

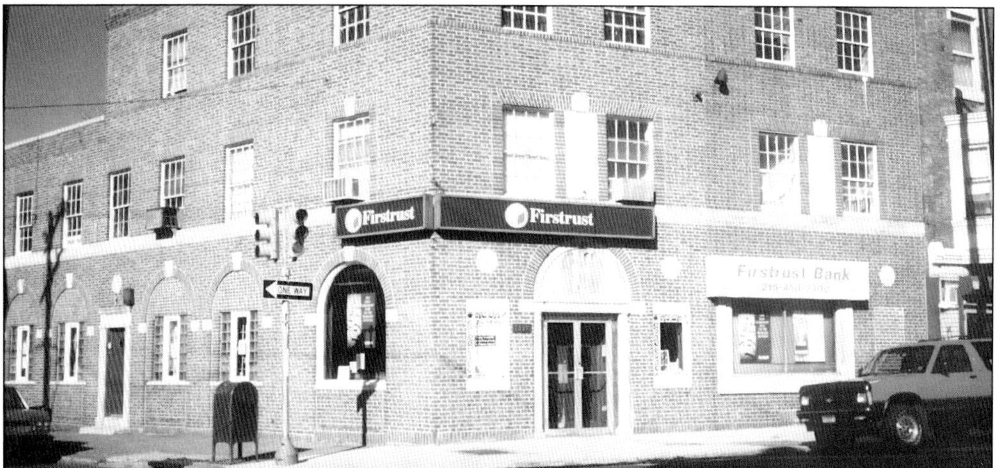


**THE FIRST FEDERAL BANK.** Sam A. Green, a Hungarian immigrant, settled on the west side of Broad Street where he established an ethnic bank (a term coined by Journalist Robert Leiter) to assist fellow Hungarians in coming to America in the 1910s. The institution became the Roosevelt Bank, located at 21st and Wharton, and received its charter in 1918 and survived the Great Depression. Dan Green, the son of Sam, born inside the house at 1332 Point Breeze Avenue where 21st and Reed Street all intersect, continued the tradition of banking when the First Federal Saving and Loan Association was founded in 1934. Today, the bank with several branches, known as Firstrust, continues to function in South Philadelphia, where Dan was born. (Courtesy of Dan Green.)

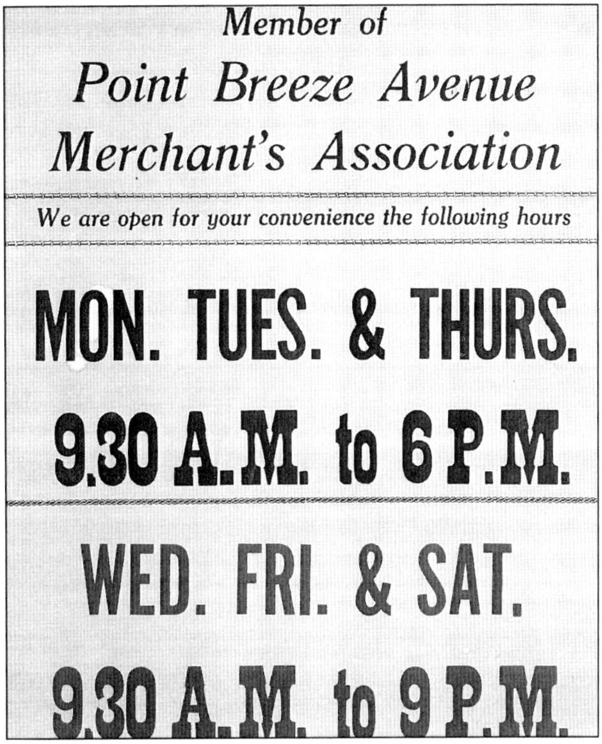


**POINT BREEZE MERCHANTS.** The Jewish community west of Broad Street developed around the 75 Austro-Hungarian merchants who lived above their stores near Point Breeze Avenue where 22nd and Wharton Streets all intersected. Rabbi Englander, a Hungarian Jew, served the business district community after he migrated from Fifth and South Streets in the 1910s to lead Congregation Shaare Shomayim. The trolley Route #7 meandered throughout South Philadelphia, from Front and Tasker to 23rd Street on its way to Strawberry Mansion where Austro-Hungarian Jewish immigrants who learned English quickly, served as merchants. (Courtesy of Selma Harris Forestater.)

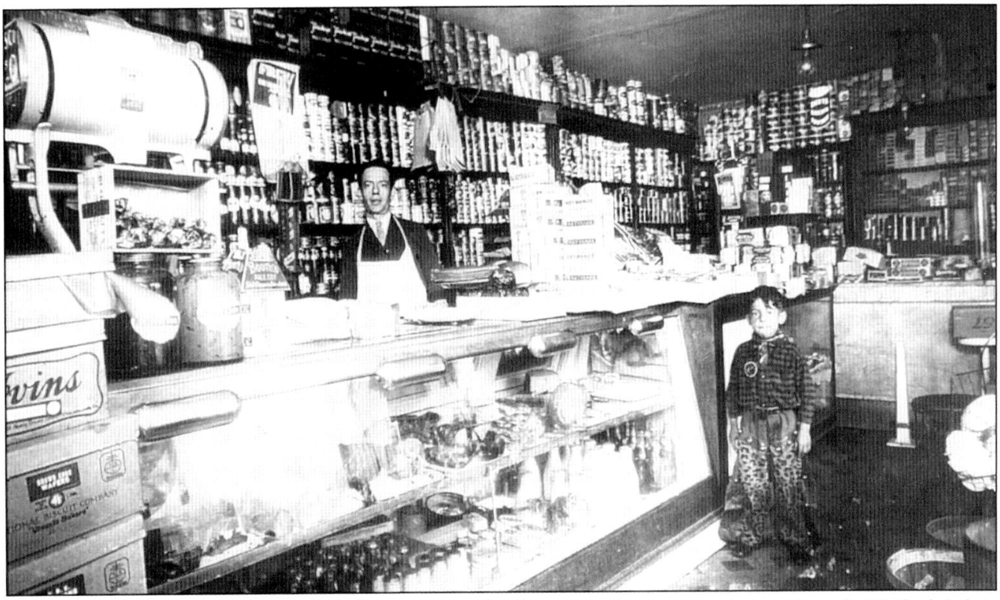

**KUPTSOW DELI.** David and Eva Kuptsow, with their son Aaron, settled in South Philadelphia west of Broad Street at 15th and Pollock Streets, one block north of Packer Avenue where the trolley Route #2 terminated. The Kuptsow family arrived from Russia in 1915, and operated a soda fountain/deli separate from the main centers of Jewish life, but connected through transportation routes to other family members. Pockets of Jewish people clustered in non-Jewish neighborhoods where all four corners were occupied by Jewish merchants, which defined their Jewish community. (Courtesy of Dr. Aaron and Anita Kuptsow.)

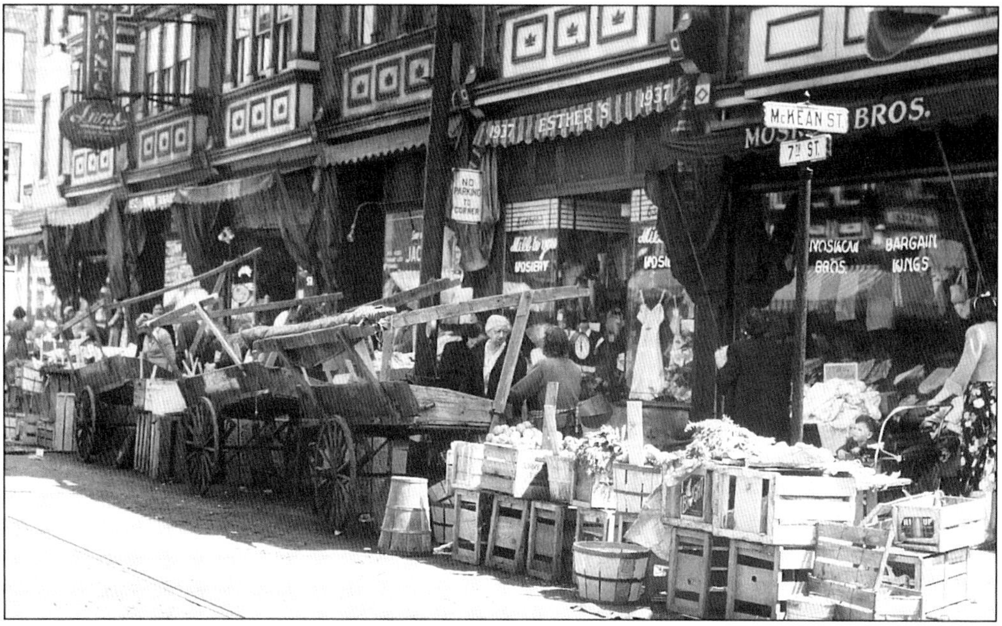


**SEVENTH AND MCKEAN STREETS.** The famous South Seventh Street open-air market came to life with the arrival of thousands of Jewish East European immigrants. The immigrant overflow in the early 1900s advanced in South Philadelphia below Washington Avenue to Oregon Avenue. Commerce began with the peddling of perishable and non-perishable items. Individual pushcarts that looked like miniature old American-western conestoga wagons, pictured above at Seventh and McKean, were taken home every night. Seventh Street served consumer needs of many ethnic groups with access by walking and riding the many transportation routes that connected it with Southwest, West, and North Philadelphia. (Courtesy of Urban Archives, Temple University, Philadelphia, Pennsylvania.)

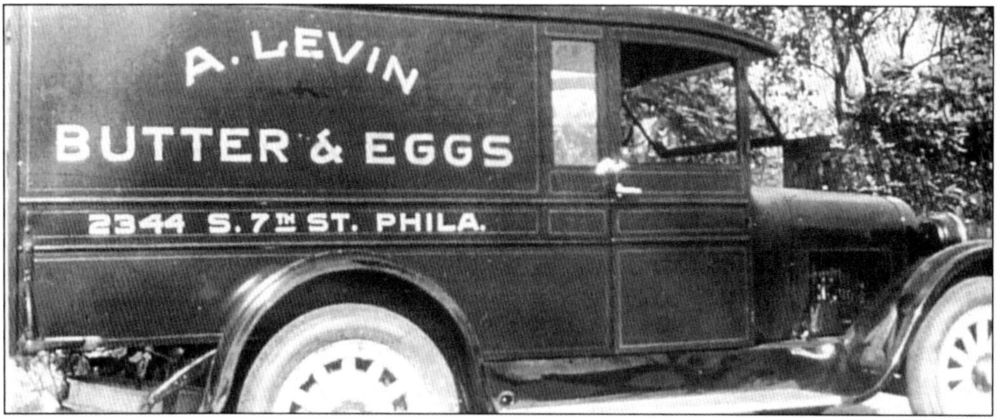


**LEVIN'S BUTTER & EGGS ON S. SEVENTH ST.** Early development of commerce on South Seventh Street depended on women as business operators. Even though the groups of merchants throughout the city formed the Business Men's Association, women ran the day to day operations while their spouses traveled as far as New York City for merchandise. Pictured above is the truck to deliver products for the Levin Butter & Egg store at 2344 S. Seventh Street, in the early 1920s. The "A" stood for the matriarch of the family, Anna, and her son David assisted when he delivered broken eggs to local Jewish and Italian bakeries in the neighborhood. (Courtsey of Sam and Gerald Levin.)

## SOUTH SEVENTH STREET
### BUSINESS MEN'S ASSOCIATION

**1600 S. 7th / below Tasker**

Dunoff shoes
Sokol Fruits
Kravitz Grocery
Cohen's Poultry
Chernoff Fish
Wolfberg Grocery
Kaplan Kosher Meats
Goldberg's Candies
Rabinsky's Bakery
Berman's Pharmacy
Blank's Wallpaper
Schwartz Printing
Flitter's Grocery
Dr. Menkowitz

**1700 S. 7th below Morris**

Kropnick's Furniture
Berry's Men Clothier
Dr. Cutler

**1800 S. 7th below Moore**

Goodman's Bridal
Goodman's Butcher
Potamkin's Fish
Margulis Candies
Soborow Butcher
Moskow's Curtains

**1900 S. 7th below Mc Kean**

Fink's Pawn Shop
Zaslow Butter/ egg
Esther's Dresses
Rabinowitz Hosiery
Cherry's Fruit Shop
Warshafsky's Shoes
Zipkin's Dresses
Fisher's Deli
Bernstein Dresses
Hymie's Banana's
Booner's Restaurant
Leibowitz Steaks
Bonze Dresses
Hoffman's 5/10 cents
Stein's Children shop
Zucker Men's clothing
Stein's Men Wear
Greenspan's Curtain
Feld's Ice Cream
Sitman's Dry Goods
Menacher's Trimmings
Saler's Butter & Egg
Michaelberg Bakery
Golub Grocery
Stillman's Hosiery
Cohen's Fruit
Sam's Clothing
Weiss Bakery

**2000 S. 7th at Snyder Ave**

Eckler's Fabric
Izzie's Hot Dogs
Lou Austin Gifts
Nutinsky Draperies
Wartenberg Meats
Saltzman's Lady Wear
Diamond's Lady Hats
Wasserman Dresses
Bell's Shoes
Leo's Fruit Store
Berger's Variety
Morris Men's Shop
Tay's Lady Wear
Bralow's Fish
Baylinson Dresses
Sitman Silks
Rosenberg's Bakery
Durlofsky Furniture
Marshall's K. Meats

**2100 S. 7th below Jackson**

Wishnoff's Corset
Rosenberg's Bakery
Wartenberg's Meats
Max's Fruit Store
Sonya's Trimmings
Yetta's Hand Bags
Durlosky Furniture
Ann's Dresses
Al's Delicatessen
Gittleman Butter/Egg
Min's Beauty Shop

**2200 S. 7th below Wolf**

Krenzel Candies
Harry's Fish
French Bootery
Becker Kiddie Shop
Postiloff Jewelry
Dave's Bargain
Evantosh Hosiery
Connell's Yarn's
Bee-Cee Boys Wear
Betty's Hosiery
Gary's Men's Shop
Cohen Plumbing
Goldstein's Shoes
Jack's Bargain
Irene's Millinery
Lilian's Dresses
Zakin K. Meats
Appel's Oil Cloth
Frelich's Shoes
Mollie's Dresses
Glickstein Saloon
Herman's Paints

**2300 S. 7th below Ritner**

Korn's Dept Store
Bonton Hosiery
Sneir Women Wear
Jacob's Hosiery
Goldis K. Meats
Abe's Smoked Fish
Ostroff K. Meats
Paul's K. Meats
Packer's Poultry
Hoffman's Lamps
Golub Oil Cloth
Portnoy Variety
Simmen's Bakery
Porter Appliances
Amish K. Meats
Levin's Butter/ Egg
Freidman Bakery
Fleishman Meats
Dimmer's Furs
Donsky Grocery
Hoffman's Gifts
Levin's Real Estate
Sonenberg's Eggs

**2400 S. 7th below Porter**

Eagle Shoes
Jacob's Candy
Duretz K. Meats
Ritkoff Bakery
Silverman Drugs
Rosenblatt Variety
Malmut Grocery
Cohen's Dry Good
Rose's Peanuts
Ostroff's Variety
Zitomer Plumbing
Varinsky Hardwar
Elias Aprons
Saunder Eggs
Weiss Slipcovers
Pollack's Gifts
Israel's Fruit s
Harvey's Dress

The stores along S. 7th Street near Snyder Avenue yielded a livelihood for hundreds of families who added a storefront to their houses and sold almost anything a consumer might need. I spent many days with the senior citzens at the Stiffel Center of the JCC at Marshall & Porter Streets in the early 1980's recalling the past. Ten years later in the early 1990's, I conducted a class, " South Philadelphia Memories and gleaned stories of the largest Philadelphia Business District in a Jewish neighborhood, merchant by merchant.

List of Merchants compiled by Allen Meyers

SEVENTH STREET MERCHANTS. The stores along S. Seventh Street near Snyder Avenue yielded a livelihood for hundreds of families who added a storefront to their houses and sold almost anything a consumer might need. I spent many days with the senior citizens at the Stiffel Center of the JCC at Marshall and Porter Streets in the early 1980s recalling the past. Ten years later in the early 1990s, I conducted a class, South Philadelphia Memories, and gleaned stories of the largest Philadelphia Business District in a Jewish neighborhood, merchant by merchant. (Compiled by Allen Meyers.)

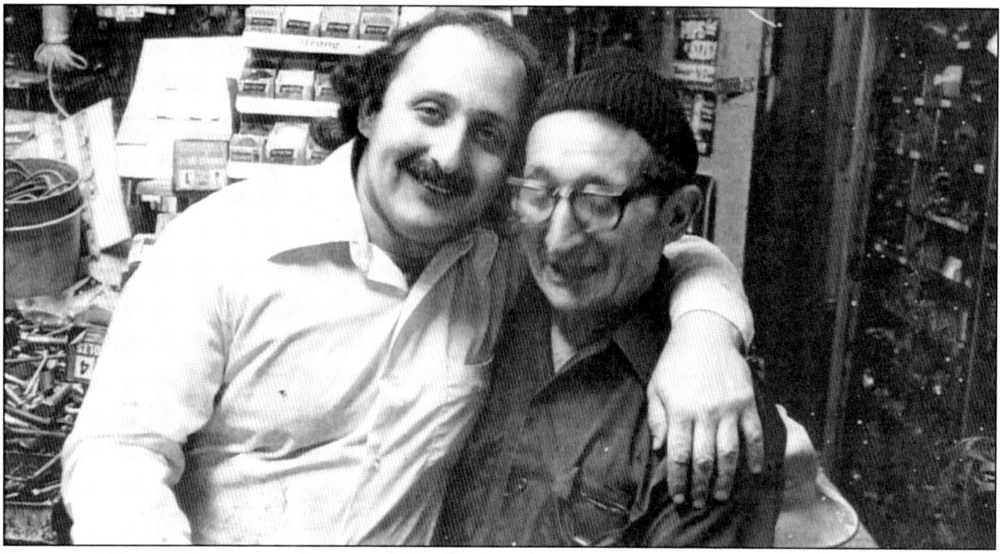

**IRV AND HARRY BRUSKIN.** Isaac and Estella Bruskin came to Philadelphia from Kiev, Russia, and settled in South Philadelphia. The Bruskins started their hardware business on the northeast corner of Fifth and Porter, and Estella ran the business in the store, while Isaac traveled and made house keys for customers. Isaac's son Harry and his wife, Gertrude, ran the business in the 1950s, when most people did not lock their doors except when they went on vacation. Pictured above are Irv and Harry Bruskin. Today, Irv runs the family business and recalls the past with pictures of people hanging in his display windows. (Courtesy of Irv Bruskin.)

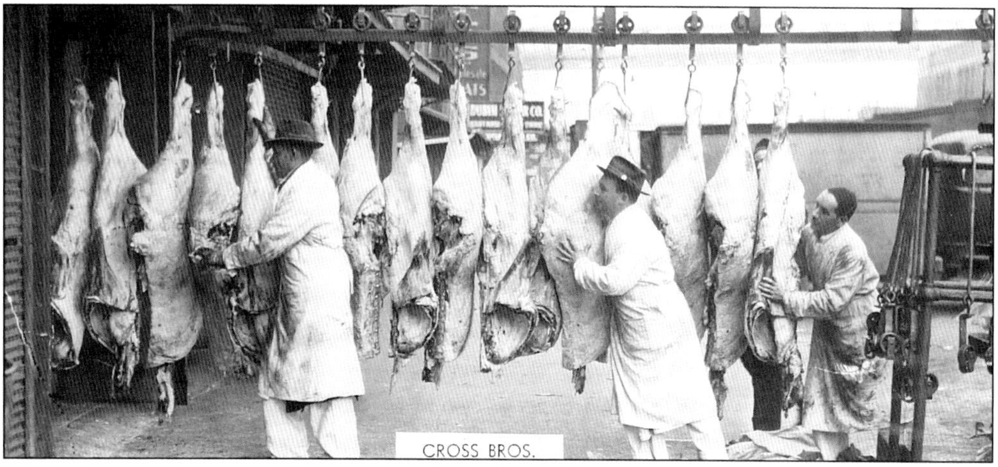


**CROSS BROTHERS MEAT PACKING COMPANY.** The Cross Brothers Meat Packing House served many Kosher Butchers across the city. The slaughterhouse located at 220 Moore Street was one of many operations overseen by Chief Rabbi B.L. Levinthal and the Vaad Hakaruth (kosher inspection staff) in the early 1940s. A neighbor on Moore Street recalled some cattle that ran loose down the middle of the street during WW II, and people went scurrying for safety jumping up on the wooden porches just like in the wild west. At one time, Cross Brothers serviced 450 Kosher Meat outlets. As times changed, so did the industry. Sam Lotman, a competitor, created Keystone Foods, which services the McDonald's restaurants with beef in the Mid-Atlantic States. (Courtesy of Urban Archives, Temple University, Philadelphia, Pennsylvania.)

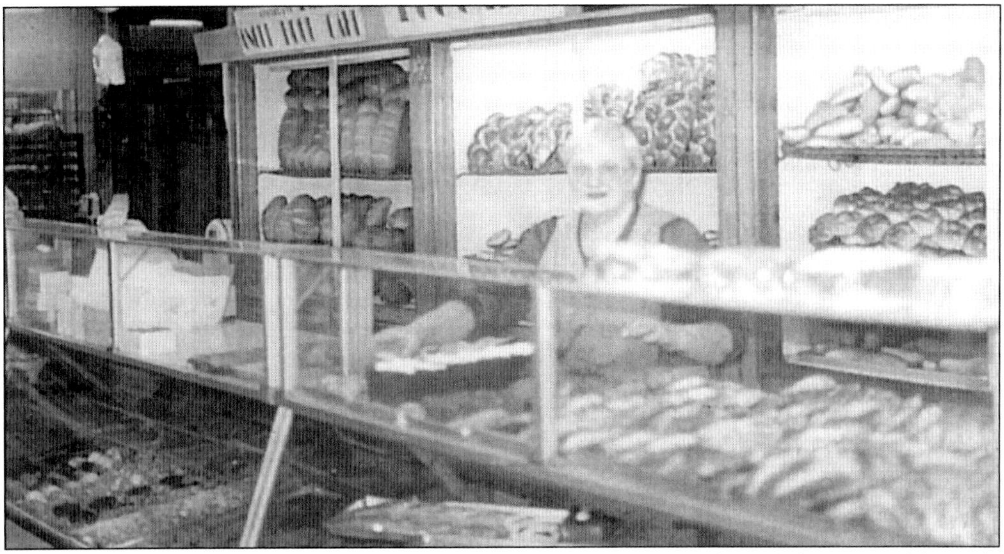

**LIPKIN'S BAKERY.** At age 15, Jacob Lipkin escaped conscription in the Polish army and he stole aboard a ship bound to America, in 1913. One day out at sea, the captain discovered Jacob and he had Jacob's one leg overboard when Jacob cried out, "I'm a baker." Jacob remained aboard the ship until it came into New York Harbor, where he was thrown overboard. He reached shore more dead than alive. Jacob migrated to South Philadelphia and opened a bakery shop at Fourth and McKean Streets, and he joined Local #6 the Bakers Union. Today, four generations of bakers including Jacob's son Abe, his sons, Mitch and Jerry, plus a nephew, David, service many ethnic groups with their daily bread and pastries in Northeast Philadelphia. (Courtesy of Mitch Lipkin.)

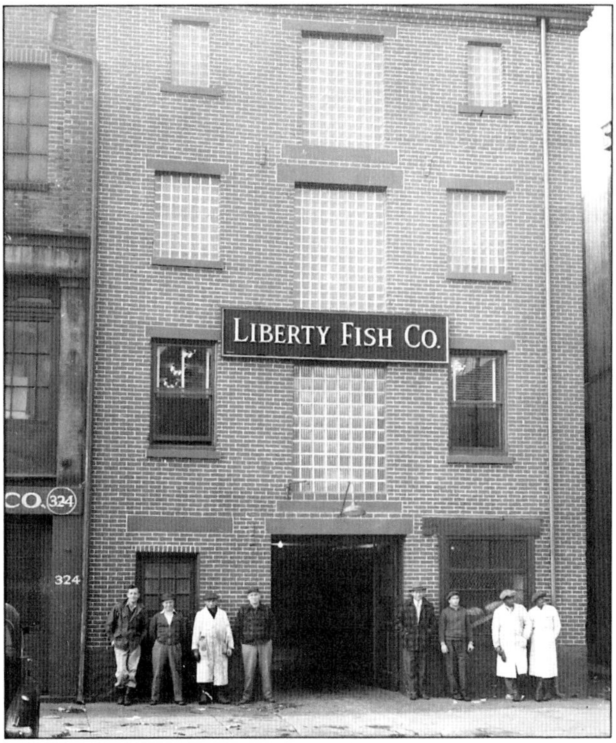


**LIBERTY FISH COMPANY.** Jacob and Ida Goldstein sold fresh fish, including carp, pike, mullet, and perch after they arrived in America from Russia, in 1908. Ida gave advice with each sale to the women, who made gefilte (stuffed) fish, a Friday night traditional meal, to avoid tasting raw fish for seasoning, to prevent a severe illness. The business, originally at 614 S. Fourth, included Jacob's sons, Lewis, Stanley, Fritz, and Sam, along with Fritz's son Jonathan, and expanded to seven stores in Philadelphia. The Goldstein boys formed the Liberty Fish Company, with a warehouse at 322 S. Delaware Avenue, off Dock Street, which moved to the Food Distribution Center on Pattison Avenue in the 1960s. (Courtesy of Fritz Goldstein.)

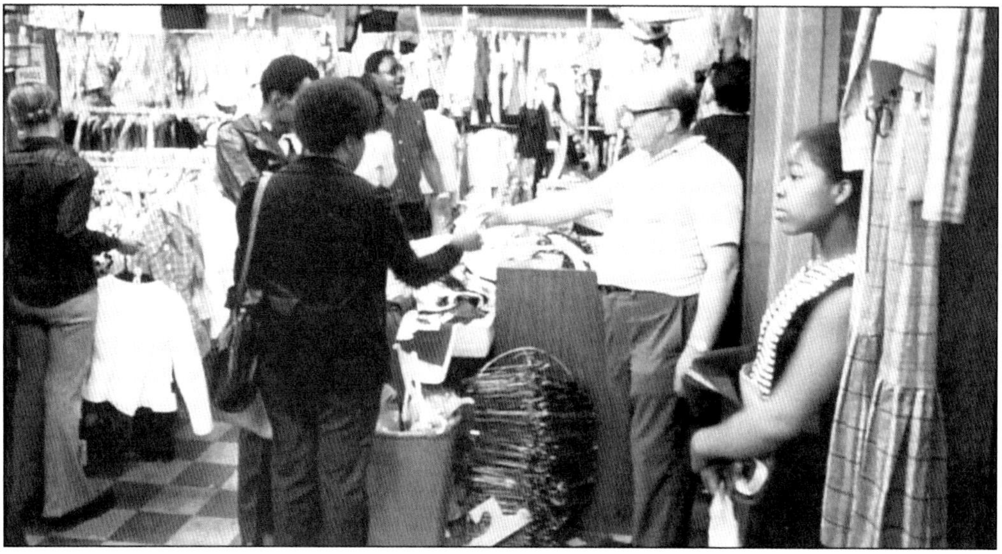

**IRV ZISS ON S. NINTH STREET.** Irv Ziss, a Yeshiva student from Galicia, stole away on a ship bound for America to escape Hitler, in 1938. After arriving in Canada, Irv entered the United States, without papers, as a salesman's assistant who traveled to New York City. Irv came to Philadelphia, married Faggie Schiff, and started his clothing business on South Ninth Street at Washington Avenue with advice from his brother-in law, Dave Black, who had a store on S. Seventh Street. Irv's new world revolved around his family in South Philadelphia. (Courtesy of Howard and Freya ( Ziss) Nemiroff.)

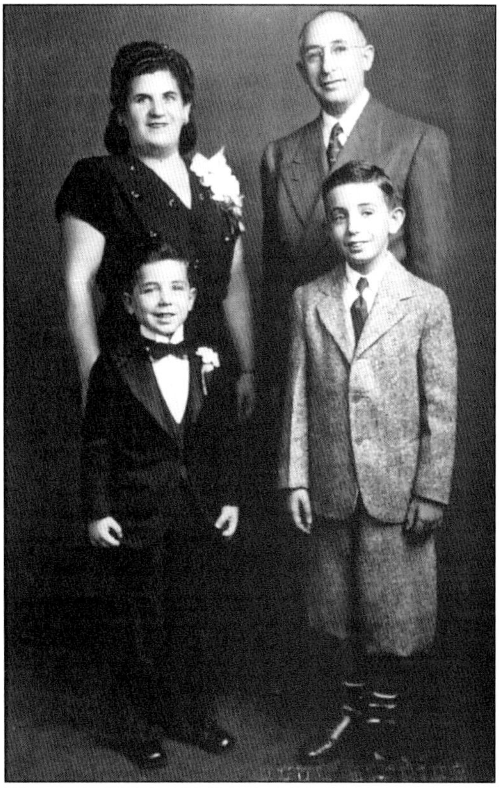

**LEIBOVITZ FAMILY, SHOPKEEPER ON S. NINTH.** Abe and Dora Leibovitz left Russia for the voyage to America, in 1923. The Leibovitz family settled at 1032 South Ninth Street above Washington Avenue where they had a children's wear shop with living quarters upstairs. The Leibovitz children, Norman and Harry, had friends up and down the Nineter (Ninth St.), an open-air market with the Route #47 trolley car running up the middle of the street. Other Jewish merchants in the 1950s included Tarlow's Chernoff Dresses, Evantosh Hosiery, Kay Dresses, Herb Dresses, Felix Syrikus (the Big Store), Silverman Dresses, Rudder's Sport Shop, Max & Morris Wilk Silks, Moskow's Children Clothes, and Sopolsky's. (Courtesy of Norman Leibovitz.)

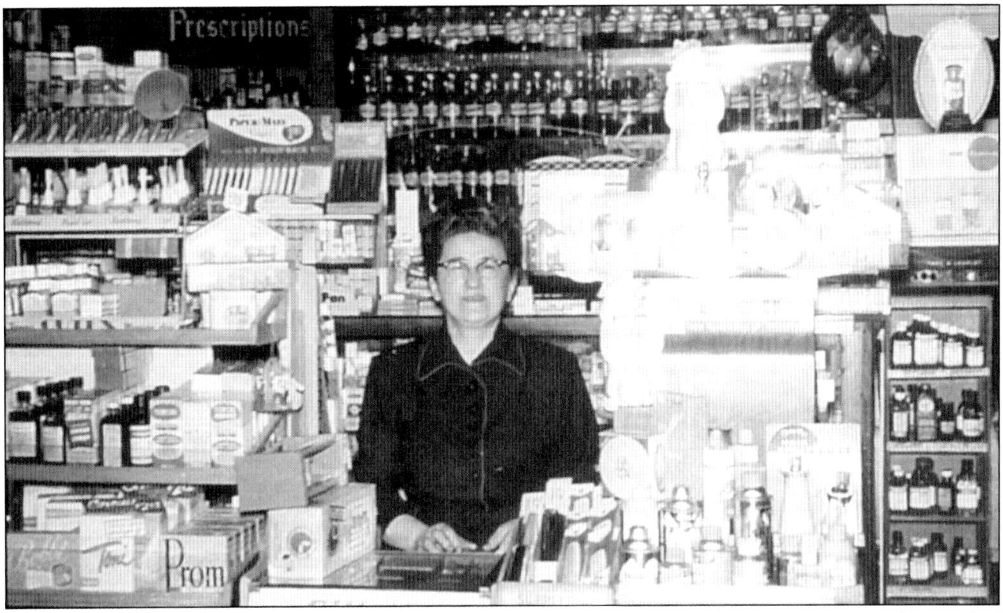


**MRS. CARTON, A PHARMACIST.** Ruth and Bernard Carton escaped Bessarabia and traveled as a young family unit to America in 1914. The Carton family settled in South Philadelphia at Ninth and Porter Streets near the new Shari Eli Synagogue. Ruth, one of several women pharmacists in South Philadelphia, opened her business with her husband during WW I to aid people who came down with the flu. The Carton Pharmacy moved in the 1940s to Fourth and Snyder Avenues. (Courtesy of Reba Carton Wallner.)

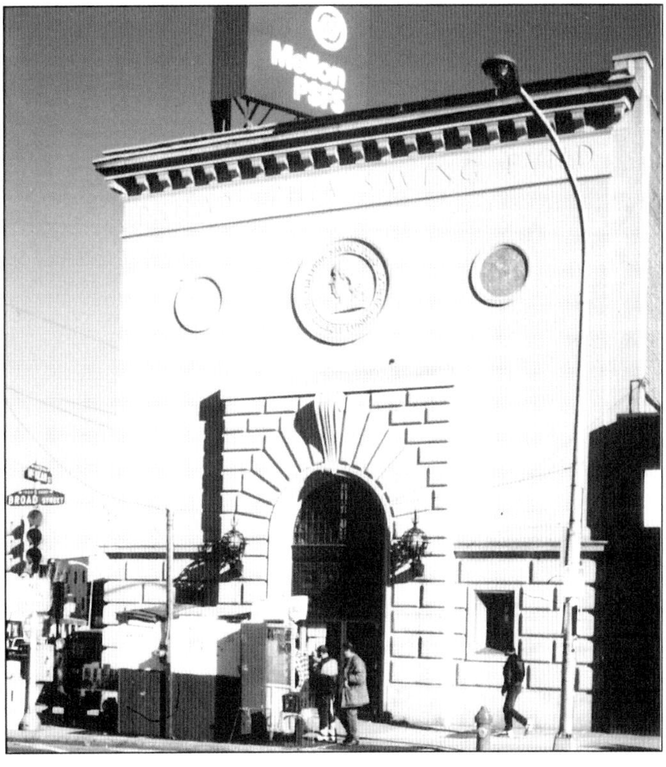


**PSFS AT BROAD AND MCKEAN STREETS.** Walking in South Philadelphia was the biggest pastime. Rose Ponnock (of blessed memory) frequently walked more than ten blocks from Sixth and Morris Streets over to Broad and McKean Streets to pay her gas and electric bills at the PSFS (Philadelphia Savings Fund Bank) and her phone bill across Broad Street. "The trip to pay bills with my bubbie (grandmother) in the summertime was a very long walk as I remember as a child. The reward for such a long schlep included a chocolate water ice purchased on South Seventh Street." (Courtesy Allen Meyers.)

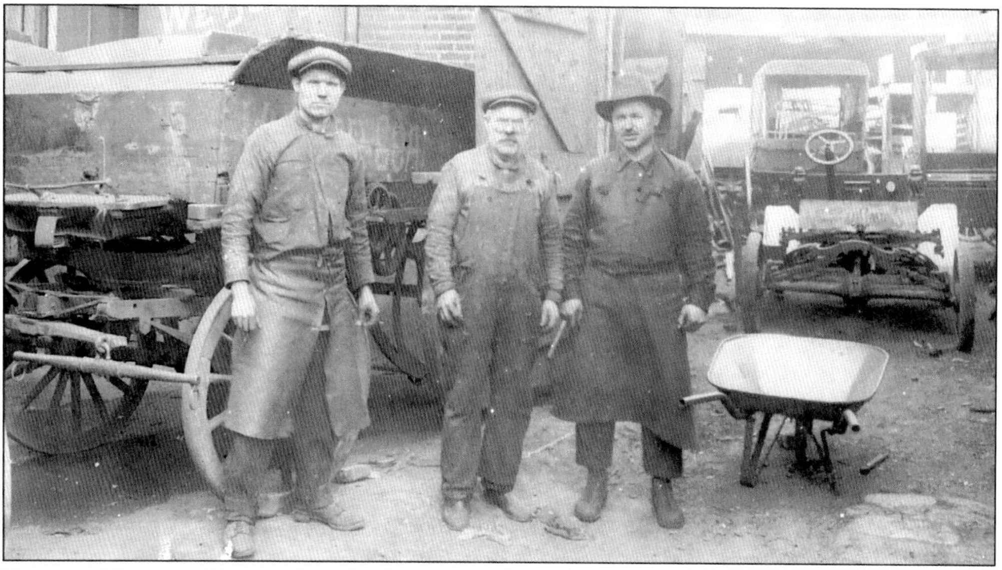

**DRIBAN WAGON WORKS.** Sam Driban came from the town of Driban in Ukraine, Russia, in 1911, where he was a blacksmith and wagon master. The Driban family, including their sons Pete and Hyman, settled near Second and Wharton Streets, where Sam built a garage to construct wagons and truck bodies. He peddled everything from Javela water (bleach), to house dresses, to fruit and produce, including freshly ground horseradish. Later, Ford Motors sold Sam's chassis, and he built up the sides of the trucks for Waldman Ice & Coal, Frank's Beverages, and Quaker Moving & Storage Co. (Courtesy of Sandy Wizov and Richard Driban.)

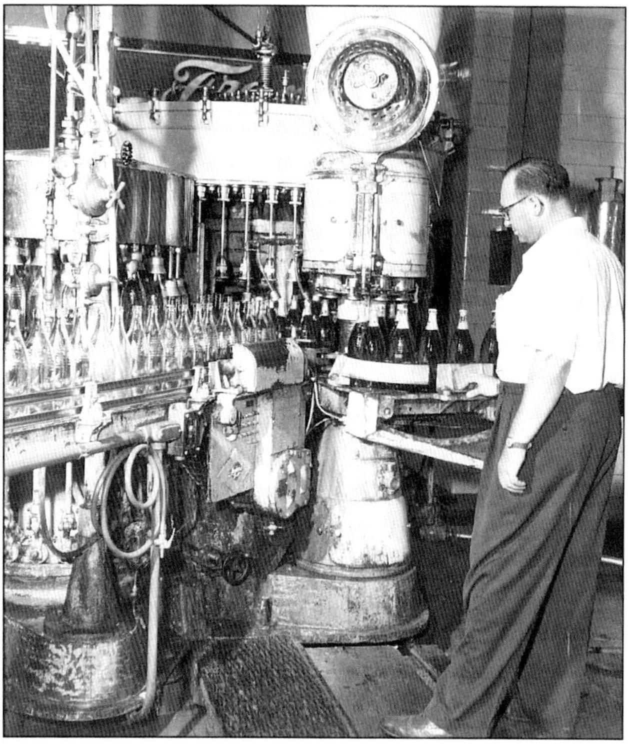

**FRANK'S SODA WORKS.** Sanford Frank joined others in Philadelphia selling his soda water product from a pushcart in the early 1900s. The Frank Soda plant was a landmark on S. Sixth Street near Moore with a connecting bottling tunnel where scores of Jews worked to create fresh fruit sodas such as Cherry Wisknak. Many members of Jerry Shatzman's family, along with Bernie Reiter and Sam Broustein, labored at Frank's. Rabbi Novoseller of Wynnefield, who placed his name with "KP" ( Kosher for Passover) on the bottle cap, to insure the lack of corn syrup in the soda water, also labored there. (Courtesy Urban Archives, Temple University, Philadelphia, Pennsylvania.)

# *Six*

# Time Out

## Sports, movie Theatres, Vacation Spots, Playgrounds, Street Activities, and Parks

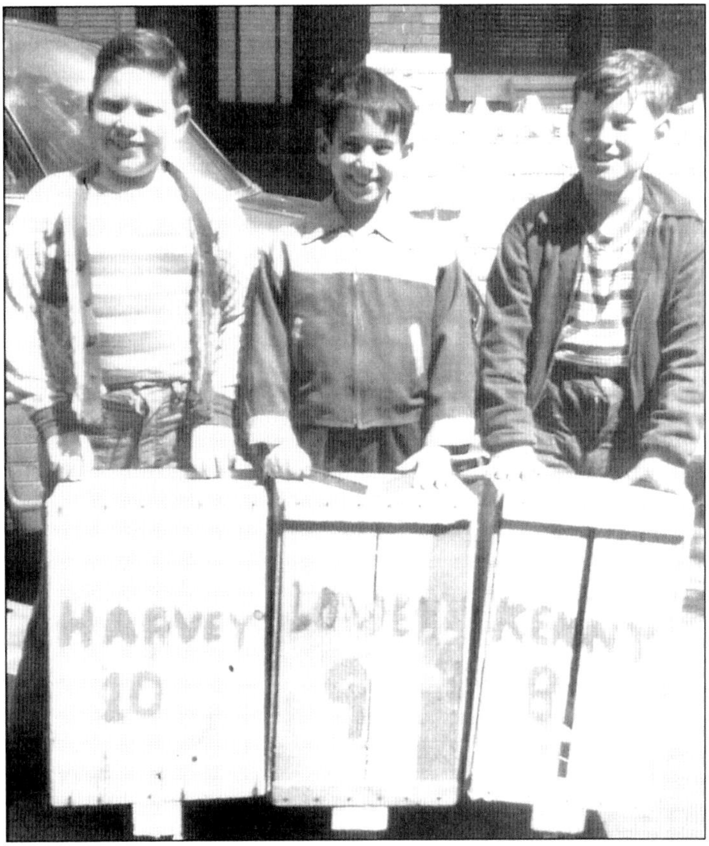


**Street Scooters.** Due to limited resources, creativity and imagination were common traits of children in South Philadelphia. The most popular and easiest item to build by young children included the street scooter. Boys went over to S. Seventh Street and collected wooden fruit crates, and with an old pair of roller skates, metal beverage caps, and a two by four piece of wood they were in business. Kenny Felstein, Lowell Green, and Harvey Warren drove the neighbors crazy with the noise from the scooters on the pavements. (Courtesy Lowell Green.)

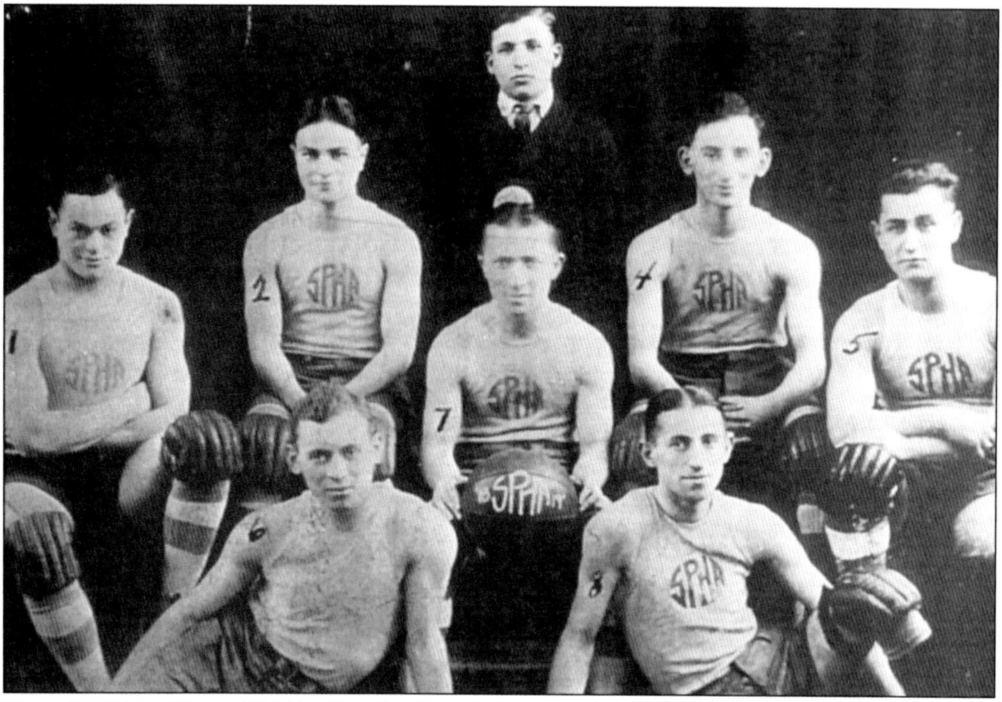


**THE SPHA'S.** The SPHA's (South Philadelphia Hebrew Association), created after its coach, Eddie Gottlieb, was graduated from Southern High in 1918, was the forerunner of the Philadelphia Warriors Basketball team. The team played double headers at the Broadwood Hotel on North Broad Street, and after the games, a citywide dance was held for Jewish singles for a $1.50. The original team included Lou Schneiderman, Chickie Passon, David Mondres, Hughey Black, Manny Davidson, Abe Radel, and Charley Newman. Many Jews from South Philadelphia played on the team, including Reds Sheer, who later owned the Saginaw Camp in the Poconos. (Courtesy of Marti Berk and the new Philadelphia Jewish Sports Hall of Fame and Museum at the Gersham Y-Jewish Community Centers of Greater Philadelphia.)

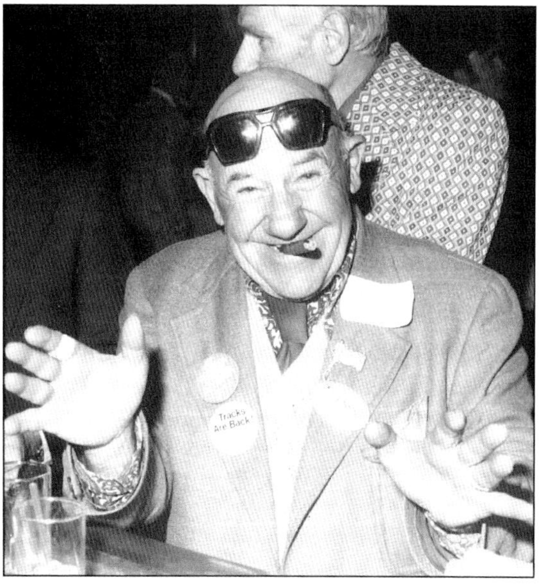

**YO YO SOUTH PHILADELPHIA CHARACTERS.** Yo Yo Schifrin, a lovable character, added color to all games with his presence and style of support for the players when he arrived at the SPHA's home games. Yo Yo hung out at various South Philadelphia retail stores, especially Lipkins bakery at Fourth and McKean Streets. At the bakery he practiced his favorite line on Mitch Lipkin as a child, "do you have have a cigareto?" Yo Yo was one of many memorable characters, including "the King of the Jews" Marvin Batoff; a big burly man, Moxie, who hung at the pool room at Ninth and Porter Streets; and Crazy May, who fought for the downtown Jews. (Courtesy of Sandy Wizov.)

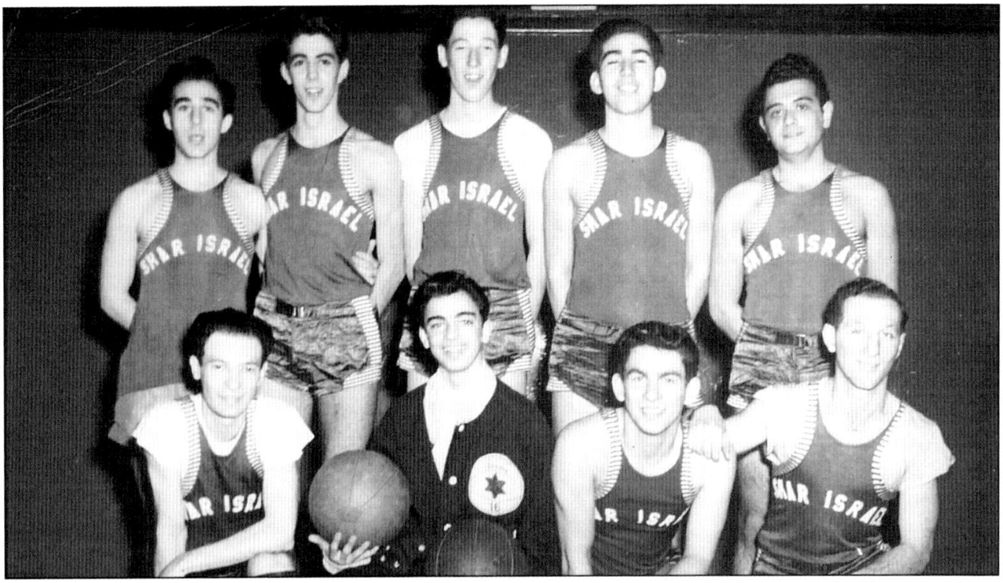


**SHAR ISRAEL BASKETBALL TEAM.** The Jewish Basketball League, composed of teams from synagogues and organizations around the city, played at the new YMHA. The YMHA was built at S. Broad and Pine Streets with its roof top courts enclosed with a chain-linked fence, in 1924. Young men who did not join the Winton Tigers or the Meteors semi-pro baseball teams near Third and Porter Streets, formed a basketball team, bought letters on S. Seventh Street, and sewed them to their jerseys. When the team won the championship, the orthodox synagogue Shar Israel at Fourth and Porter officially adopted them. (Courtesy of Sandy Wizov.)

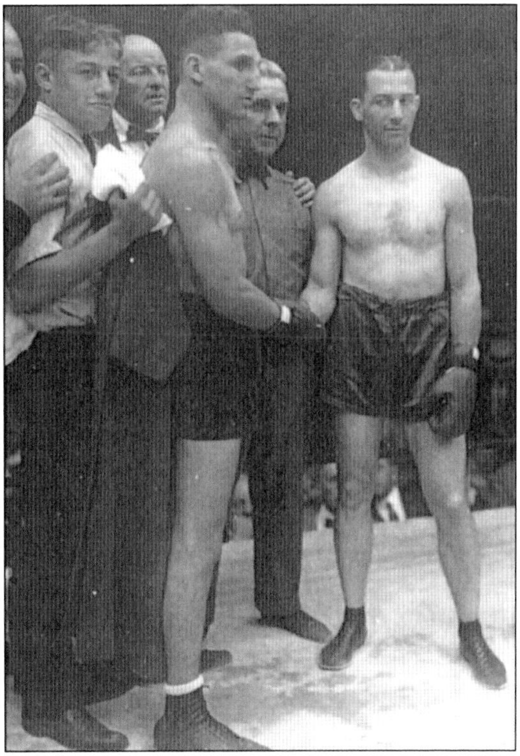

**LOU TENDLER.** Sports activities gave many children an opportunity to dream and later execute their ambitions in South Philadelphia. The selection of one sport, whether it be basketball, baseball, football, or street games, was exceeded only in popularity by the sport of boxing. Some areas in South Philadelphia demanded the ability to fistfight in order to survive on the way to school. Lou Tendler, from South Philadelphia, provided that role model. His career included a match up with Benny Leonard in 1923 at Yankee Stadium, which drew a large crowd of 59,000 spectators. (Courtesy of J. Russell Peltz.)

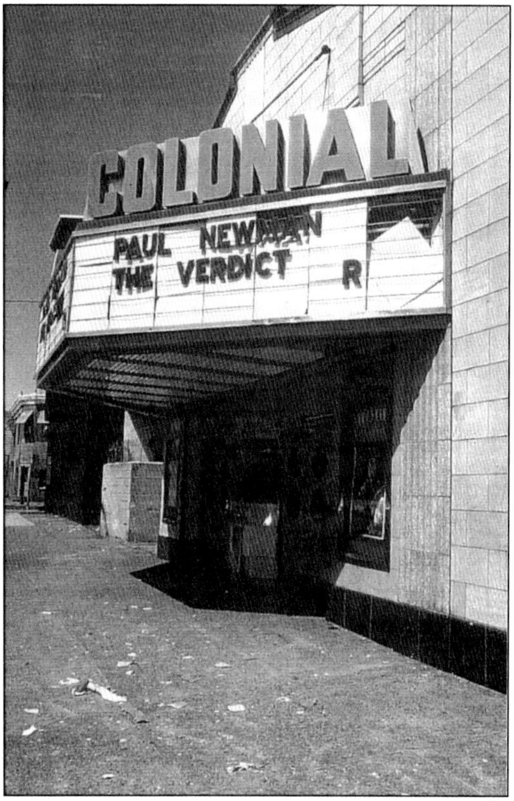


**The Colonial Movies.** The era of vaudeville, silent movies, and talkies (movies with sound), provided the Jewish East European immigrant families in South Philadelphia a form of entertainment and education. Whole auditoriums, including the Colonial Movies at Tenth and Moyamensing Avenues were filled with young children supervised only by older siblings in the 1920s, 30s, and 40s. The popularity of the movie theater was not universal. Observant Jews denied their children permission to patronize the movie houses on Saturdays to prevent the desecration of the Sabbath. (Courtesy of Rick Spector.)

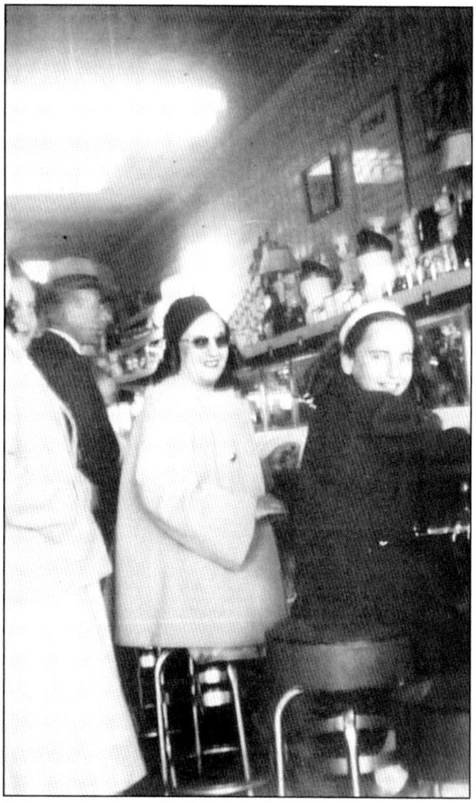

**Soda Fountain Shot.** The familiar soda fountain snapshot took place throughout South Philadelphia and included Feldman's Ice Cream parlor at Fourth and Snyder, Allen's 24-Hour Diner at Fifth and Reed, Tartak's at Sixth and Dickinson, Goldberg's candy store at Seventh and Mountain, Koniver's Sandwich Shop at Fourth and Synder, Kramer's and Nate's both at Eighth and Porter, and many other family-style stores. Ice cream sodas became a tradition after the movie theaters let out, but drinking soda water was reserved for special occasions because it was very dear in the family's weekly budget. When the order was given, children gladly ran with a 25¢-piece in one hand and a tall pitcher in the other to have filled at their favorite soda fountain. (Courtesy of Arnold Needleman.)

## South Philadelphia Movie Theatres

A Threatre is a building for rent according to Irv Glazer. The facility must have some seats and a stage. Orginially the vaudeville acts were performed in South Philadelphia for the immigrant audiences with only action and no dialog. Then the introduction of the silent films filled the same halls of recreation and orchestras were hired to accent the activity in the movie Finally, the talkies came into voque and still many Jewish people only went to see the pictures because their English was weak.

Many Nickelodeons were nameless and they only occupied a store front. If the business was brisk and they lasted more than six months a name was adopted. The admission was a mere nickel and thus the term *Nickelodeon* was coined in the early 1900's

**Aurora Picture Parlor 5$^{th}$/ Morris**
a converted stable designed by
Louis Fein in 1913

**Colonial Theatre 1025 W. Moyamensing**
One of five theatre around the city with same name

**Crystal Palace 1706 S. 7$^{th}$**
Originally it was a nickelodeon

**Empress Theatre 1811 S. 7$^{th}$**
This movie house was third or fourth run place
which meant usually a year passed before it
was first shown on South Broad Street

**Grand Theatre NW cor 7$^{th}$ & Snyder**
Originally the building was a church.
Seats ranged in price....from 5 to 11 cents

**Jackson Theatre 513 - 519 Jackson**
This was a family film house and
original Jazz Singer was shown
over and over again here

**Jerry Theatre 2029 S. 3$^{rd}$**
Orginally it was called the Southern
The gimmick during the depression to
lure patrons began with free dishes
as gifts every Tues night

**Ideal Theatre 2203-2207 S. 6$^{th}$**
Originally it was known as the Academy
This was known as the *I-Dump*
Jewish films of with sub titles in Russian
and Yiddish often were shown
Bea Schwartz won a pair of roller skates
from the Ideal, which became *community property*

**Lyric Theatre 201 Morris**
Originally known as the Gregory
Jay Eichler fell asleep in the theatre
and he was locked in all night when
he was a kid

**Mirror Theatre 5$^{th}$ & Reed**
This theatre was popular due
to it closeness to the Mt. Sinai Hospital
and the 24 hour Allen's Luncheonette

**Morris Theatre 2029 S. 10$^{th}$**
This theatre observed the blue laws
which meant it was closed on Sunday
until the repeal of the laws in the late 1930's

**Penn Theatre 1426 S 4$^{th}$**
On Saturday afternoons, the children and
adults were treated to an organist who
played music to accompany the silent films

**Strafford Theatre NE cor 7$^{th}$ & Dickson**
During the Depression the children collected
the three union labels from the ends of
Jewish rye bread and received a free pass

**The First Run Theatres on South Broad Street**
Included South Theatre at 1412 S Broad Street,
Savoia at 1709 S. Broad Street and the Comique
at 2408 S. Broad Street

**The Broadway Theatre 2042 S. Broad Street**
Movie Stars with new cars often appeared
to promote their films at the largest movie
house on South Broad Street

**LIST OF MOVIE THEATERS.** The movie houses were more organized than the vaudeville and silent film/talkies establishments. A preview of coming attractions spread across the darkened auditorium. Newsreels informed the viewers of world-wide current events. Cartoons came next, and then the serials about the Wild West with a featured cowboy, or science fiction shows that featured Flash Gordon. Finally, after two hours, the feature film came on and the children clapped their hands as their childhood stars appeared bigger than life on the silver screen. (Compiled by Allen Meyers with aid of the Senior Adults at the Stiffel Center, at Marshall and Porter Streets; a member of the Jewish Community Centers of Philadelphia, where I conducted the class "South Philadelphia Memories" from 1991-1993; and an interview with Philadelphia's Movie Theater Historian, Ivr Glazer (of Blessed Memory) on June 1, 1992.)

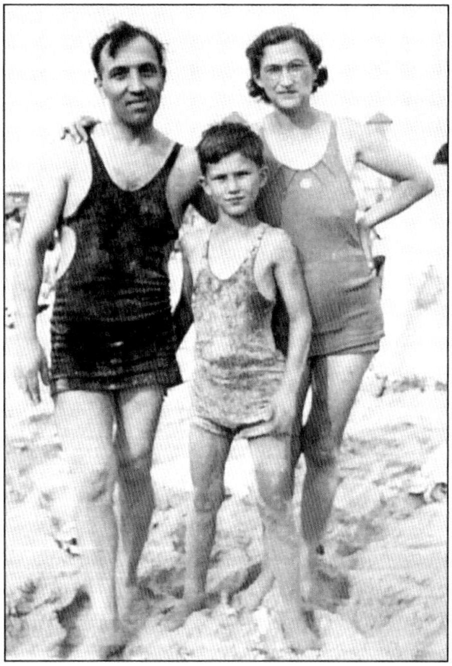

**EVANTOSH FAMILY IN ATLANTIC CITY.** Bernie Evantosh enjoyed the summertime trips to Atlantic City with his parents, Harry and Fanny, in the 1930s. The beach by day was hot, and sometimes the woolen bathing suits shrunk so much people had to buy new ones everyday while at the beach. At night, Atlantic City was full of fun with live shows performed by Yiddish actors at the Stratmore, Schuman, Chorney, and Stein's Royal Palms Hotel. (Courtesy of Bernie Evantosh.)

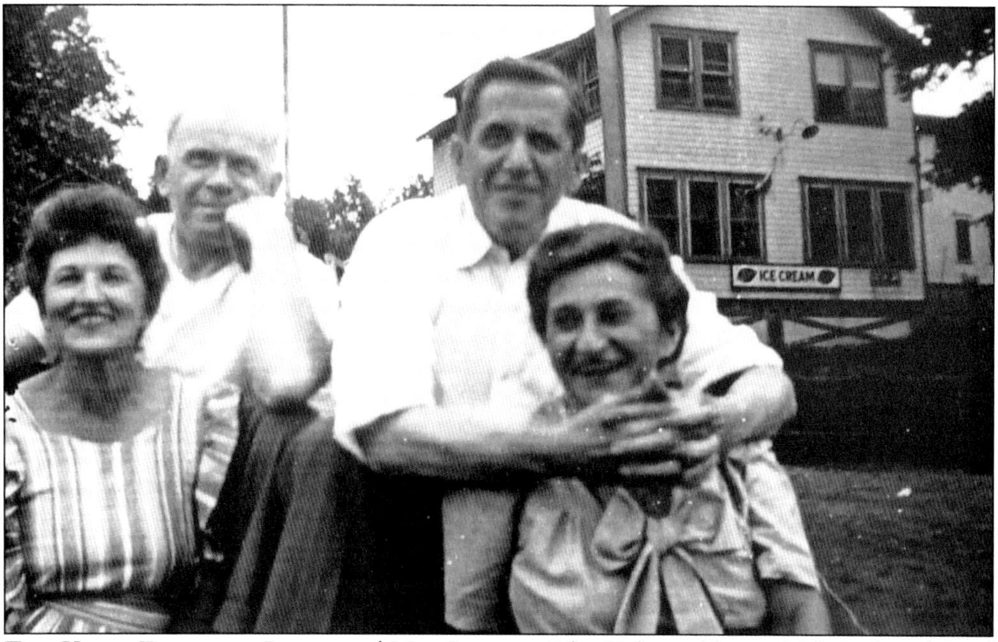


**THE KAHN FAMILY IN JEWTOWN/ MT. LAUREL.** The Kahns, Abe and Mary, founders of the Southwark Paint Company at 801 S. Fourth Street, spent time with their friends, Ann and Walter Weiss, in Jewtown. Walter was an active South Philadelphia politician, who migrated every year to Jewtown (a Jewish summer resort on Hartford Road in Mt. Laurel, New Jersey) during the 1930s. Jewish families from Philadelphia stayed at Jewish farm summer resorts in Norma and Blackwood, New Jersey, plus Collegeville, Willow Grove, and Warrington, Pennsylvania, until the end of WW II when air travel became popular. (Courtesy of Kenneth Kahn.)

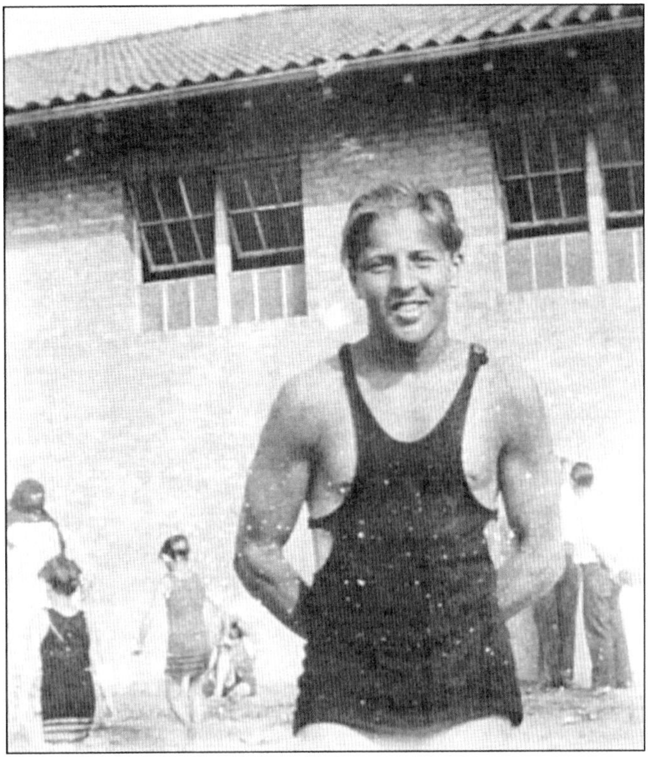

**THE SWIMMIES.** South Philadelphia had several public swimming pools nicknamed the swimmies after WW I. Hy Soll joined his friends at Tenth and Moore for swim meets and competed with swimmers from the Carpenter Street pool near Eighth Street. The kids at Edward O' Malley recreation center bypassed the rules for getting into the swimming pool more than one time per day by changing into their street clothes and then placing their swim trunks in the middle of Fourth Street where car traffic squeezed all the water out of them until they dried. The lifeguard only allowed children into the pool if their swim trunks were dry. (Courtesy of Arthur Soll.)

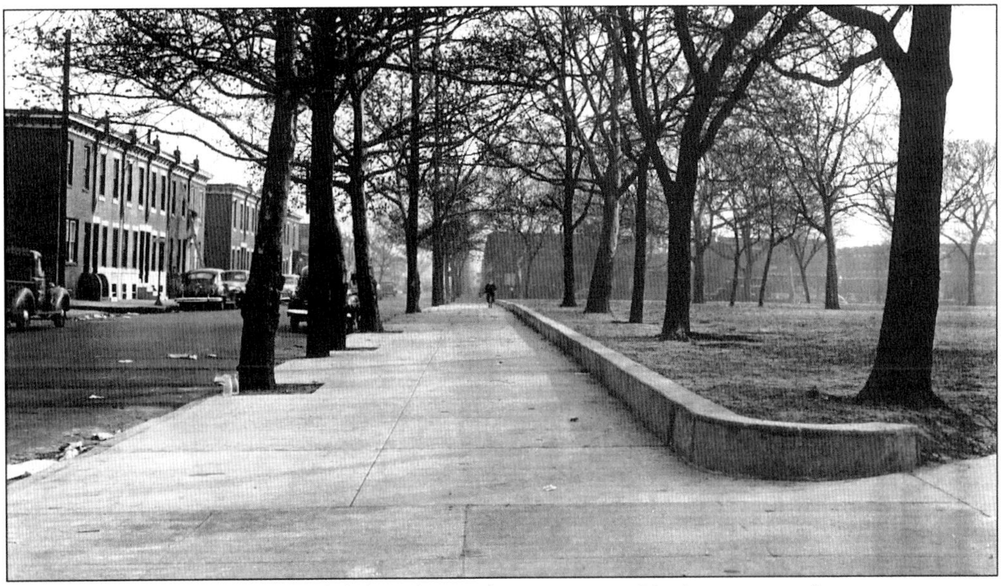

**MIFFLIN PARK.** South Philadelphia devoted one square block to one of its green spaces including Mifflin Square Park bounded by Fifth and Sixth and Ritner and Wolf Streets. The park served as the end of the trolley Routes #9 and #50 terminal. Synagogues faced the park and clusters of old Jewish men sat on the wooden benches under the shade of the maple trees arguing their interpretations of the Talmud, while young mothers with infants strolled nearby. The immigrants enjoyed the seasonal changes, especially the burning of leaves. (Courtesy of the Philadelphia City Archives.)

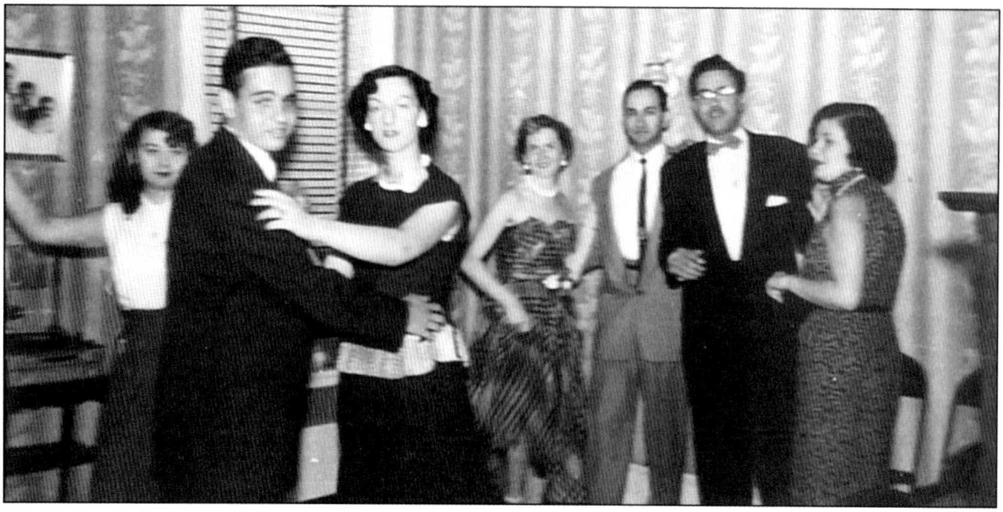

**GATHERINGS/PARLOR MEETINGS.** The popular way to meet other Jewish people in South Philadelphia included the parlor meetings (gatherings) on Saturday nights. The girls customarily invited the guys to 1612 S. Seventh Street for potato chips, pretzels, ice cream, dancing, and socializing, while their parents took long walks on S. Seventh to browse and visit their friends. The circle of friends often led to courtships and weddings. (Courtesy of Zachary Kaplan.)

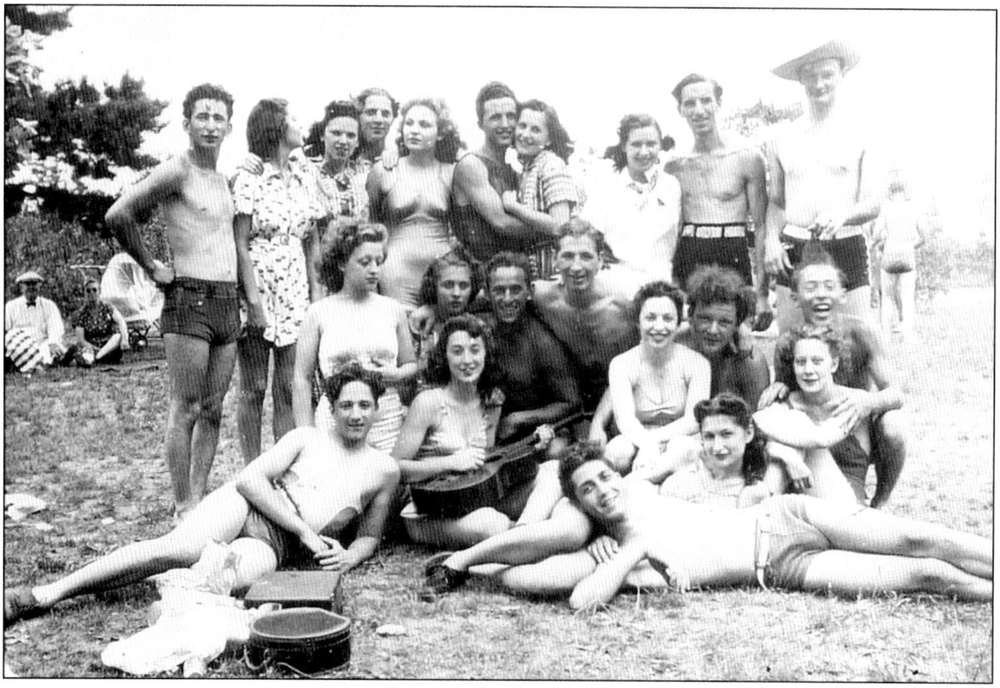

**LEAGUE ISLANDS-THE LAKES.** Day trips to amusement parks around the city organized by high school groups, included Sigma Alpha Rho Fraternity. They established Theta, their third high school chapter, at Southern High School in 1921. Nearby League Island, below Pattison Avenue and accessible by the trolley Route #2, served as the most popular South Philadelphia spot with a swimming pool, picnic grounds, and outdoor pavilion. The girls always brought the food as part of the contract. (Courtesy of Morris Grossman.)

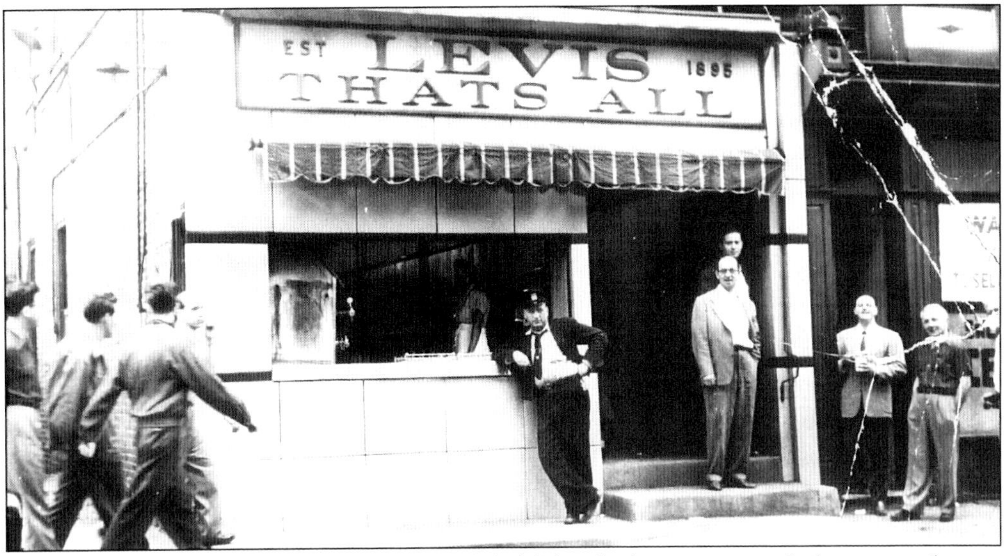


**LEVIS HOT DOGS.** Abe Levis was sent to Philadelphia by his parents in Lithuania at the age of 14, to escape conscription into the Czar's army. In 1892, at age 21, he married Anna Solo, and two years later, they started a lifelong hot dog business in the immigrant neighborhood on S. Sixth below Lombard Street. The simple menu of hot dogs, fishcakes, Champ Cherry, and chocolate sodas was an immediate success. Abe is credited with inventing the long hot dog bun, and his business served as the unofficial headquarters of the Republican Party in the Fifth Ward for many years into the 20th century. (Courtesy of Marc Polish, last owner of Levis Hot dogs.)

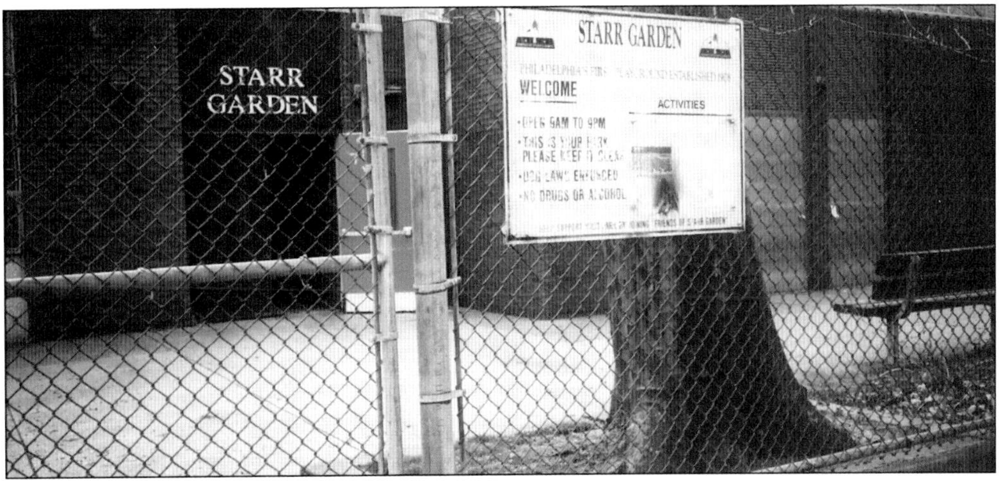


**STARR GARDEN PLAYGROUND AND PARK.** Starr Garden Playground opened as the first municipal recreation center throughout America, in 1908. The one-square block originally designated as a park, became a second home to many children of various ethnic groups who lived in the area across from Levis Hot dogs. The playground sponsored the Jewish Basketball League, which fielded a neighborhood team in 1908. Dorothy Weiner(t), daughter of Jacob and Reba, won the runner's contest which preceded the Penn Relay races in 1912, and Sam Weiner(t) came from Rosenhayn, New Jersey, to play baseball. He later made the Philadelphia Phillies, in the 1920s. (Courtesy of Allen Meyers.)

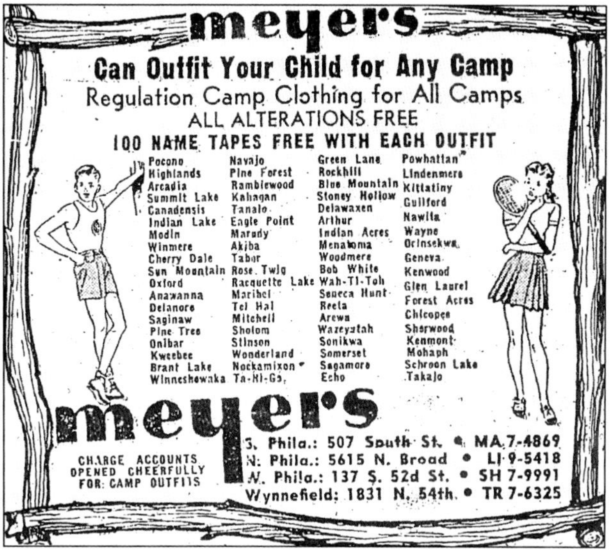


**MEYERS CAMP OUTFITTERS.** The thrill of going to camp included the selection of the proper boys' or girls' attire for overnight camps throughout Philadelphia, the Pocono Mountains, and New Jersey. The Meyers clothing store, at 507 South, along with the sale, counseled the children on their first experience to an overnight camp. Many of the summer camps were run by organizations such as Brith Sholom, while others were independently owned by South Philadelphia Jews, such as Camp Saginaw. What summer camp do you remember attending as a child? (Courtesy of Irv Bruskin.)

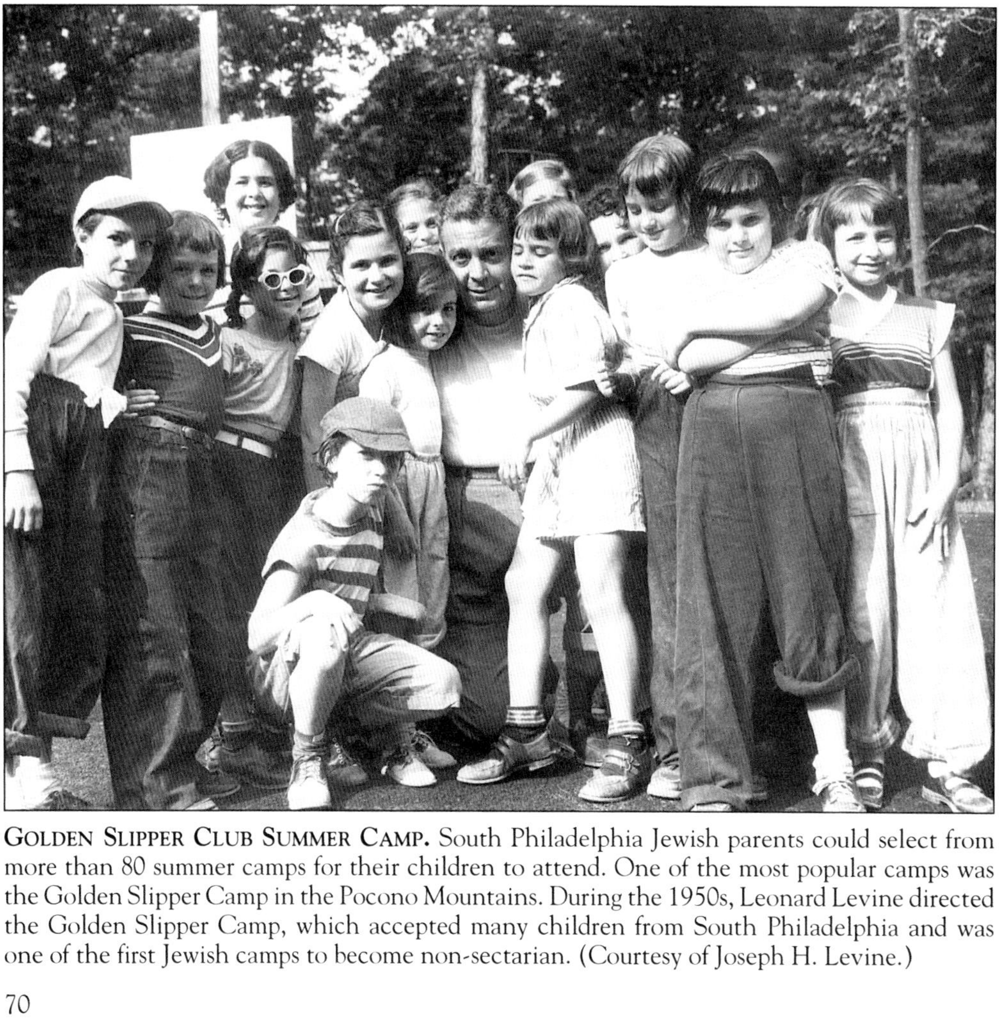

**GOLDEN SLIPPER CLUB SUMMER CAMP.** South Philadelphia Jewish parents could select from more than 80 summer camps for their children to attend. One of the most popular camps was the Golden Slipper Camp in the Pocono Mountains. During the 1950s, Leonard Levine directed the Golden Slipper Camp, which accepted many children from South Philadelphia and was one of the first Jewish camps to become non-sectarian. (Courtesy of Joseph H. Levine.)

**SOUTH PHILADELPHIA JEWISH STREET PARTY.** Street parties, another Philadelphia tradition, were adopted as a form of entertainment and served as a fund-raiser for Jewish organizations and synagogues in South Philadelphia. The Ladies Helping Hand Society engaged Dr. Louis Sorokin's Concert Band to play at the gala street affair that closed off Moyamensing Avenue in front of Joey Bishop's family (Gottlieb) bicycle shop in the early 1930s. The street party was different from the block party which helped to bond individual blocks together for a common cause such as the benefit of an individual family in desperate straits. (Courtesy of Hillard Sorokin.)

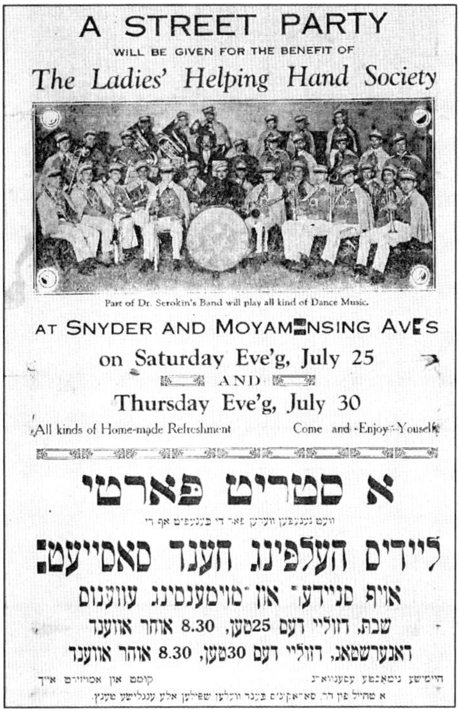


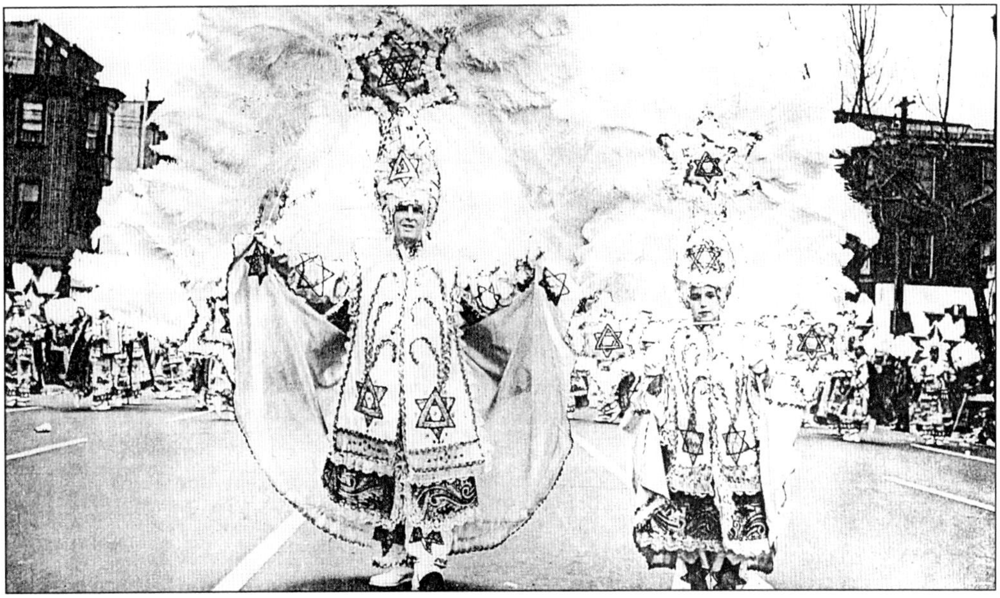

**MUMMERS AND JEWISH PARTICIPATION.** Contrary to popular belief, Jews participated in the Mummers Parade, which has ushered in the New Year in Philadelphia since 1901. The James Durning String Band, pictured above, marched up Broad Street in 1965 to the tune of Hativah, the Israeli National Anthem, led by Captain Arthur Gardner in a presentation of the Star of Israel. Students of the Music Settlement School at Fifth and Queen Streets added to the largest street pageantry in Philadelphia. Participation in the Mummers Parade by Jews conferred acceptance by their fellow Philadelphians as part of a greater community. (Courtesy of the Mummers Museum staff, Jack Cohen, Palma Lucas, Syd Kramer, and Bill Conners.)

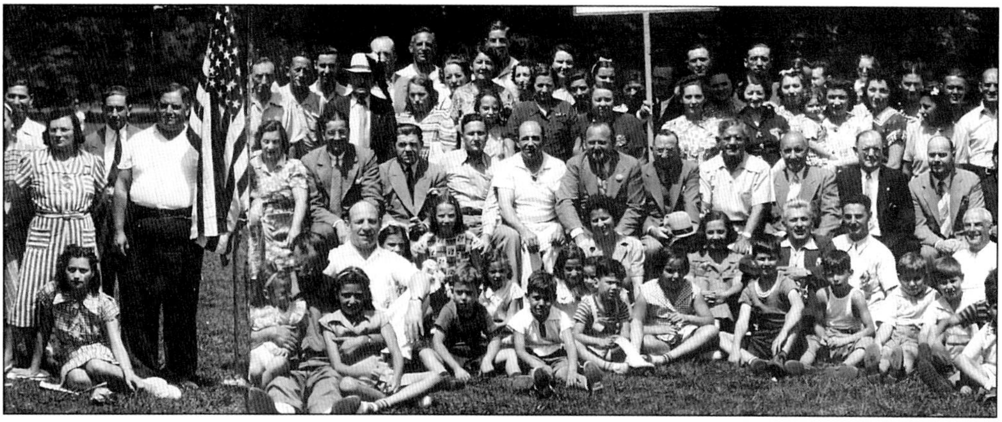

**SHOMRIM PICNIC IN THE PARK.** The Shomrim of Philadelphia represented the Jewish policemen and fire department personnel as a familiar society since 1937. The most revered local station house in South Philadelphia existed at Fourth and Snyder Avenues. The officers held social activities that revolved around their families to bond the Jewish personnel into one unit. A picnic was held in Woodside Park, on the west side of the Schuylkill River, in 1939 to unite the families before the outset of WW II. The ranks of the police and fire department swelled with Jewish personnel during the Depression, when jobs were hard to find. (Courtesy of Leonard Block.)

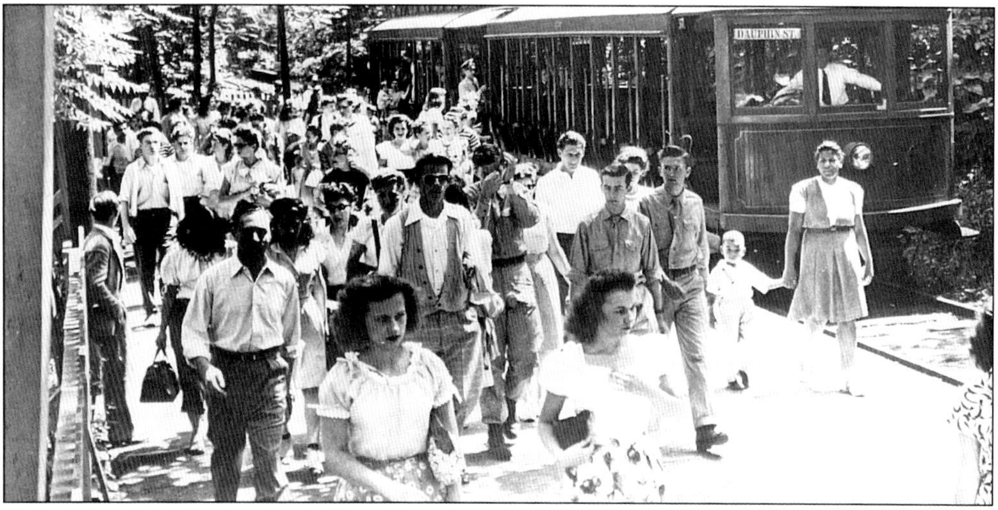

**PARK TROLLEY.** The open-air Fairmount Park Trolley, Philadelphia's greatest outdoor venue, connected Strawberry Mansion and the Parkside neighborhoods annually from April until October dating back to the late 1890s, via a ride through the most scenic terrain in the city. The trolley loop from Cherry's famous restaurant at 33rd and Dauphin Street stopped at ice cold water springs, the Robin Hood Dell (summer home to the Philadelphia Orchestra), an open-air amphitheater, the Schuylkill River to watch the regatta boat races, then crossed the river like a roller coaster before it entered Woodside Amusement Park and Crystal Pool next to the Philadelphia Country Club and Polo Grounds. The park trolley traveled over the great Belmont Plateau picnic area to its terminal near Memorial Hall (the Centennial Fairgrounds). The Fairmount Park Trolley bridged the generation gap with its famous Saturday and Sunday excursions for old and young alike. Although it stopped running in the 1950s, the trolley is etched in our memories forever! (Courtesy of the Urban Archives, Temple University, Philadelphia, Pennsylvania.)

# *Seven*

# The Education System: Public and Jewish Schools

## Talmud Torahs, Yeshiva, Private Chederim, and Meladim

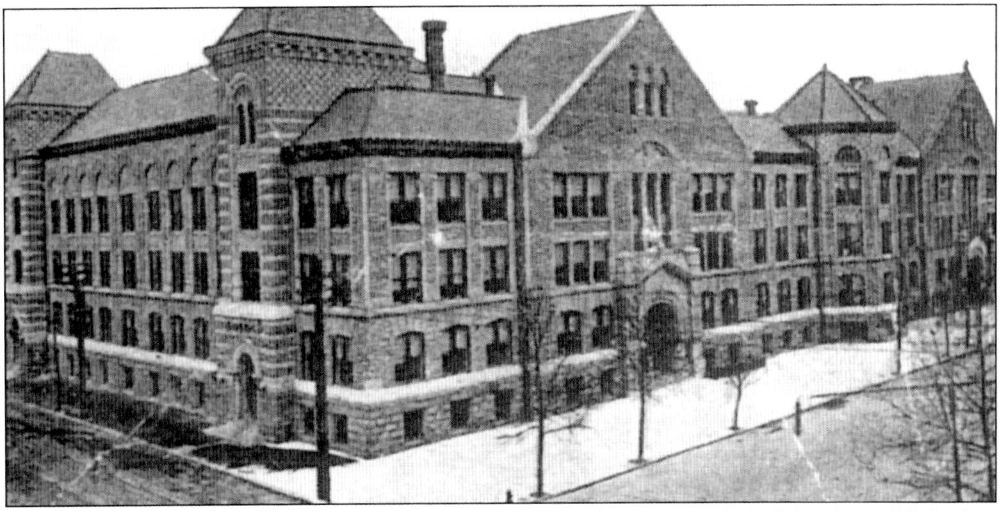

SOUTH PHILADELPHIA HIGH SCHOOL. Southern Manual Training High School, established in the late 19th century, developed into a large facility at Broad and Snyder Avenues. The school supplied academic discipline to both boys and girls through separate classes. The educational system in South Philadelphia assisted the Jewish East European immigrant's children to assimilate into the mainstream of American life by combing the best of both worlds—secular and Jewish—through the virtues of education and Jewish identity. Although many children, boys and girls alike, desired a diploma, more worthy goals, such as helping the family survive financially, took precedence over completing high school. Southern High School proudly produced Dr. Israel Goldstein, a 1911 graduate who became a nationally recognized Rabbi as well as the founder of Bradeis University, a Jewish sponsored institution (non-sectarian) of higher learning in Boston, in 1947. The Southern High School song started, "I'm glad I came to Southern; I wish the days were longer. . . " (Courtesy of Bill Esher, president of the Southern High School Alumni Association.)

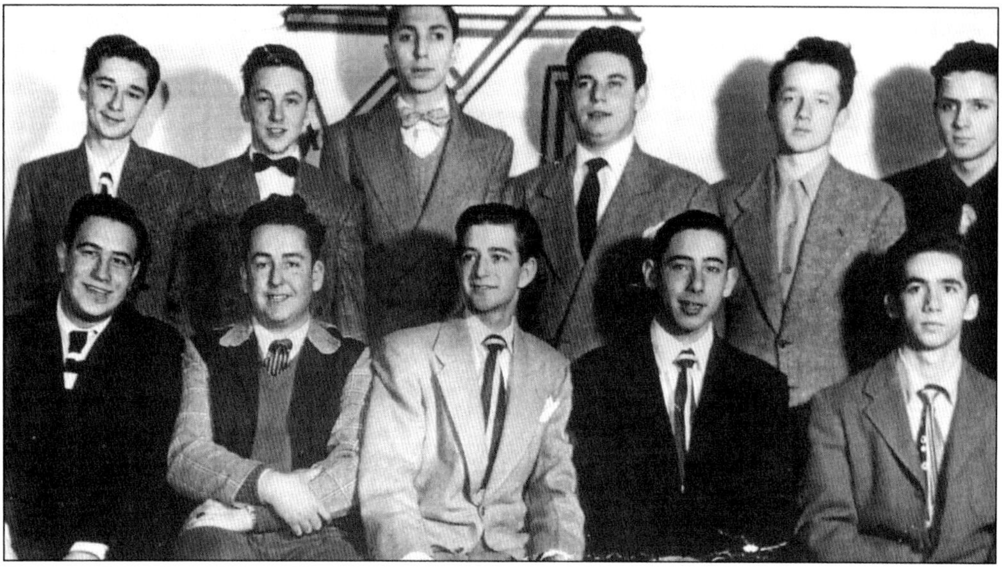

JEWISH FRATERNITY ALPHA BETA GAMMA. Pictured is the Alpha Beta Gamma Fraternity, one of five citywide chapters opened at Southern High School in the late 1930s. The "Nu" chapter rivaled the Sigma Alpha Rho Fraternity for loyalty. Sigma Alpha Rho competed by giving out scholarships, which Jay Meyers, Esq. was a recipient. Listed from left to right are as follows: (front row) Bobby Block, Arnold Kramer, Al Fox, Marshell Greenstein, and Al Katz met at the Neighborhood Center at Fifth and Bainbridge Streets on Sunday mornings. (Back row) Marvin Malnick, Eddie Merow, Murray Ginsburg, Jordan Demarsky, Carry Gurst, and Irv Goldsmith. Membership was the key function of the fraternity where recognition was considered Koved (an honor). (Courtesy of Bobby Block.)

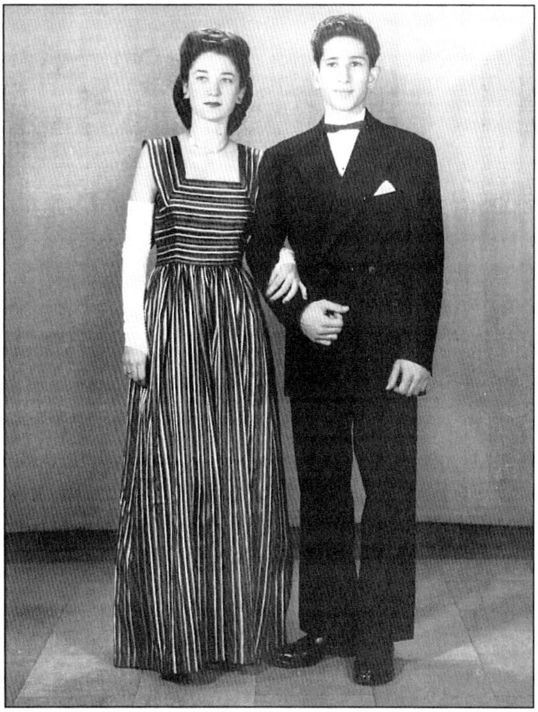

SOUTH PHILADELPHIA PROM PICTURES. A night to remember is what the students called their prom night. Sy Abramson and Ann Cohen posed at Jack's Roof Garden Room atop the Ritz Carlton near Rittenhouse Square at 19th and Walnut Streets during 1944. After the dance, the couple met two dozen friends and fellow students for breakfast at 4 a.m. at the Melrose Diner (15th and Passyunk Avenue). Strict rules of dating applied by parents included the selection of a Jewish date in order to attend the prom. (Courtesy of Bettyann Abramson Gray.)

## South Philadelphia Public Schools

### What Public School did you attend ?

| School | Location | Year |
|---|---|---|
| Alcorn, James | 34th & Wharton | 1889-1932 |
| Baldwin, Matthias | 16th & Porter | 1899 |
| Baugh, Joseph | Marshall & Dickinson | 1892-1924 |
| Binny, Horace | 6th & Spruce | 1872 |
| Benson, Matthias | 27th & Wharton | 1896 |
| Bok, Vocational High School | 9th & Wolf | 1938 |
| Calhoun | 10th & Synder | 1871 |
| Campbell, James | 8th & Fitzwater | 1900 |
| Catto, Octavius | 20th & Lombard | 1878-1913 |
| Chillds, George | 17th & Tasker | 1894 |
| Columbus, Christopher | 9th & Carpenter | 1913 |
| Durhan, Thomas | 16th & Lombard | 1910 |
| Fell | 9th & Oregon | 1913 |
| Florence | 8th & Catherine | 1875 |
| Furness, Jr. High School | 3rd & Mifflin | 1914 |
| Hawthorne, Nathaniel | 12th & Fitzwater | 1907 |
| School | 23rd & Federal | 1866-1923 |
| Lee, Richard | Front & Christian | 1913 |
| Levin, Handy Smith | 5th & Snyder | 1876-1913 |
| Key, Frances Scott | 8th & Wolf | 1914 |
| Kirkbride, Eliza | 7th & Dickinson | 1925 |
| Mc CallVocational | 6th & Delaney | 1911 |
| Mc Daniel, Delaplaine | 21st & Moore | 1892 |
| Meredith, William | 5th & Fitzwater | 1876-1930 |
| Morse, Sam | 2nd & Morris | 1866-1930 |
| Mt. Vernon | 3rd & Catherine | 1874-1930 |
| Nebinginger, George | 6th & Carpenter | 1924 |
| Nichols, Jermemiah | 16th & Wharton | 1876 |
| Pierce, William | 24th & Christian | 1874 |
| Poe, Edgar Allen | 22nd & Ritner | 1914 |
| Point Breeze | 26th & Ritner | closed 1926 |
| Read, Francis | Sartain & Moore | 1917 |
| Southern High School | Broad & Snyder | 1893 |
| Southwark | 9th & Mifflin | 1911 |
| Taggart, George | 5th & Porter | 1895-1916 |
| Taggart, George, II | 4th & Porter | 1927 |
| Thomas, Jr. High School | 9th & Johnson | 1918 |
| Wayne, Anthony | 28th & Morris | 1909 |
| Vare Middle School | 24th & Snyder | 1916 |
| Vare, Abigail | Morris & Moyamensing | 1912 |
| Washington, George | 5th & Washington | 1913 |
| Wharton, George | 3rd & Lombard | 1900 |
| **Normal School | 13th & Spring Garden | 1875 |
| **High School for Girls | 15th & Spring Garden | 1892 |
| **Central High for Boys | Broad & Green | 1897 |

** Schools outside of South Philadelphia - school teachers went the Normal School

**List of Public Schools in South Philadelphia.** The general population in South Philadelphia swelled to three hundred thousand people by WW I. Increased public school enrollment demanded a steep increase in school facilities to accept the load and educate a new group of mostly non-American born children. Older schools were torn down, and new ones were built in the community. The cost was low in comparison to what the educated immigrant masses contributed to the community as they took their respectful places in society by earning an income, paying their taxes, and owning a home as adults in the early and mid-20th century. (List compiled courtesy of the School District of Philadelphia-Pedagogical Library.)

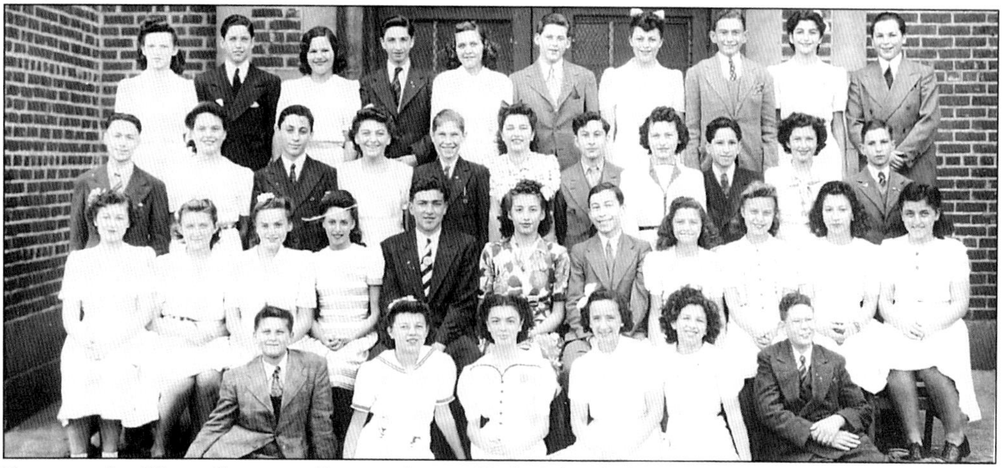

**FURNESS JR. HIGH SCHOOL.** Furness Junior High School, located at Third and Mifflin across from the Tasker Street park, accepted children as students in the seventh grade. The first section of the year became known as 7a until January 31st, 7b started the second half of the year. The park was off limits even though the students were allowed to leave the school grounds for lunch, which they went home to eat. The Furness Class of 1943, January 9B1 included Fred Bell, Marvin Kirchner, Cy Abramson, Ken Syken, Sylvia Goldberg, Jack Litz (now a lawyer), and Evelyn Love. All thought that junior high school was the best years of people's lives. (Courtesy of Bettyann Abramson Gray.)

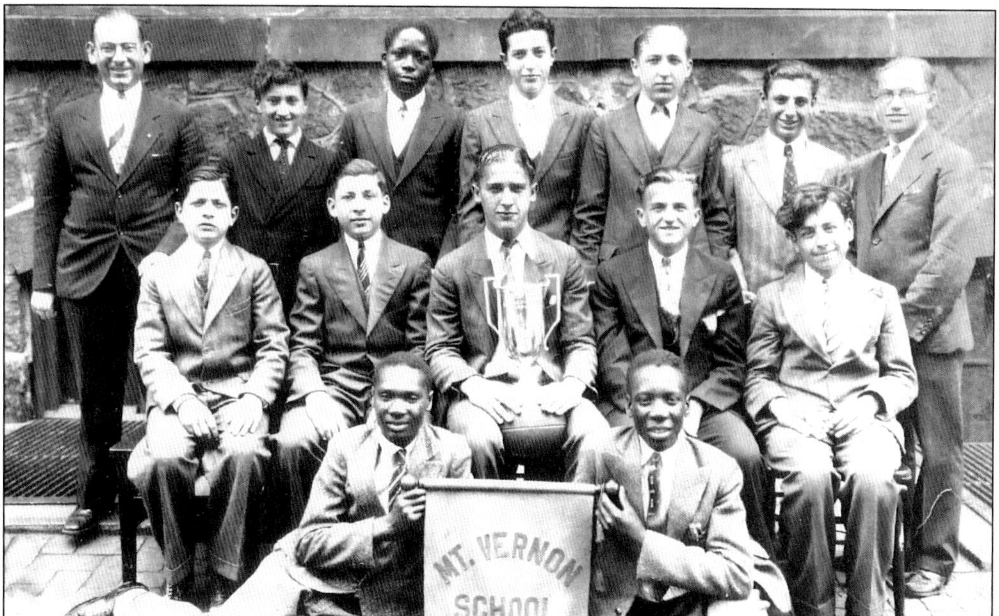


**MT. VERNON SCHOOL.** The 1929 Mt. Vernon Elementary School Volleyball championship team photograph included the teacher, Frank Raphael, on the far right. Listed from left to right are as follows: (first row) O. Ulmpkin; (second row) Abe Mersky, Charlie Mersky, B. Brady, J. Boturo, and Dominic De Rossi; (third row) Nate Katz, Walter Utley, Harry Greenfield, A. Gouch, and M. Goldfarb. When the school closed in 1932, the students attended the Meridth School at Fifth and Fitzwater Streets and then went to Bartlett Junior High School at 11th and Catherine Streets. (Courtesy of Monte Pearson.)

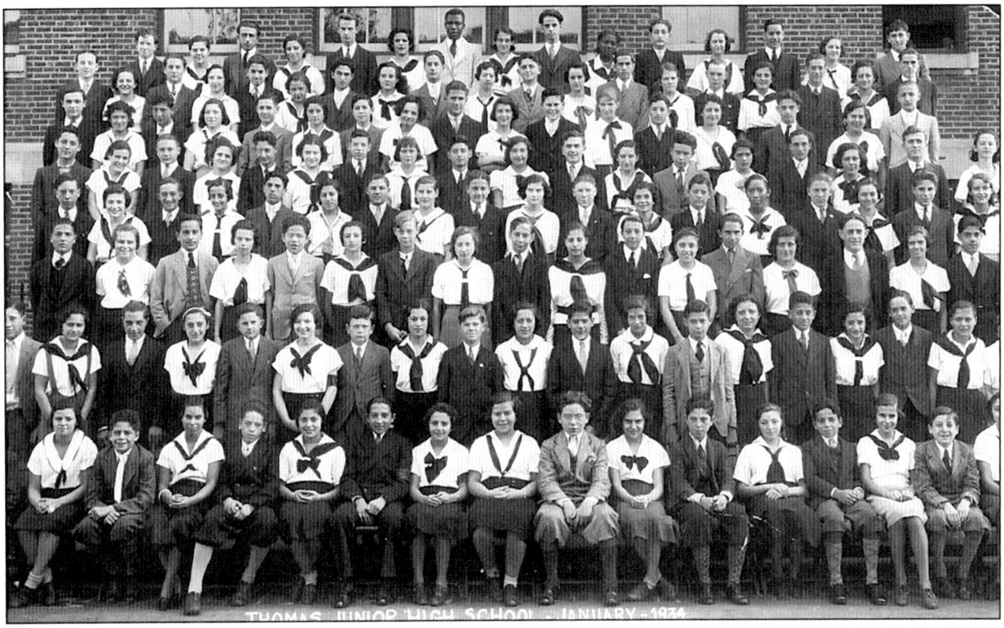


**THOMAS JUNIOR HIGH SCHOOL.** Ida Zutomer was born in the house at 2438 S. Eighth above Porter Street. She attended the Frances Scott Key Elementary School, one block north of her house, at Eighth and Wolf Streets in the late 1920s. When Ida grew older, she walked in the southern direction toward Thomas Junior High School at Ninth and Johnson, which shared a recess yard with the Fell School. Uniforms at Thomas were required when this photograph was taken in January 1934. Many South Philadelphians remained in the community they were raised in to start their own family. Today, Ida Zutomer Holshin still lives on S. Eighth Street where she was born. Passing of property from one generation occurred regularly in the Shtetls of East Europe. (Courtesy Ida Zutomer Holshin.)

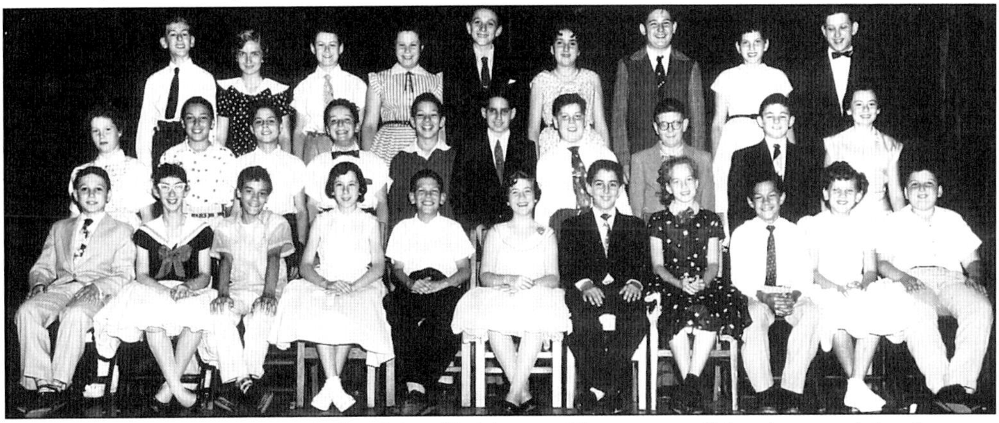

**TAGGART SCHOOL.** In 1916, the John H. Taggart Elementary School opened its doors to Jewish East European immigrants and their children. The school held English classes from 8 a.m. until 8 p.m. daily. The adjacent Benjamin Rush School for unruly children shared a common recess yard only separated by a red line. A constant message told to Jewish youngsters who left everyday for school included, "do not shame the family's name." The very fear of causing a shandah (a shameful incident) became a code of ethics observed religiously every day. A shandah was after the fact, and you could not erase pain and sorrow once it happened. (Courtesy of Sandy Wizov.)

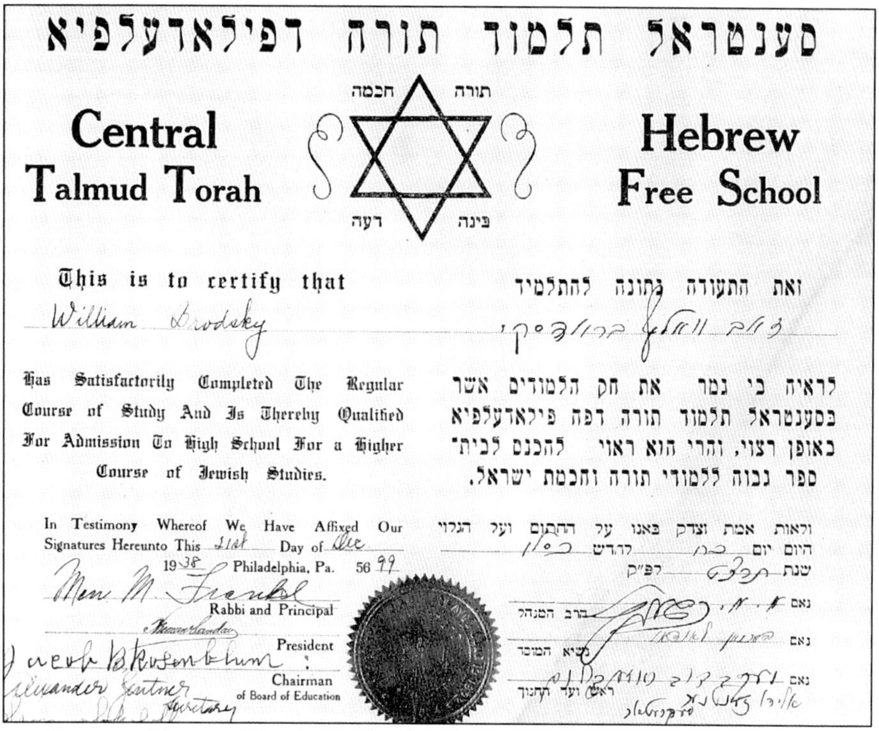

סענטראל תלמוד תורה דפילאדעלפיא

תורה חכמה

# Central Talmud Torah

# Hebrew Free School

פינה דעה

This is to certify that
זאת התעודה נתונה להתלמיד

William Brodsky

Has Satisfactorily Completed The Regular Course of Study And Is Thereby Qualified For Admission To High School For a Higher Course of Jewish Studies.

לראיה כי נמר את חק הלמודים אשר בסענטראל תלמוד תורה דפה פילאדעלפיא באופן רצוי, והרי הוא ראוי להכנס לבית ספר גבוה ללמודי תורה וחכמת ישראל.

In Testimony Whereof We Have Affixed Our Signatures Hereunto This 21st Day of Dec 1938 Philadelphia, Pa. 5699

ולאות אמת וצדק באנו על החתום ועל הגלוי היום יום לחדש שנת לפ"ק

Rabbi and Principal

President

Chairman of Board of Education

נאם הרב המנהל

נאם נשיא המוסד

נאם ראש ועד החנוך

**CENTRAL TALMUD TORAH.** The Central Talmud Torah, located on Catherine Street between Third and Fourth Streets, served thousands of Jewish children who lived in the immigrant districts of South Philadelphia from the 1890s until the late 1930s. Chief Rabbi B.L. Levinthal, upon his arrival in Philadelphia in 1891, insisted that a central school teach the immigrant's children their Jewish history, in English. The four-story building with a swimming pool became home for many children, four days a week, and on Sundays. William Brodsky received his education from Rev. M. Aaronberg, Mr. Hoffman, Jacob Penn, Esq., and Rabbi Frankel. He received his diploma on December 28, 1938, during a special commencement at 8:30 p.m. (Courtesy of William Brodsky.)

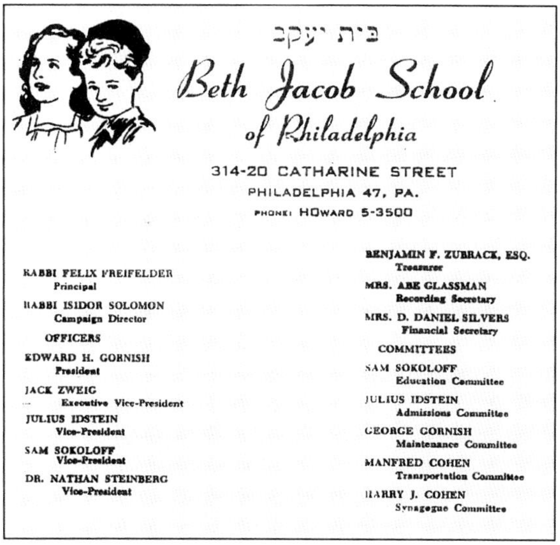

בית יעקב

# Beth Jacob School of Philadelphia

314-20 CATHARINE STREET
PHILADELPHIA 47, PA.
PHONE: HOward 5-3500

RABBI FELIX FREIFELDER, Principal
RABBI ISIDOR SOLOMON, Campaign Director

OFFICERS
EDWARD H. GORNISH, President
JACK ZWEIG, Executive Vice-President
JULIUS IDSTEIN, Vice-President
SAM SOKOLOFF, Vice-President
DR. NATHAN STEINBERG, Vice-President

BENJAMIN F. ZUBRACK, ESQ., Treasurer
MRS. ABE GLASSMAN, Recording Secretary
MRS. D. DANIEL SILVERS, Financial Secretary

COMMITTEES
SAM SOKOLOFF, Education Committee
JULIUS IDSTEIN, Admissions Committee
GEORGE GORNISH, Maintenance Committee
MANFRED COHEN, Transportation Committee
HARRY J. COHEN, Synagogue Committee

**THE BETH JACOB SCHOOL.** During the 1940s, the Jewish population migrated from South Philadelphia to other neighborhoods throughout the city. The orthodox community created a Jewish all-day school to enrich the children's appreciation of Jewish culture and history as they left the primary settlement district. Secular studies were taught along with courses to acquaint the children with daily obligations set forth in the Bible. Beth Jacob represented the start of the Jewish day school movement in the Philadelphia region with bus transportation to its schools. (Courtesy of the Philadelphia Jewish Archives Center at the Balch Institute.)

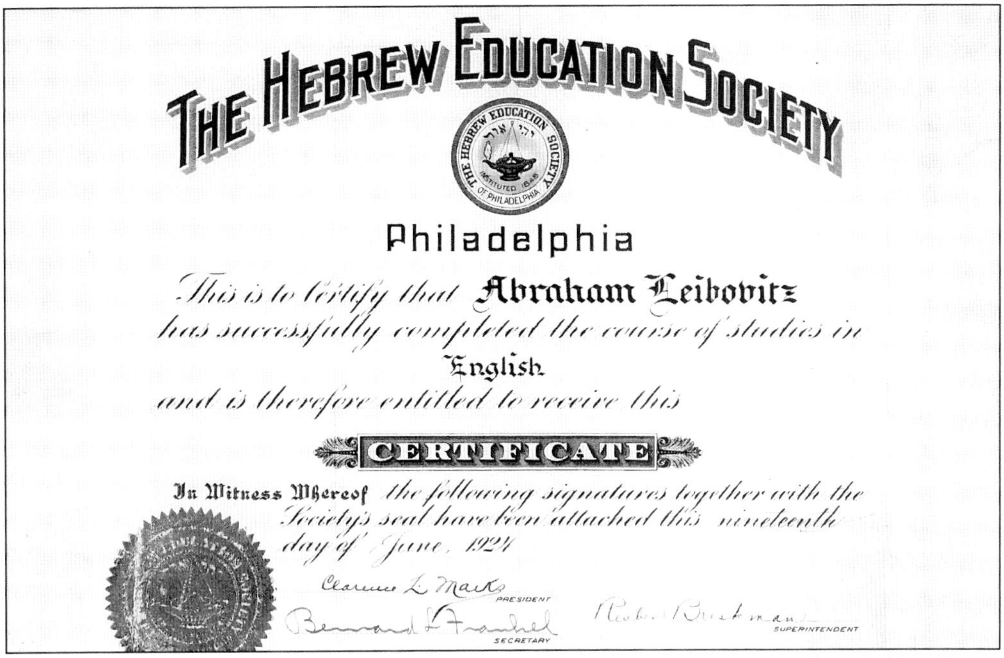
THE HEBREW EDUCATION SOCIETY

Philadelphia

This is to Certify that Abraham Leibovitz has successfully completed the course of studies in English and is therefore entitled to receive this

CERTIFICATE

In Witness Whereof the following signatures together with the Society's seal have been attached this nineteenth day of June, 1924

PRESIDENT

SECRETARY

SUPERINTENDENT

**HEBREW EDUCATION SOCIETY.** In 1891, the Hebrew Education Society, founded by Rabbi Isaac Leeser from Congregation Mikveh Israel, moved its headquarters from Seventh and Wood Streets to its new location at Tenth and Carpenter Streets. It was to serve the growing Jewish East European immigrant population in South Philadelphia. Touro Hall featured a swimming pool, religious services, and manual trades for men and women, including cigar-making and sewing. Abraham Leibovitz, a S. Ninth Street merchant, learned English at night at Touro Hall, in 1924. Touro Hall came into disuse with the end of immigration and was demolished in the early 1930s. (Courtesy of Norman Leibovitz.)

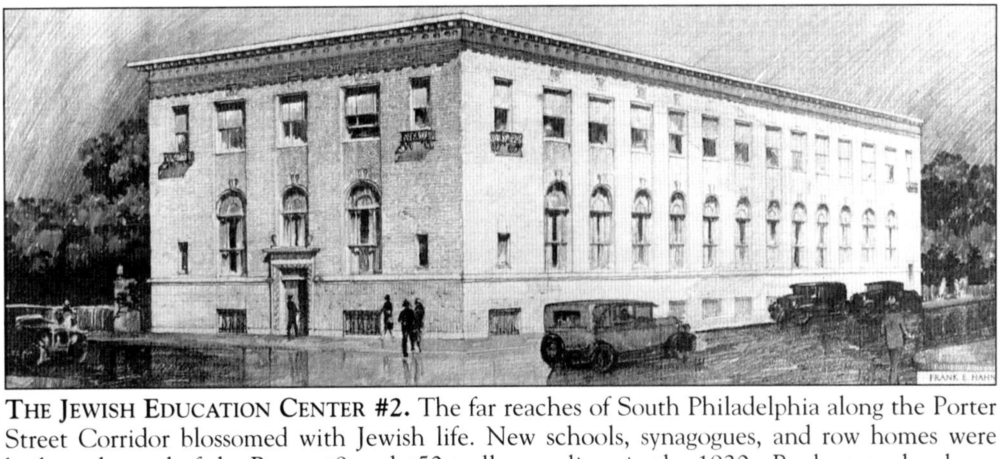


**THE JEWISH EDUCATION CENTER #2.** The far reaches of South Philadelphia along the Porter Street Corridor blossomed with Jewish life. New schools, synagogues, and row homes were built at the end of the Route #9 and #50 trolley car lines in the 1920s. Real estate developer magnate, Albert M. Greenfield, financed the construction of a center for the downtown Jews and their children, in 1928. Architect, Frank E. Hahn, designed the facility to blend in with the neighborhood. Recreation, education, and religious activities attracted hundreds of nearby families to the Jewish Education Center #2 at Marshall and Porter, which is still in operation today as the Stiffel Senior Center of the Philadelphia Jewish Community Centers. (Courtesy of the Philadelphia Jewish Archives Center at the Balch Institute.)

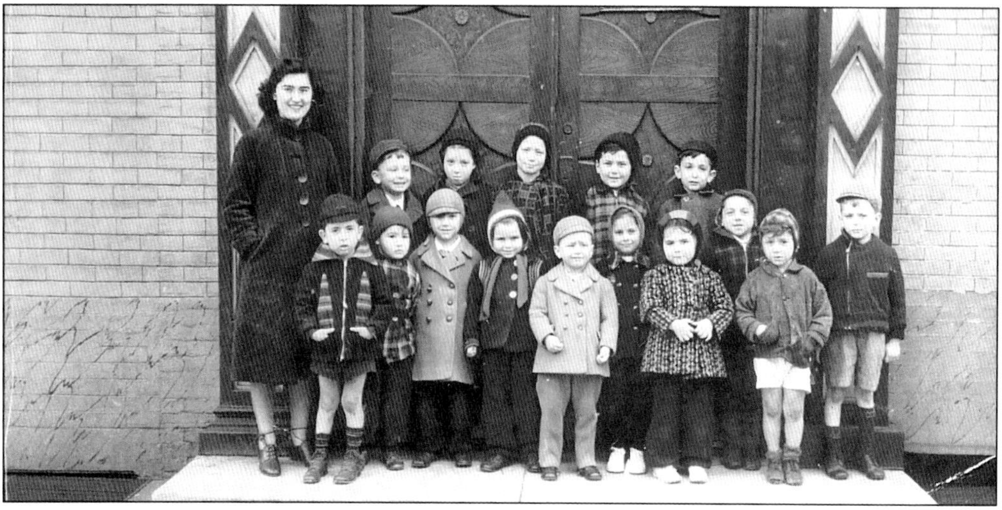

**YESHIVA MISHKAN ISRAEL.** Yeshiva Mishkan Israel, at 506 Wharton Street, offered pre-school programs, Hebrew Sunday School Society chapter (founded in 1838 by Rebecca Gratz), and a high school for Jewish learning. The Hativah Club met here with Israel Goldstein, Gershon Agronsky, Louis Feinberg, David Gaiter, Louis Leveinthal, David C. Matt, and Samuel Noah Kramer as children to discuss a Jewish homeland in Palestine. Local Philadelphia Rabbi Abraham Israelitean studied at Yeshiva Mishkan Israel. He later attended Gratz College before studying for the rabbinate and serving Temple Menorah (the NE Jewish Community Center), which served Mayfair and Tacony. (Courtesy of Rose Davis Lakier.)

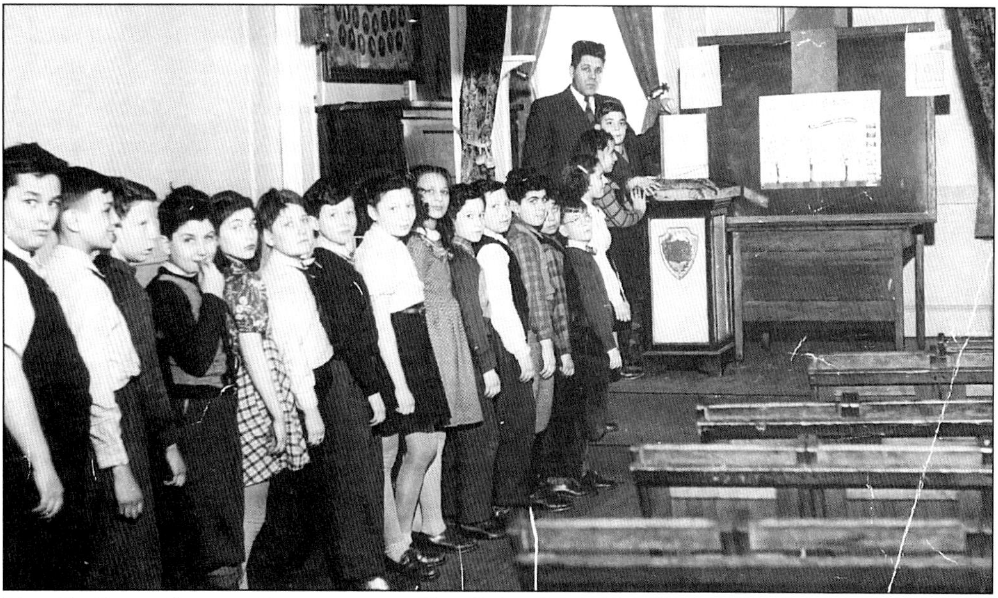

**THE S. SIXTH STREET FOLKSHULEN.** The S. Sixth and Mifflin Street Folkshulen offered a popular alternative to religious education under the supervision of the Workman Circle. The children observed the Jewish holidays and gained an appreciation for a Jewish homeland under teacher Chaver Dashevsky. Some of the students lined up for Jewish National Fund Day, celebrated in January, included Marty Robbins, Betty Stein Pearlman, Rose Davis, Stanley David, and Howard Eveloff. The folkshulen represented secularists in South Philadelphia. (Courtesy of Rose Davis Lakier.)

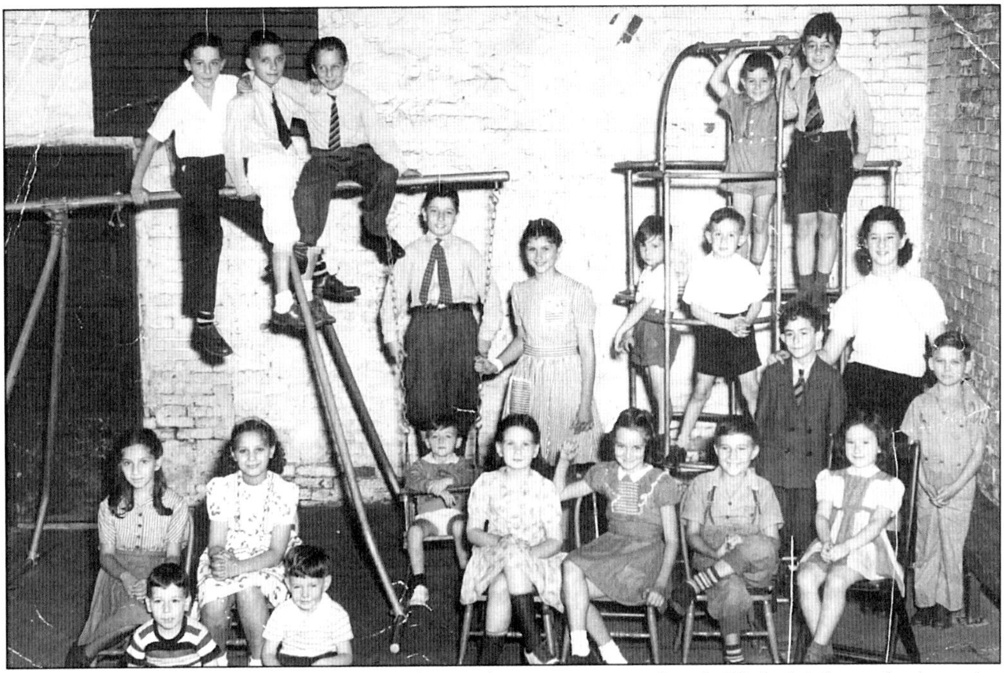

**The Jewish Day Nursery.** Daycare for working parents in South Philadelphia relied on the Jewish Day Nursey at 1514 S. Sixth Street. The director, Cecilia Shupak (in the above picture), supervised Batty Ann Abramson, Rose Davis, and the Berman boys, whose father worked for the Sandler Kosher Sausage Company in Strawberry Mansion. The nursery was a constituent of the Red Feather agency, a predecessor of the United Way. (Courtesy of Rose Davis Lakier.)

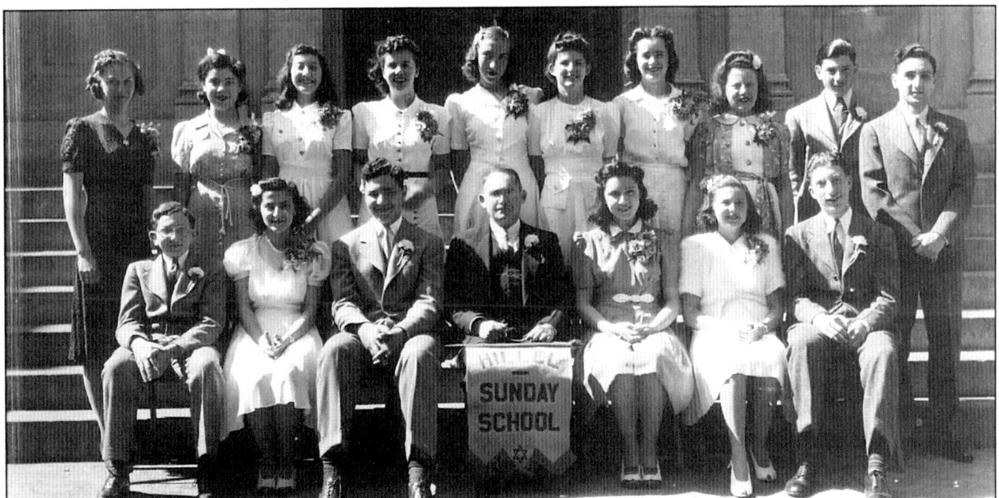


**Hillel Sunday School.** The Hebrew Sunday School Society ran several chapters in South Philadelphia for the children of immigrants. Jewish education took place for many children in Jewish institutions, which the Jewish community supported, thus these institutions remained free to the public. The Hillel Sunday School met at the Jewish Education Center I, located at 508 Moore Street. The two teachers in the above 1939 photograph are Sadie Shapiro and Milton Kahn. Courses to become a Sunday School teacher were held at Broad and Pine Streets inside the YMHA. (Courtesy of Edith Weinstein.)

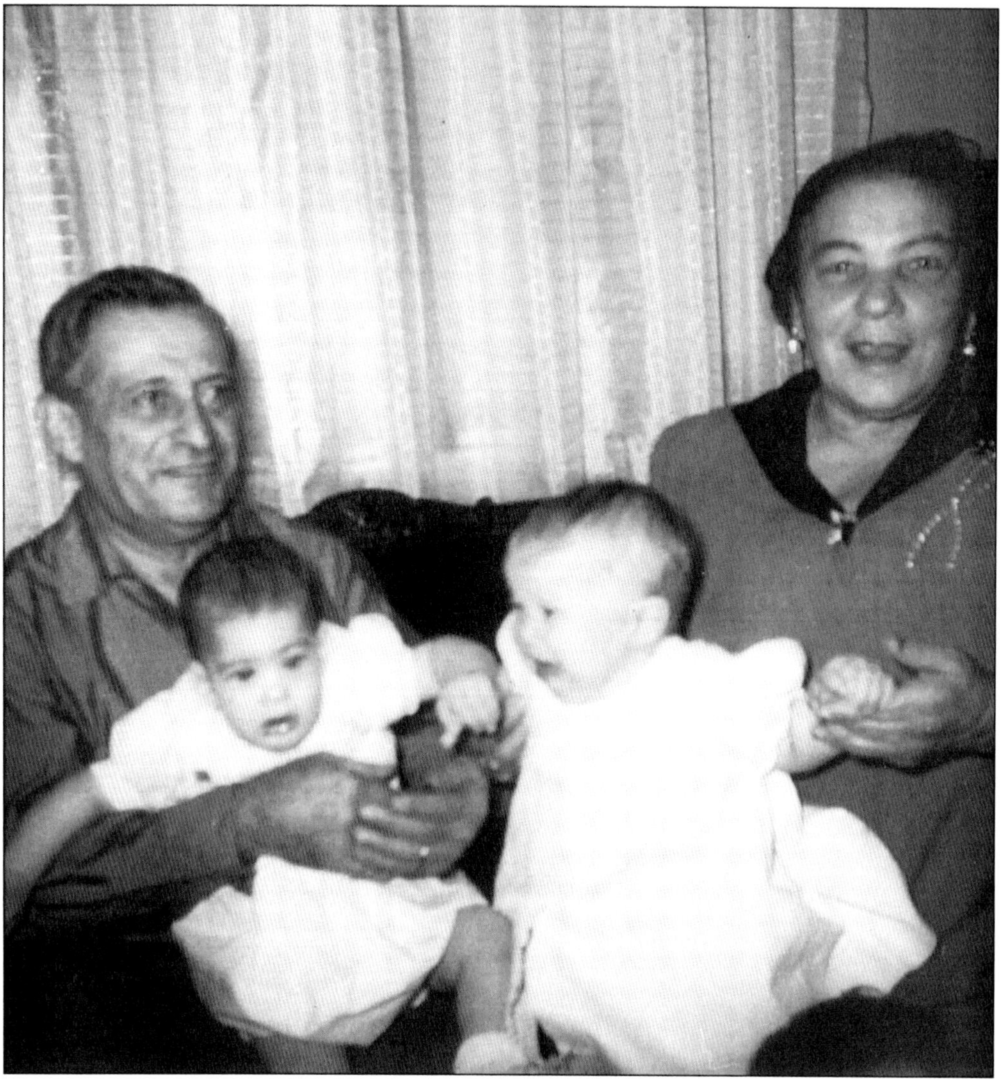

**ROSE AND BEN MAGNESS.** You have to love children the way Rose and Ben Magness did in South Philadelphia. Christian missionaries became active in the neighborhood, and Rose decided to create a satellite of the Neighborhood Center from Fifth and Bainbridge, on the southeast corner of Sixth and Mifflin. The community institution known as the Neighborhood House offered classes in English, Dramatics, and Arts and Crafts in a safe environment. Milk was sold every morning to the children, in 1929. Rose reversed the decline of Jewish apathy in her neighborhood with the formation of the Mother's Club. (Courtesy of Libby Magness Weisberg.)

# *Eight*

# COMMUNITY INSTITUTIONS

## TRADIONAL JEWISH INSTITUTIONS, SERVICE ORGANIZATIONS, FEDERATION OF JEWISH CHARITIES, AND INDIVIDUALS AS ICONS

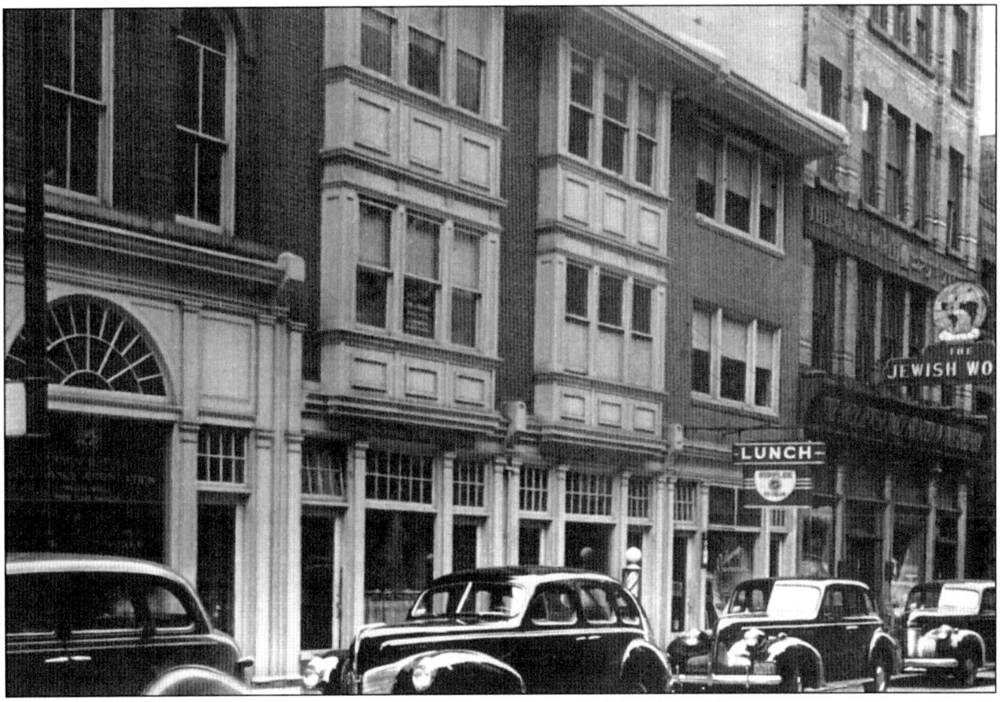


THE JEWISH WORLD. Philadelphia developed into a Yiddish/Jewish Newspaper Capital with the publication of five daily papers. The center of the activity took place at Fifth and Pine Streets, where the Jewish newspapers had their printing presses that included the *Yiddishe Velt* (*Jewish World*), the *Forward*, the *Tag* (the *Day*), the *Freiheit*, and the *Morning Journal*. Jewish people bought and sold the Jewish newspaper routes, and according to Simcha Gersh, who owned one of two routes in South Philadelphia, "it was like a union that provided a steady income with no possibility of competition." (Courtesy of the Atwater Kent Museum, Philadelphia, Pennsylvania.)

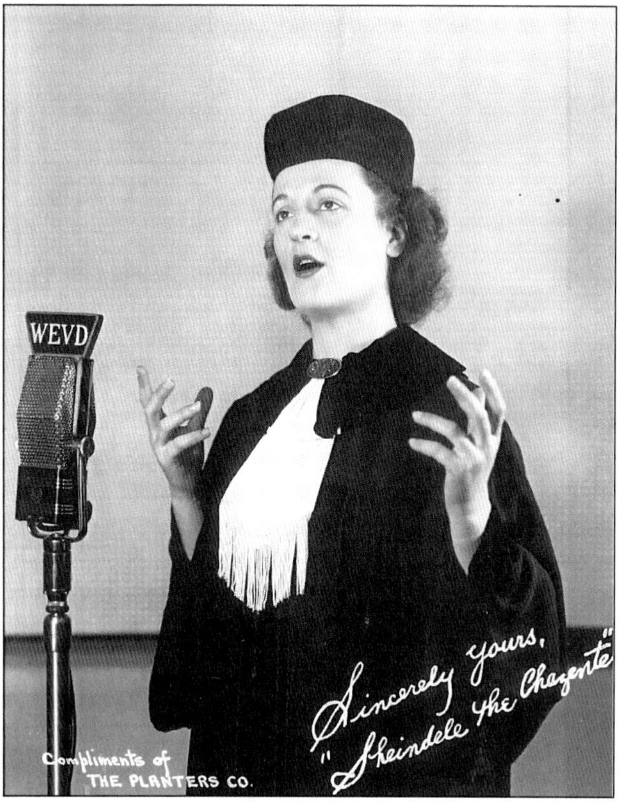


**SHANDEL THE CHAZENTE.** Sheindele the Chazente (Jean Gornish), an orthodox woman with a powerful voice, had something to sing. Sheindele lived at 426 Lombard Street, in the early 1920s she miraculously survived in a sand pile that had been run over by a trash wagon. The lady cantor, under the direction of her manager, Ben W. Gottlieb, sang on the radio on Sunday afternoons after Nathan Fleischer delivered the news. Sheindele could not render her service of liturgical music to any conservative or orthodox congregation due to tradition which did not allow women on the pulpit and choirs in synagogues consisted of male voices only. (Courtesy of Barry Reisman.)

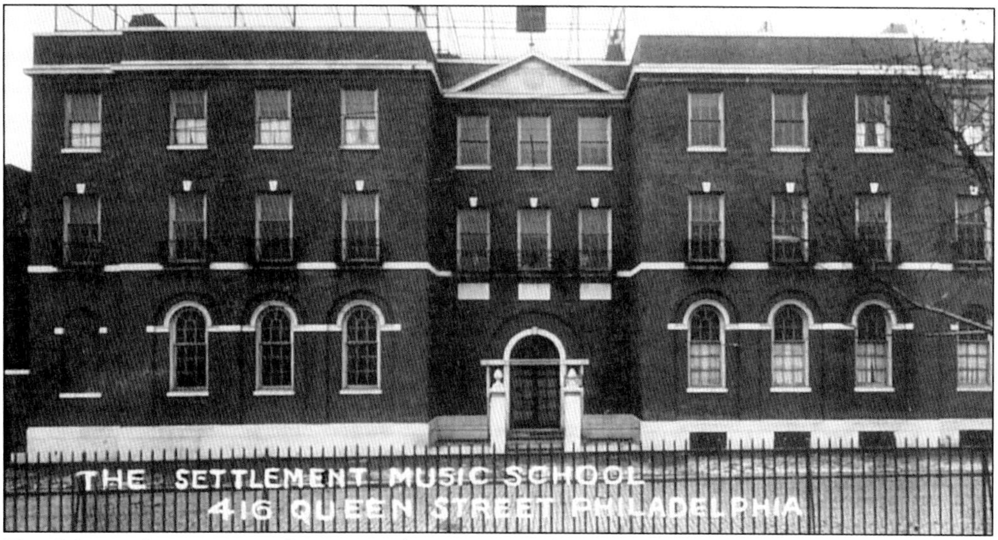


**THE MUSIC SETTLEMENT SCHOOL.** The Music Settlement School, founded by Blanche Wolf Isidore and Jeanette Selig Frank in 1908, provided music lessons to Jewish East European immigrants and other ethnic groups in the area. Mrs. Edward Bok provided funds to erect its current facility at 416 Queen Street, in 1917. Many children who received training at the Music Settlement School became professional musicians. The thousands of mummers who played musical instruments owed a debt of gratitude to the dedicated teachers at the school. (Courtesy of the Jewish Exponent, Philadelphia, Pennsylvania.)

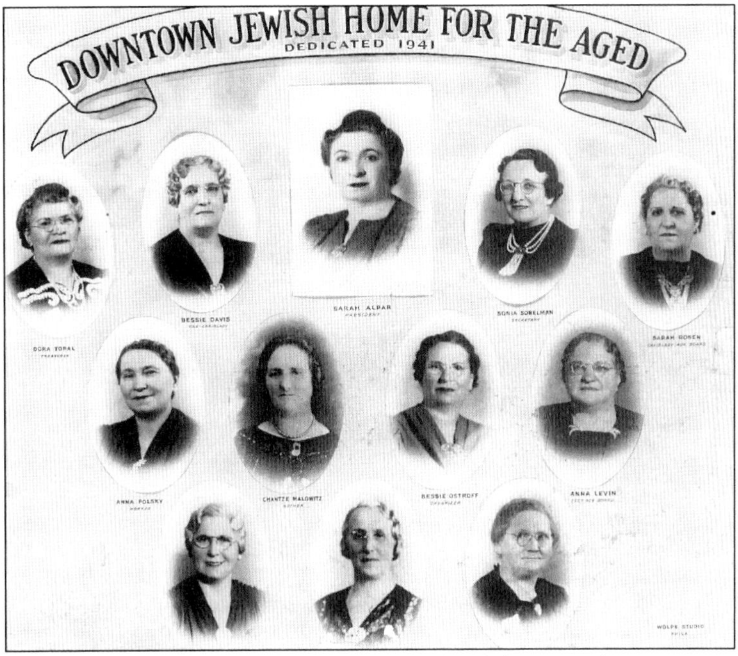


**The Downtown Home for the Aged.** South Philadelphia Jewish institutions multiplied in number as the community migrated farther south of the original settlement area. The neighborhood below Washington Avenue in South Philadelphia demanded and received communal attention between the World Wars. The neighborhood below Washington Avenue demanded and received youth, recreational, cultural, and geriatric institutions. As the Jewish Education Center at 508 Moore Street closed its doors, the Downtown Jewish Home for the Aged emerged in 1941. Sarah Alpar and Sam Dubin ran the home for many years until it moved to Ford Road out in Wynnefield Heights. (Courtesy of Bernard Klevan.)

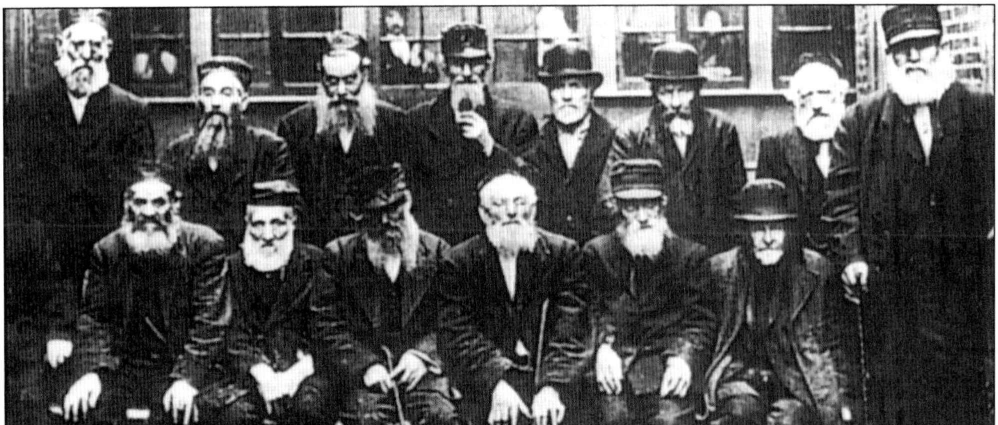

**Women's Society's Jewish Sheltering Home.** Look at all those Zaydes (grandfathers)! According to Biblical writings, Jewish children as adults are held responsible for the welfare of their elderly parents and they shall not forsake, forget, or abandon them! The care of the elderly along with many institutions in the Jewish community came under the supervision of women. The Women's Society Jewish Sheltering Home existed first at 235 Delancey Street before it moved to 315 S Third Street during the early 20th century. (Courtesy of the Philadelphia Jewish Archives at the Balch Institute.)

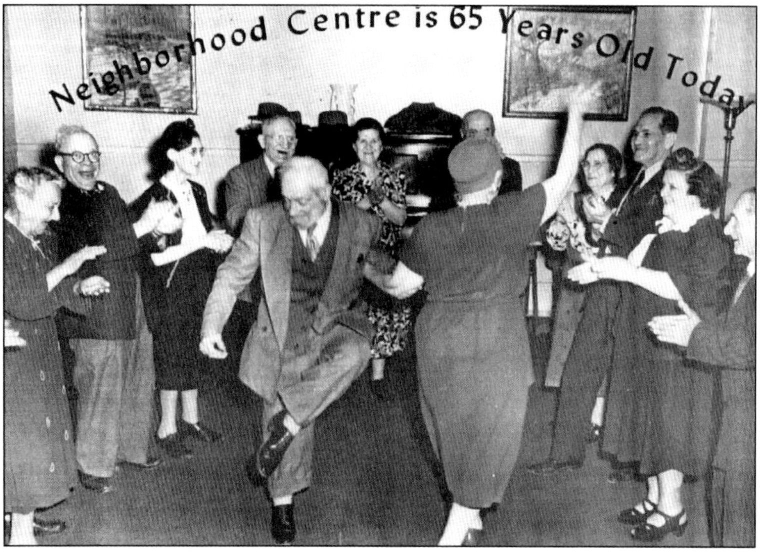


**The Neighborhood Centre.** The Jewish immigrant district near Fourth and Bainbridge overburdened with requests for help by individuals for many different services, created a self-help agency. The Neighborhood Centre, located at 428 Bainbridge Street, aided the immigrants in their adjustment to American life and provided help that included cultural, recreational, and literary activities, as well as manual training courses in the early 1910s. (Courtesy of Julian Greifer (of blessed memory) and the Philadelphia Jewish Archives Center.)

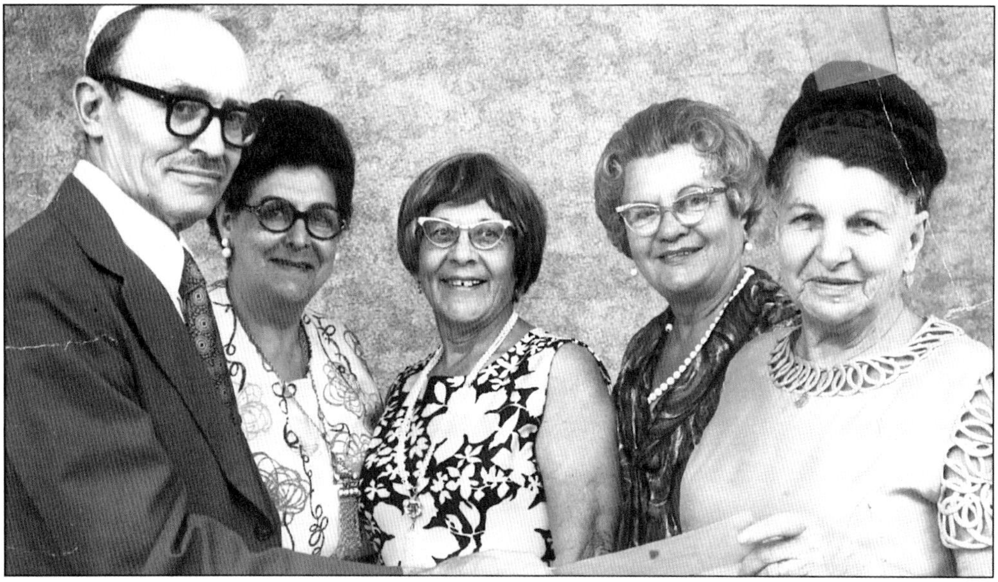

**Hindas Goodis Downtown Free Loan Society.** According to Jewish Law, loans by people to others had to bear no interest. The self-help institution that refused to call itself a bank in South Philadelphia was known as the corporation, and it allowed Jews to buy homes, invest in a business, and take a vacation in the 1930s. The period of the loan depended on how much an individual put in as collateral. Sarah Stillman, founder and president of the Hindas Goodis Downtown Free Loan Society at 401 Mifflin Streets, received a check from well-known South Philadelphian Harry Beitchman (Torah Reader for three synagogues), in 1960. (Courtesy of Sam Stillman.)

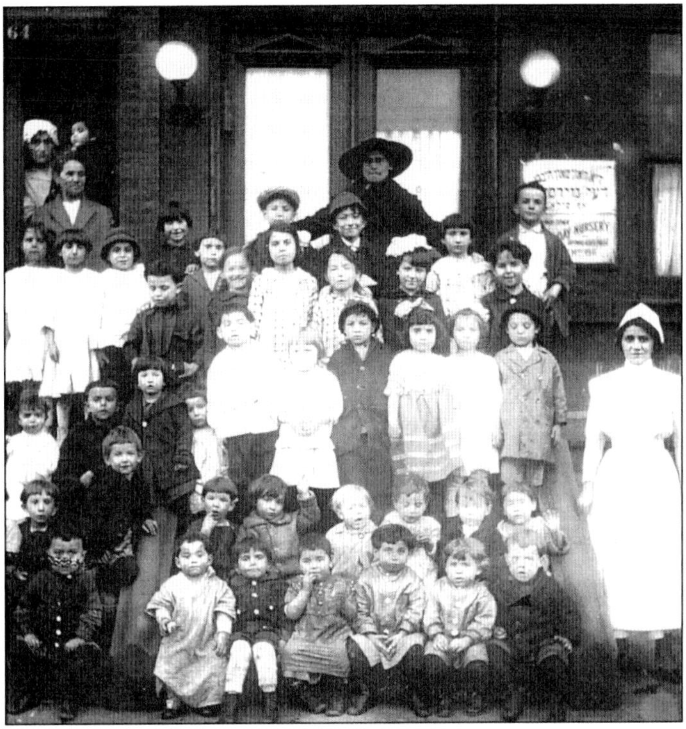

**The Downtown Hebrew Day Nursery.** Yetta Bernstein, founder of the Downtown Hebrew Day Nursery stood with the children on the steps of the institution at 366 Snyder Avenue. Charles Bernstein supported his wife's ambition with a flyer that read, "Don't forget these small down-trodden children who have to look for help from strangers-give as much as you can." The Downtown Hebrew Day Nursery cared for children as their parents worked everyday. Today, the agency is known as the Downtown Children's Center. (Courtesy of Ben Bernstein.)

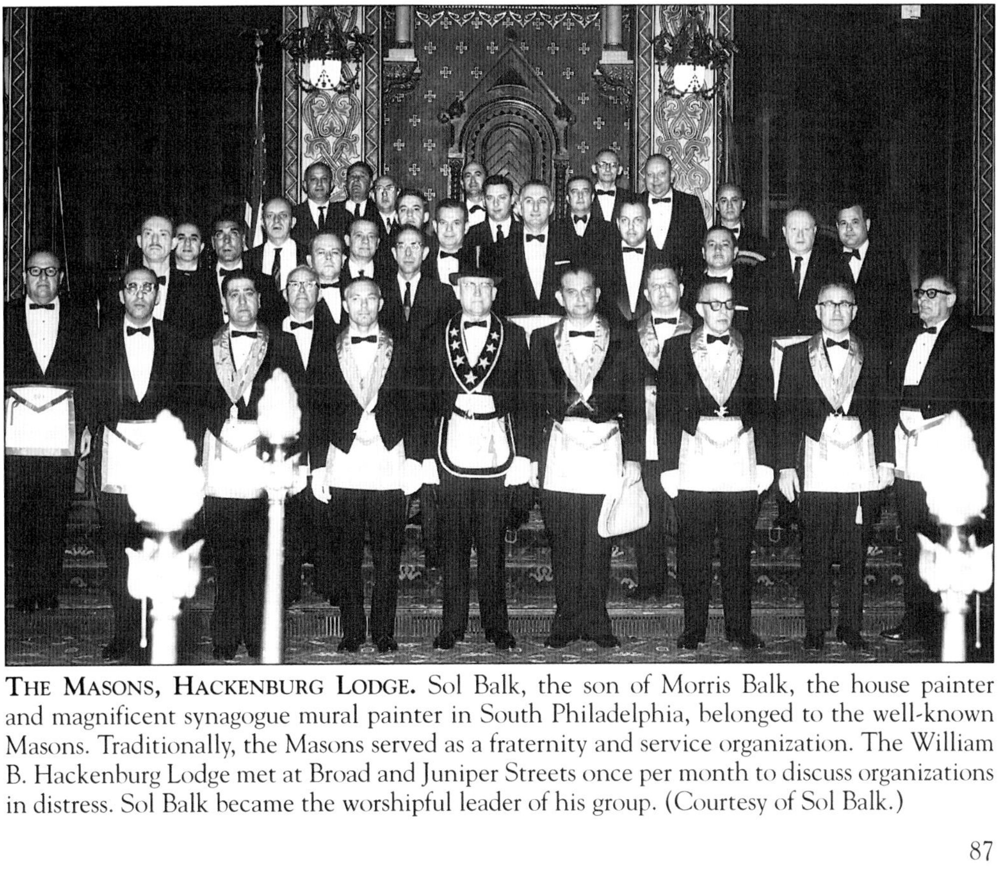

**The Masons, Hackenburg Lodge.** Sol Balk, the son of Morris Balk, the house painter and magnificent synagogue mural painter in South Philadelphia, belonged to the well-known Masons. Traditionally, the Masons served as a fraternity and service organization. The William B. Hackenburg Lodge met at Broad and Juniper Streets once per month to discuss organizations in distress. Sol Balk became the worshipful leader of his group. (Courtesy of Sol Balk.)

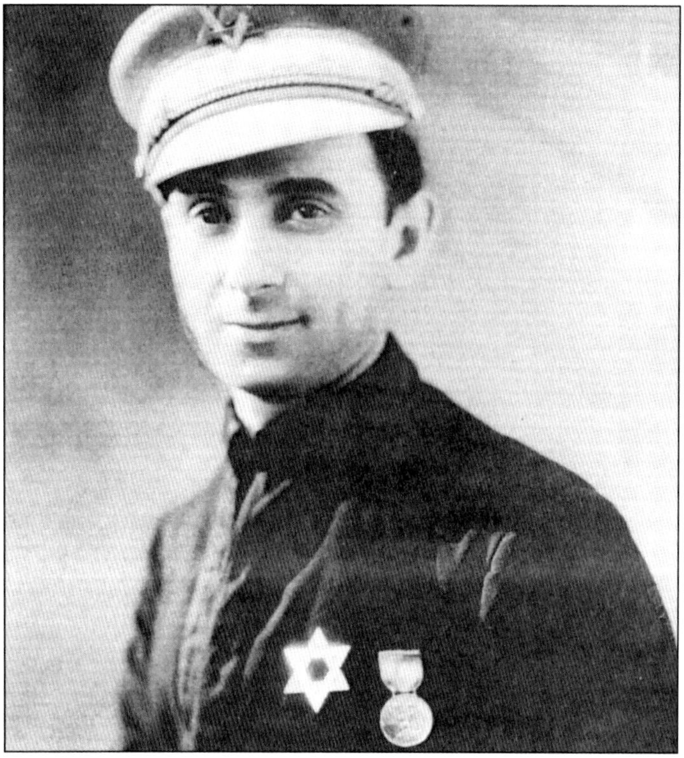

**Dr. Louis Sorokin.** Louis Sorokin, born in Rostov, Russia, in 1906, left his place of birth with his parents for Philadelphia at the age of 11 . The idea to form a concert band emerged after Louis became a dentist in the mid-1920s. Proud of his heritage, Louis decided to create his own uniforms, complete with Mogen Davids (stars of David) and hats that looked like the trolley drivers of the day. The concert band consisted of 36 Jewish children who were taught by Louis and the staff at Music Settlement House. (Courtesy of Hillard Sorokin.)

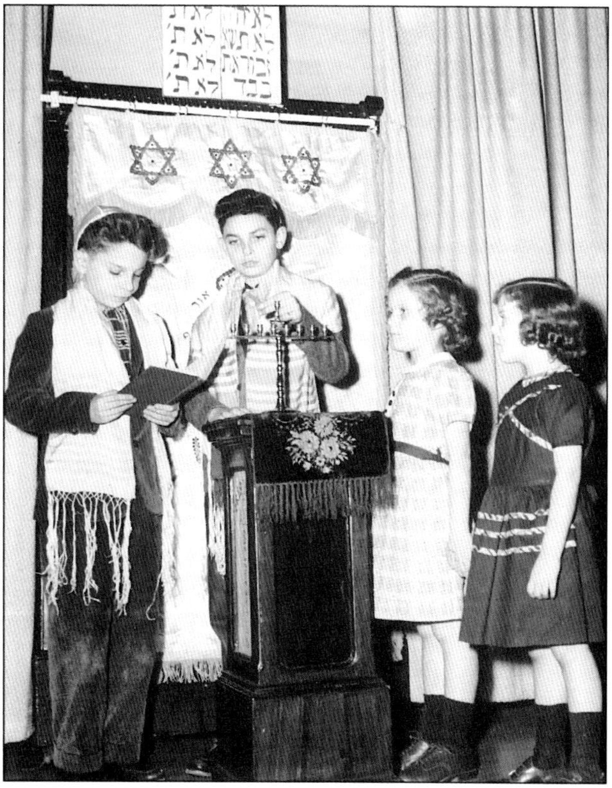

**The Downtown Jewish Orphanage Home.** The Downtown Jewish Orphanage, located at Ninth and Shunk Streets, dedicated its new building in 1924. During the Depression, Jewish families split apart and the orphanage allowed Jewish children placed in their care special visiting rights by one parent. The Jewish orphans were fully integrated into all aspects of the community, which included religious, recreational, and educational groups. Saul Resnick, Murray Itzenson, and Darlene and Sarah Markowitz celebrate Chanukah at the orphanage in 1952. (Courtesy of the National Museum of American Jewish History, Philadelphia, Pennsylvania.)

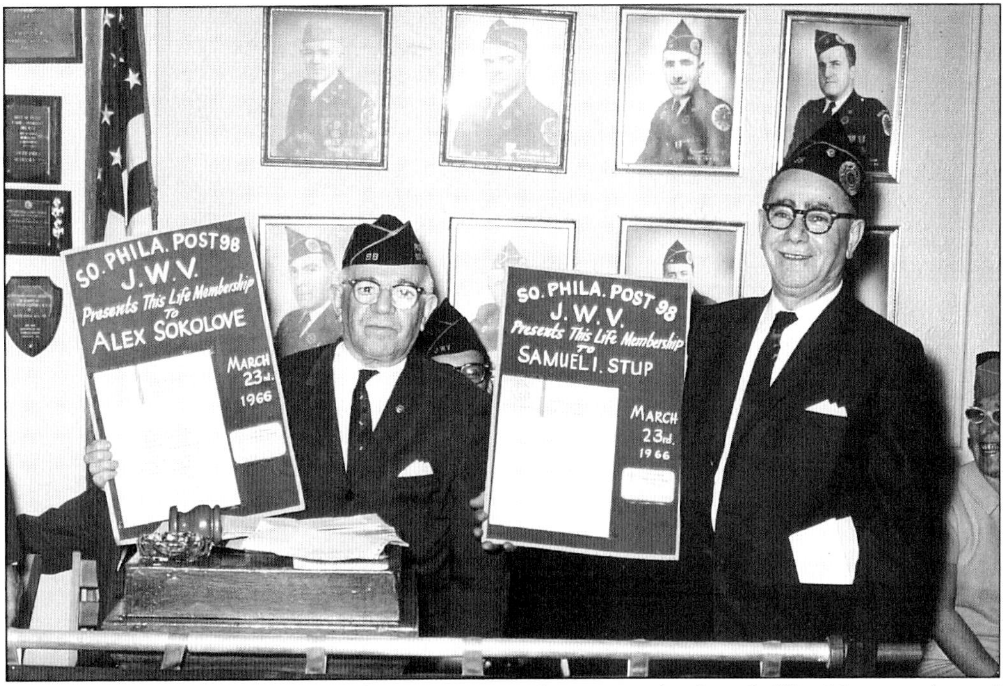


**The Jewish War Veterans.** The organization known as the Jewish War Veterans formed Post #98 during the late 1910s. The veterans met at their post home on the southeast corner of Fifth and Morris Streets for many years. Two well-known officers included Alex Sokolove and Sam Stup. Both men encouraged the women to form a ladies auxiliary, which became very active during WW II. (Courtesy of Jack Litz, Commander Post #98.)

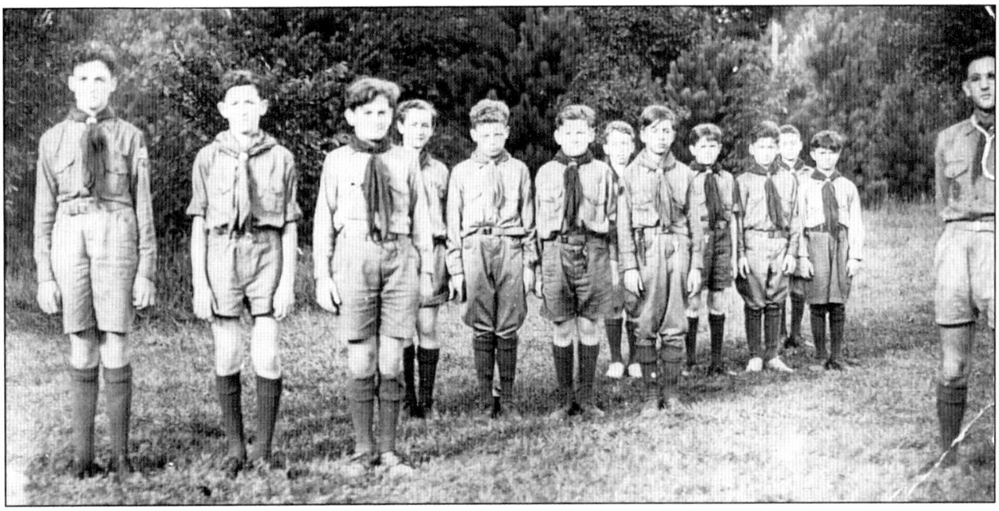

**Boy Scouts Troop #253.** South Philadelphia had several Jewish Boy Scout Troops, including troops #42, 55, and 253. The Scouts met at synagogues, Jewish institutions, and the police station at Fourth and Snyder Avenues. Troop #253 (above), led by scout master Victor Silverman, met at the Jewish Education Center #2 at Marshall and Porter Streets, and was sponsored by the Hebrew Sunday School Society. The boys camped out at Scouts Triangle in Woodside Park where Sam Moskowitz, age 13, snapped this picture in 1931. (Courtesy of Sam Moskowitz.)

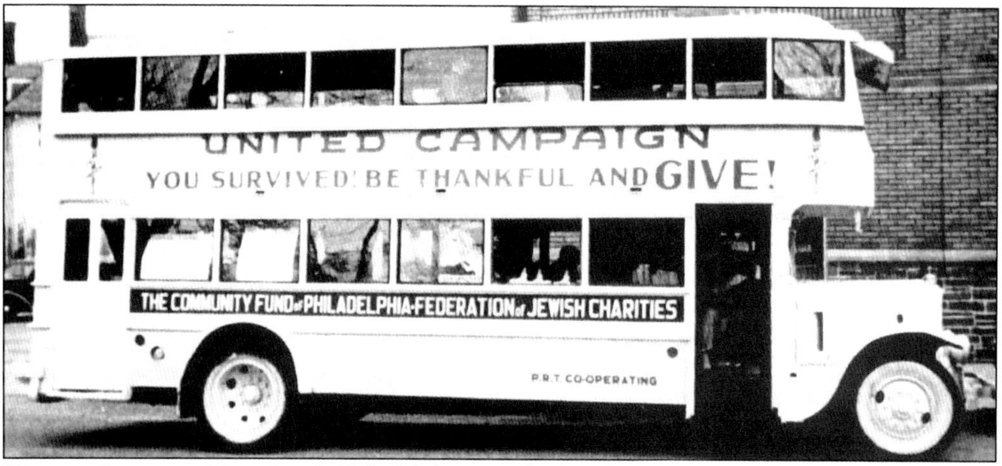


**UNITED CAMPAIGN BUS.** South Philadelphia Jews displayed their commitment to the community with pride when they participated in the Federation of Jewish Charities traveling band. WW I ended, and a double-decker bus filled with local South Philadelphia musicians traveled to constituent agencies to play concerts in appreciation of increased charitable acts of giving in the early 1920s. (Courtesy of the Philadelphia Jewish Archives Center at the Balch Institute.)

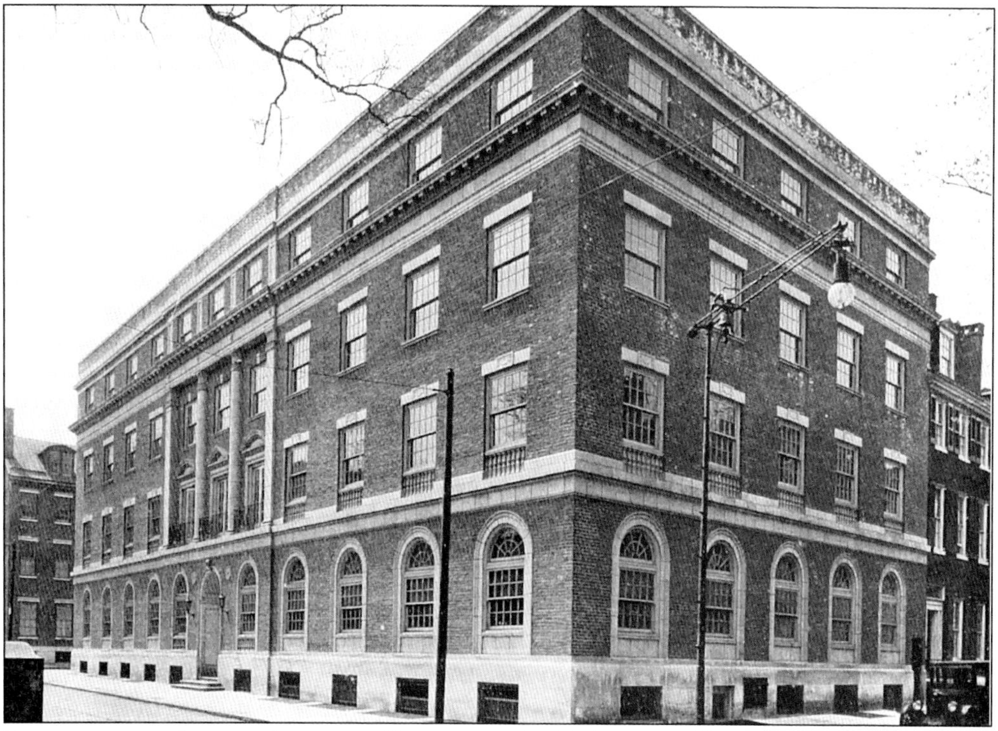

**FEDERATION OF JEWISH CHARITIES BUILDING.** The Federation of Jewish Charities, organized in 1901 to prevent the duplication of services, met in various downtown facilities to plan and coordinate fund-raisers for the many constituent agencies. A new headquarters for the federation opened on the northwest corner of Ninth and Pine Streets, in 1922. The building designed by well-known architect Frank E. Hahn had stately features similar to the Curtis building at Sixth and Walnut Streets. (Courtesy of Frank E. Hahn Jr.)

South Philadelphia
Jewish Community Institutions
buildings and architects
1891 - 1937

Courtesy of the American Institute of Architects / George Thomas

The references are for buildings completed by architects and dates listed in the Building Guide ( BG ) manual according to the last four digits. For example 0591 = May 1891

Emunath Israel Congregation
NE cor 5$^{th}$ & Gaskill
S. Mulligan BG 061913 0591

Kesher Israel Congregation
420 Lombard
J. Stuckert BG 0814 050593

B'nai Abraham Congregation
527 Lombard
M. Silberstein BG 124220 01097

Hebrew Union House
422 Bainbridge
Baker & Sallet BG 141611 090499

Hebrew Orphanage House
SW cor 1000 Bainbridge
A. Miller BG 15352 090800

Central Talmud Torah
314-320 Catherine
J. Jackson BG 1826 010703

B'nai Reuben Congregation
S. 6$^{th}$ below Kater
C. Bolton BG 19111 060304

Hebrew Literature society
312 Catherine
Wilson & Richards BG 19133 0304

Ahavath Chesed Congregation
322 Bainbridge
C. Rahn BG 19336 070904

Jewish Sheltering Home
230 Lombard
F. Furness PI 11 - 080605

B'nai Moishe Congregation
5$^{th}$ & Watkins
B. Medoff 0304 1910

Cohen's Bath House
504 Morris
Anderson & Haupt BG 263530 08 1911

Bessarbia Talmud Torah
1625 S. 6$^{th}$ above Morris
B. Medoff 0206 1912

Quaker Maid Dairies
220 Manton
B. Medoff & son BG 295123 1914

Bogeslofsky Bakery
5$^{th}$ above South
F. Greisler BG 29342 0608 1914

Jewish Sheltering Home
315 S. 3$^{rd}$
M. Haupt 0210 1915

Toras Israel Congregation
728 W. Moyamensing
J. Fieldstein 07 01 1915

Immigrant Station
Washington and Delaware
A Stand 07 1915

Jewish Sheltering House
235 Delancey
L. Magaziner BG 3028 071415

Silverman Bridal
6$^{th}$ & South
L. Magaziner 0908 1916

Adath Jeshurun Talmud Torah
2113 S. 6$^{th}$
A. Kline 0121 1917

Grand Theatre
7$^{th}$ & Synder
F. Greenstein 1104 1917

Brith Sholom
506 Pine
E. Rothchild BG 3437 09 1919

I. Kranser Business
7$^{th}$ & Sigel
H. Kline 0107 1920

Beth Jacob Congregation
6$^{th}$ & Wolf
H. Kline BG 3627 0607 1921

Federation of Jewish Charities
NW cor 9$^{th}$ & Pine
F. Hahn BG 372231 95 1922

YMHA
Broad & Pine
F. Hahn BG 3733 0111 192

Boslover Hall
7$^{th}$ & Pine
W. Charr BG 394322 10

Downtown Jewish Orphanage
SE cor 9$^{th}$ & Shunk
J. Fieldstein 0203 1924

Joseph Levine Funeral Home
513 Pine
F. Hahn Bg 39140 0204 19

Rossman's Turkish Bath House
741 Porter
I. Levin 0511 1924

Jewish Community Building
8$^{th}$ & Wolf
E. Rothchild 0104 1925

Jewish Education Center No. 1
508 Moore
E. Rothchild BG 41461 0711

Jewish Education Center No 2
Marshall & Porter
F. Hahn Bg 42241 0506 1

Beth Samuel Congregation
Marshall & Ritner
M. Bernhaqrdt 04 1927

Shaare Shomayim Congregation
23$^{rd}$ & Wharton
W. Charr 0803 1928

Row Houses
500 Ritner
W. Charr 07 1935

S. Himmelstein Restaurant
5$^{th}$ & South
H. Kline BG 52342 0909 19

**List of Architects for Jewish Communal Buildings.** The large concentration of Jewish people in South Philadelphia led to a building boom for that section of Philadelphia from the 1890s until the late 1920s. Buildings housed a variety of communal institutions such as bathhouses, bakeries, synagogues, and old age homes. Bids for design and construction for the 40 buildings became very competitive for many Jewish architects. (List compiled by Allen Meyers—courtesy of George Thomas and the American Institute of Architects.)

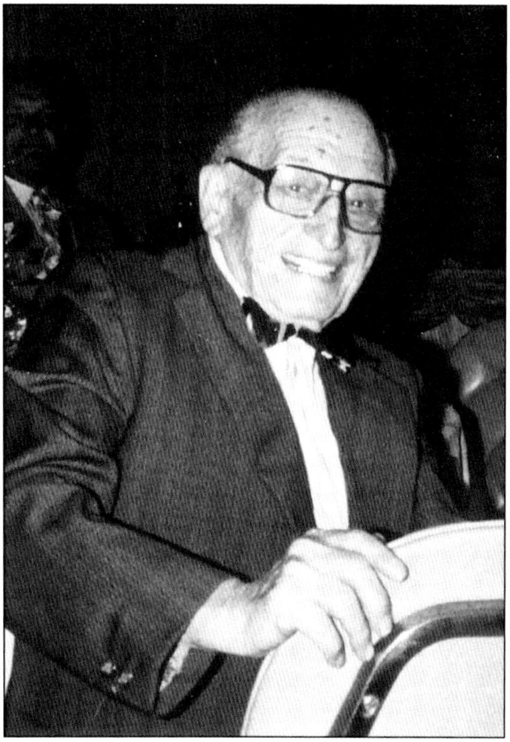

**DR. JACOB MAKLER.** Dr. Jacob Makler served the community west of Broad Street at an office on 22nd and Passyunk for more than 50 years. Colleagues often said that Dr. Makler had a soothing way to take the pain away from a person just by the way he said hello. At age 95, Dr. Makler passed, and his reputation for never taking a vacation and walking to his office during blizzards established him as a well-respected person in the community. (Courtesy of Helen Graham Konstance.)

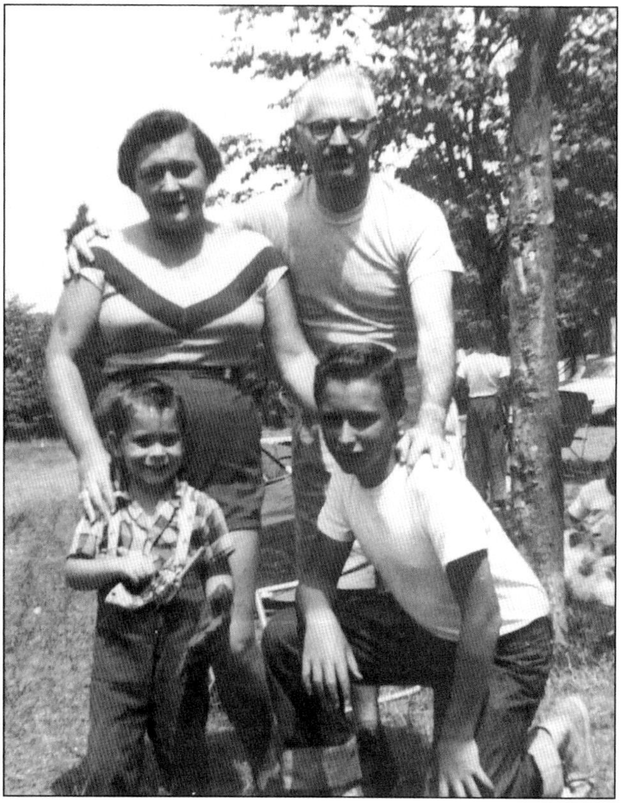

**DR. ABE GLICK.** Dr. Abe Glick represents the old-fashioned family physician—a person with a heart! Before WW II, Dr. Glick married his wife, Sylvia, who lived near Wolf and Reese Streets. He built his office on the southeast corner of Fifth and Wolf Streets. Dr. Glick spent 50 years tending to the sick and frail and he made daily calls at the Mt. Sinai Hospital at Fifth and Reed Streets. Dr. Glick rarely left his neighborhood except to go on vacation to Mr. Sharp's farm in Rockydale, Pennsylvania, with his wife and two sons, Seth and Richard (right). Dr. Glick refuses to leave South Philadelphia, where he was born close to 90 years ago, in 1909. (Courtesy of Dr. Abe Glick.)

**DR. MILTON KITEI.** Dr. Milton Kitei grew up at Tenth and South Streets and loved to enrich people's lives. Rabbi Israelitean tutored Milton with his Hebrew lessons as a child and in turn, he became a Hebrew Sunday School teacher at Shaare Shomayim at 23rd and Wharton Streets. Dr. Kitei continued his practice from his father-in-law, Dr. Robert Rubin's, office at 2243 Ninth Street for the past 30 years. The South Philadelphia neighborhood is family to Dr. Kitei, who recently lost his wife, Janet (of blessed memory), and his patients look in on him to console as a courtesy. (Courtesy of Dr. Milton Kitei.)

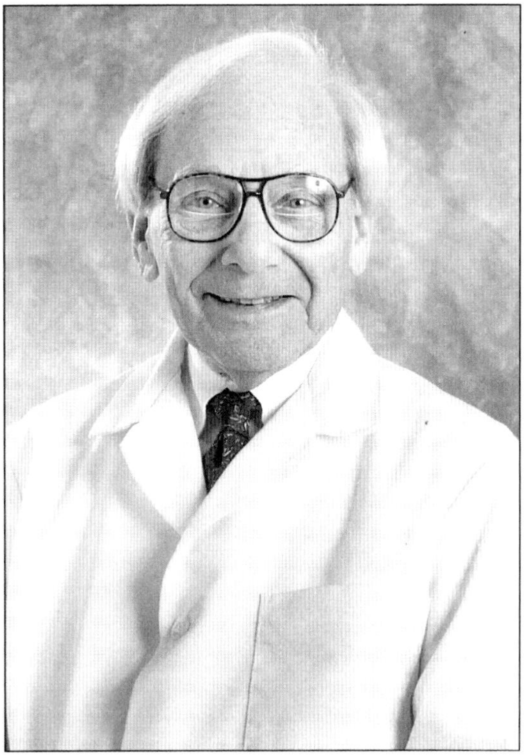

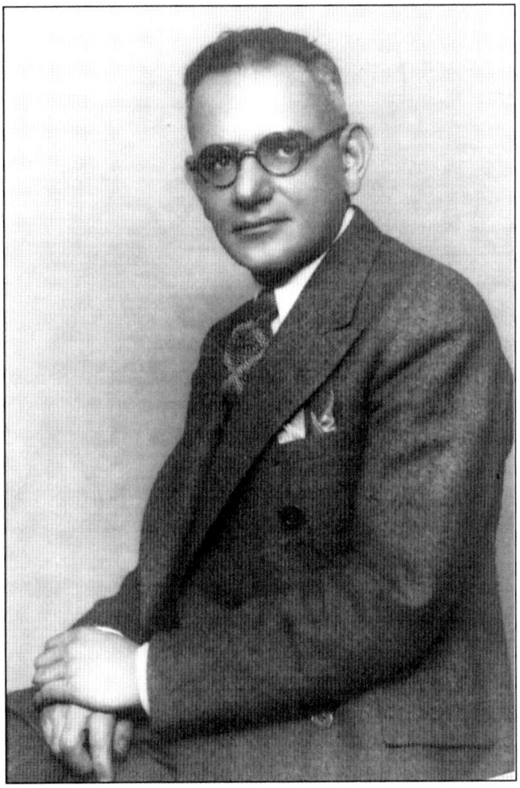

**DR. ROBERT RUBIN.** Family doctors in South Philadelphia had deep roots. Dr. Robert Rubin lived above his family's bakery shop at 413 Fitzwater Street, and as a child, he delivered bread with a horse and wagon. Dr. Rubin came from a family that treasured life since Robert's brother succumbed to the 1918 Flu epidemic. When Robert first started out at 2243 S. Ninth Street, he waived the 50¢ visit for people who could not afford to pay, and he supported the rabbi at the small shul located on Ninth above Porter Street. (Courtesy of Milton Kitei.)

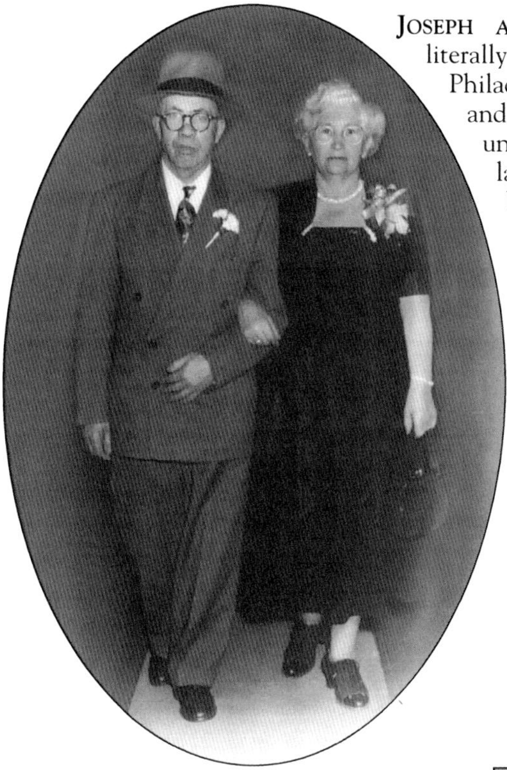

**JOSEPH AND LIBE KLEIN.** Joseph and Libe Klein literally added to the popular saying, "Watch South Philadelphia Grow." Joe came from Russia, in 1913, and he immediately changed his name in an unusual fashion when he adopted Klein as his last name after he ate a Klein's chocolate bar. New houses on S. Seventh Street and the small streets below Oregon Avenue had a trademark of Joseph Klein since he was a carpenter in the old country and an independent builder in Philadelphia in the 1920s. (Courtesy of Tsipoprah Klein Strauss.)

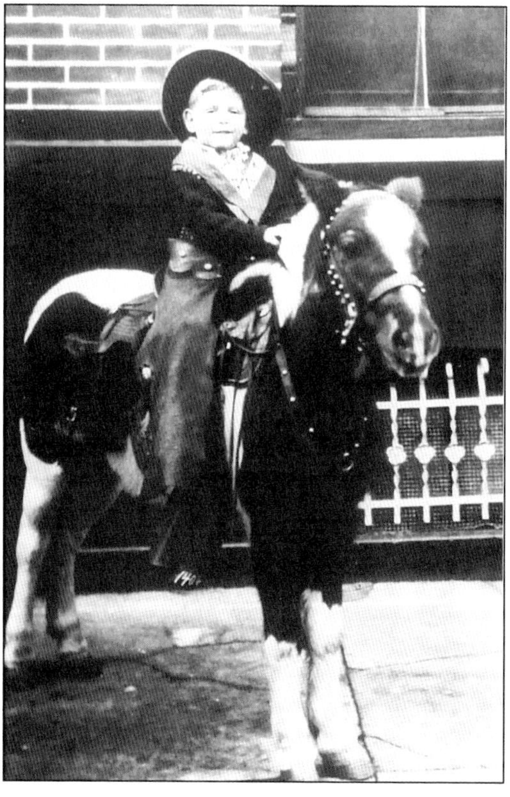

**BRUCE SCHWARTZ.** Many adults can recall their pony pictures. Bruce Schwartz, age 5, the son of Sam and Sallie Schwartz, was entrusted with Izzy Pearlman who ran Izzy's hot dogs on Seventh Street. Upon returning from a bar mitzvah luncheon affair, Mr. Pearlman lit the stove and the ensuing gas explosion, felt throughout the neighborhood, killed little Bruce Schwartz and Izzy. Young Bruce had a short life, but he was remembered for all time by his family, sitting tall in the saddle, atop a pretty pony on the sidewalk in South Philadelphia. (Courtesy of Sunny Rosenstein.)

**LEYBELE SATANOFFSKY.** Leybele (the shprekher) Satanoffsky transferred his folk-healing methods along with his family to South Philadelphia in the late 1890s. Folk medicine performed according to tradition swept the evil eye away from the person and thus perfectly healed many sick souls with prayers and potions that included a whipped egg and bonkunis (heated glass cups). East European Jews flocked to Leybele who lived on Monroe off Fourth Street instead of a visit to the modern Mt. Sinai Hospital for a treatment. Leybele's livelihood came to an end when he was required to have a license and refused to comply, in 1936. (Courtesy of the Philadelphia Jewish Archives Center at the Balch Institute.)

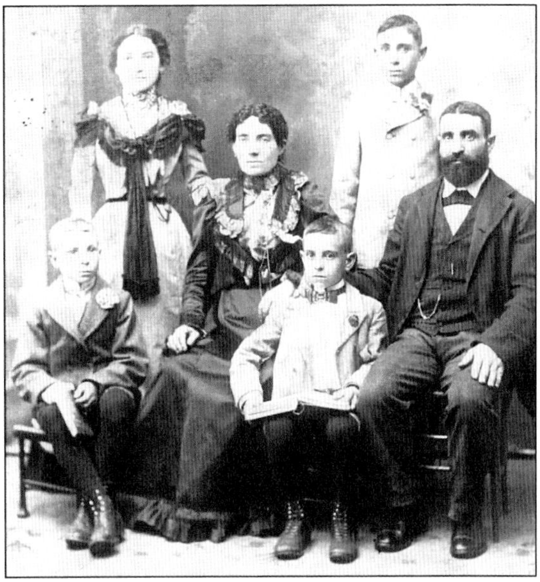

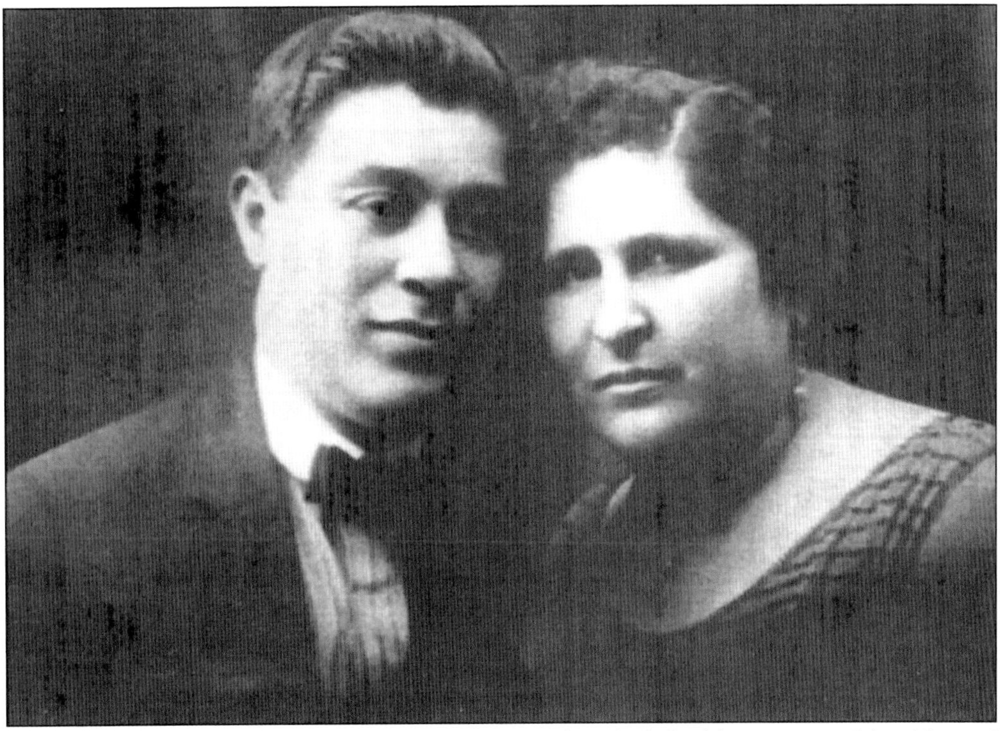

**ABE AND RACHEL KRETCHMAN.** Abe's Russian and Turkish bathhouse, owned by Abe and Rachel Kretchman at 317-321 Monroe Street in South Philadelphia, was divided into areas for both men and women, which made sense at a time when indoor bathrooms did not exist in many South Philadelphia homes. Towels and soap cost a nickel. Everyone brought a lunch along to enjoy. Four other bathhouses in South Philadelphia included one at Fifth and Lombard Street, Cohen's at Fifth and Morris, Tener's at 730 Snyder Avenue, and Rossman at 741 Porter Street, which also had a (Mikveh) or purification pool for the ladies. (Courtesy of Lillian Kretchman Abrams.)

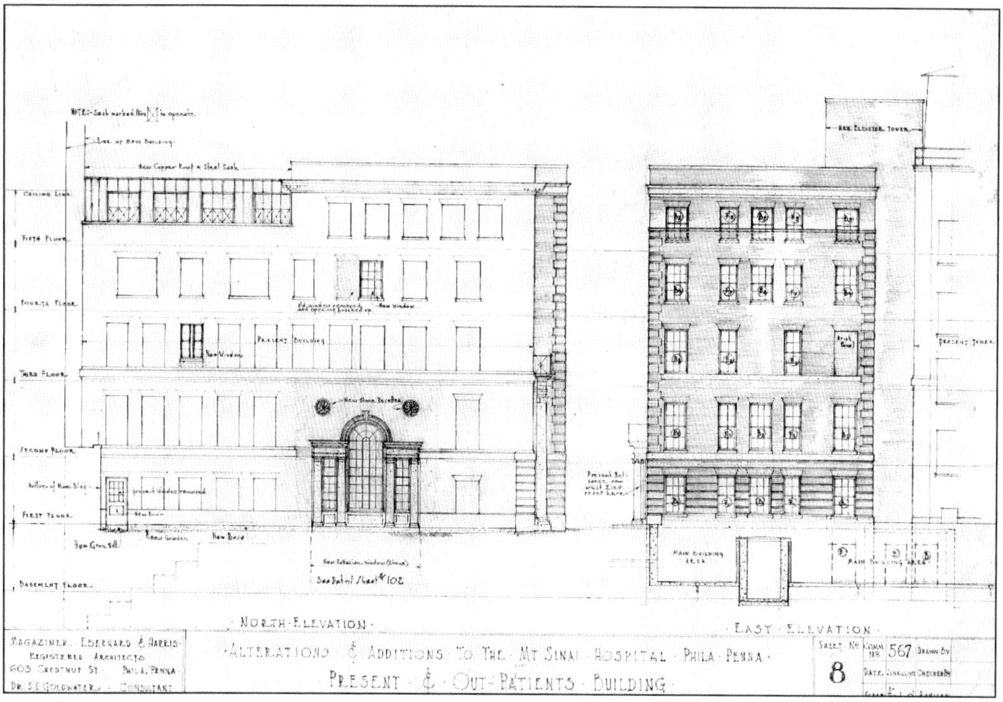


**MT. SINAI HOSPITAL.** The Mt. Sinai Hospital, organized and built in 1900, at Fifth and Reed Streets in South Philadelphia, towered as the largest landmark in the area. It was more than ten floors tall. In 1927, a new out-patient's wing designed by the most successful early 20th-century Jewish architect, Louis Magaziner, opened with the new Babies Club in use. The new out-patient program was the first of its kind in America with emphasis on babies' wellness and the prevention of disease. (Courtesy of the Athenaeum of Philadelphia.)

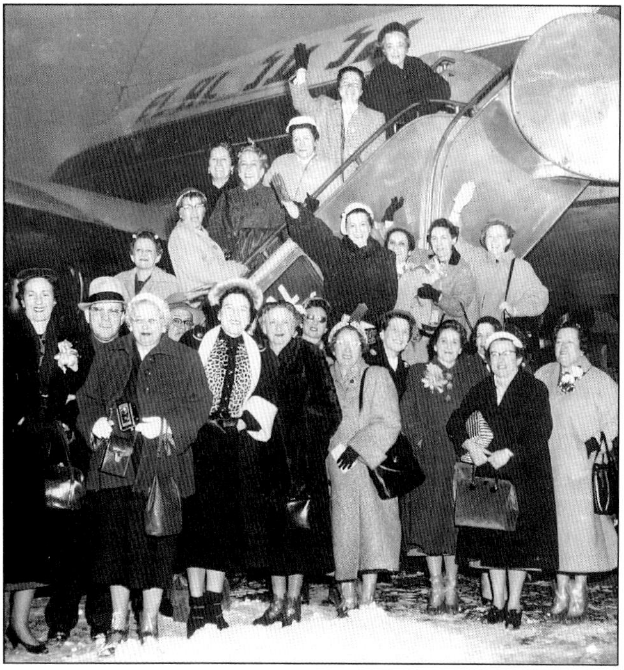

**HADASSAH.** South Philadelphia developed Zionist agency branches to support the development of Jewish projects in Palestine. Hadassah, the women's branch of the Zionist movement, founded in 1912, organized a South Philadelphia chapter led by Mrs. Rose Glider, in 1915. South Philadelphia Hadassah met in the Zionist Hall located at 1514 S. Sixth Street. A Junior Hadassah group led by Mrs. Joseph Litvin, played a critical role in expanding membership in the years after WW II. They traveled to Israel in the early 1950s to see their efforts at fund-raising. (Courtesy of Hadassah, the Women's Zionist Organization of America, Inc.)

*Nine*

# SOUTH PHILADELPHIA JEWISH PERSONALITIES

## MUSICIANS, ENTERTAINERS, AND ARTISTS

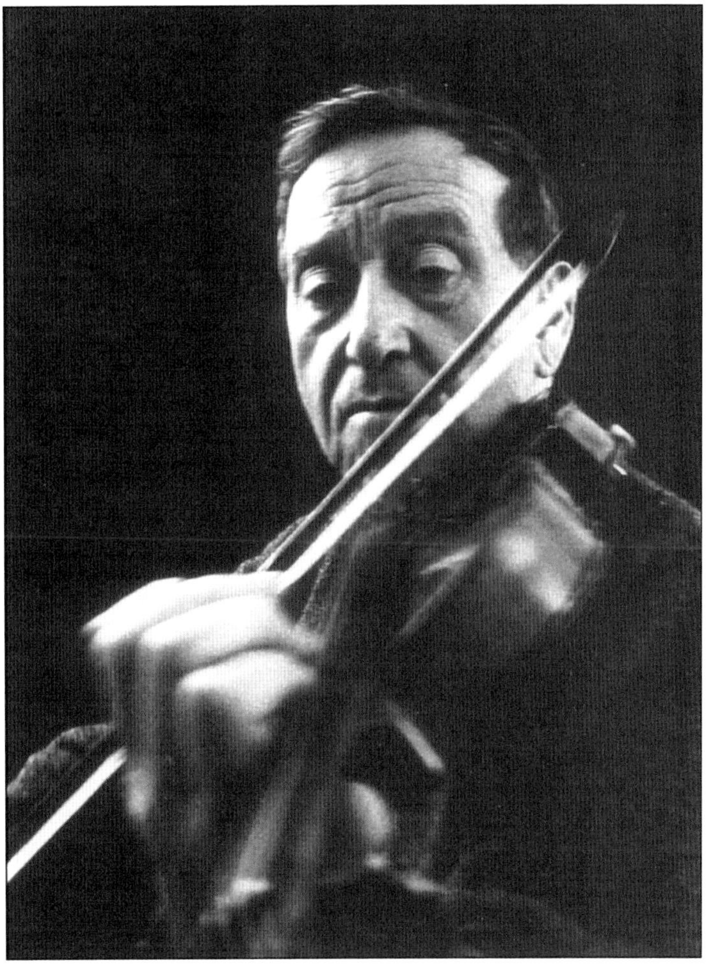

**MORRIS SHULIK.** Morris Shulik, a native South Philadelphian born at the Jewish Maternity Hospital on Spruce Street, learned to play the violin at an early age. William and Rose Shulik provided their son Morris with violin lessons at the Settlement Music School at Fourth and Queen Streets for 50¢ per week in the 1920s. Morris earned a scholarship to the Curtis Music Institute, and since WW II, he played for the Philadelphia Orchestra for more than 50 years. (Courtesy of Morris Shulik.)

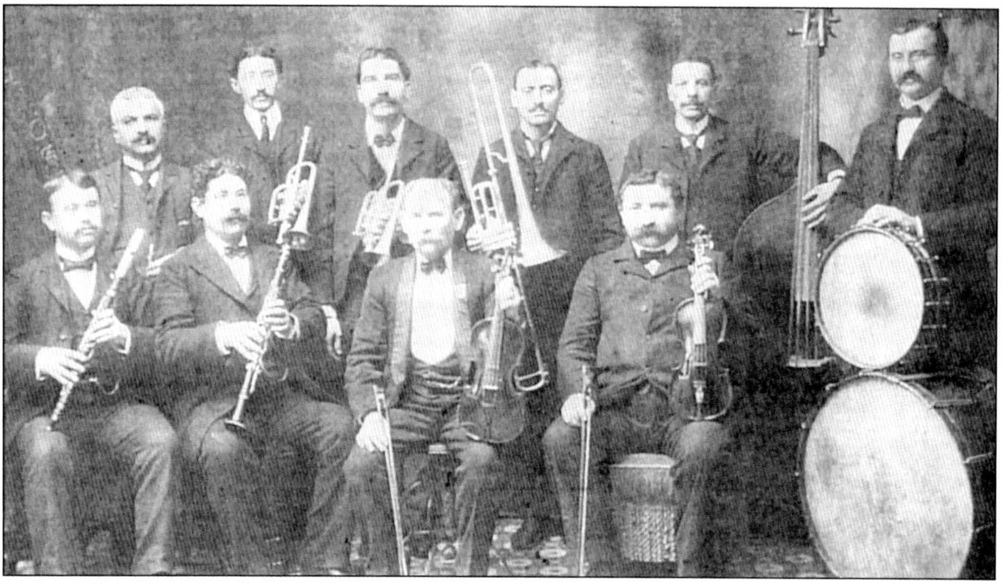

**Meyer Swerdlow's Orchestra.** The Meyer Swerdlow Orchestra originated from a group of men who lived near Fourth and Snyder Streets in the early 1900s. Meyer Dimmerman, pictured on the top row (third man from the right) led the wind section of the popular ten-person orchestra. Jewish frelochs (old world compositions) were read from bulgars (manuscript sheet music), which circulated among the old-time Jewish musicians. In the 1920s, bulgars bound into books sold for $15 in Freedman's Music Store, at Sixth and Morris Streets in South Philadelphia. (Courtesy of Marvin Katz.)

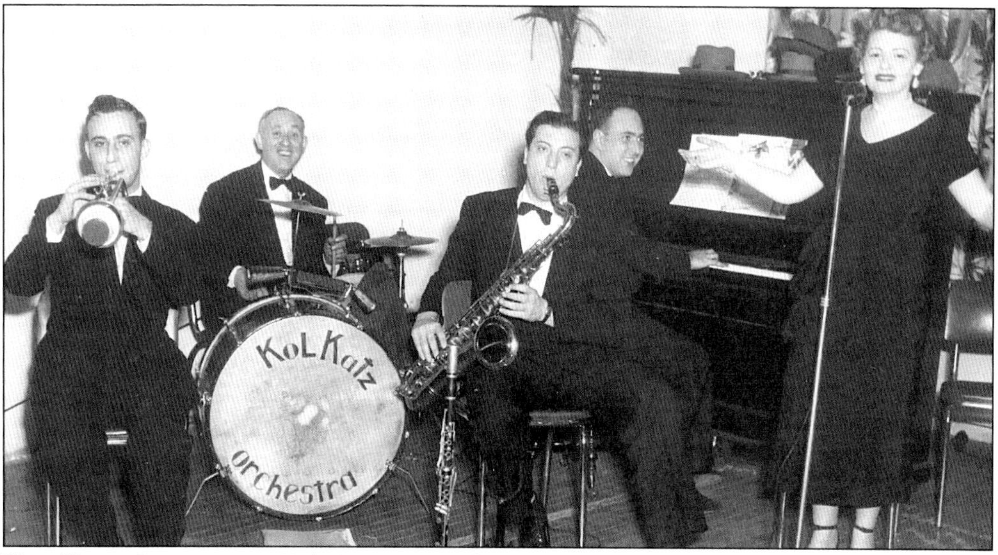


**Kol Katz Orchestra.** Kol "Man" Katz from 425 S. Fourth Street formed an orchestra in the 1920s. The Musician Union, Local #77, regulated the industry that featured other musicians, including Al Small, Mel Davis, Jerry Adlur, and Danny Shanken who played at Uhr's, Himmelsteins, and the Colonial Restaurants near Fifth and South Streets. The orchestra employed many musicians over the years. Pictured above in this 1950s photograph, from left to right, are as follows: Marvin Katz, Kol Katz, Joe Borock, and Harold Katz accompanied by singer Lynn White. (Courtesy of Marvin Katz.)

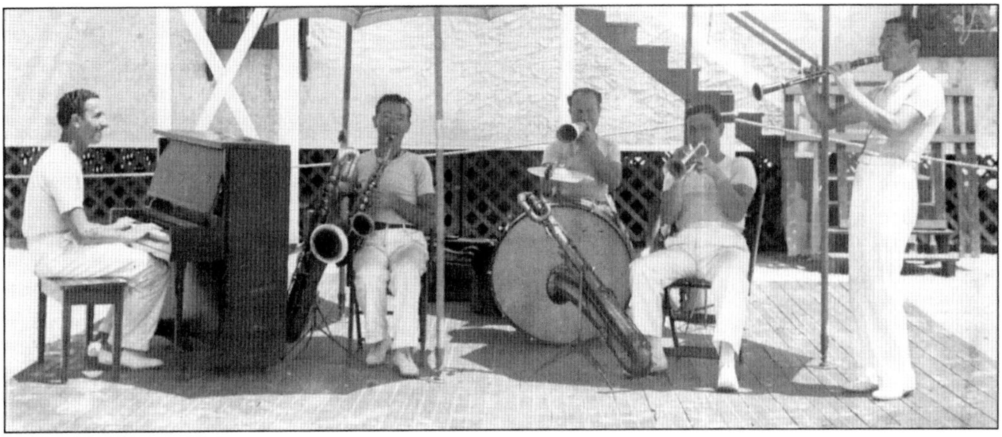

**Danny Shankin.** Danny "Cardboard" Shankin grew up in South Philadelphia, where he received world-class training from his music teacher, legendary Jay Speck, at Southern High School. The nickname of "Cardboard Danny" stuck to Danny Shankin for his unusual talent to play music that sounded like a trumpet from behind a large rolled up Jewish-theater poster. Danny Shankin played at weddings and bar mitzvahs in the well-known hotel ballrooms on Broad Street, which included the Majestic, the Broadwood, the Ambassador, the Savoy, the Bellevue, the Coronet, and later the Shelron. (Courtesy of Bobby Shankin.)

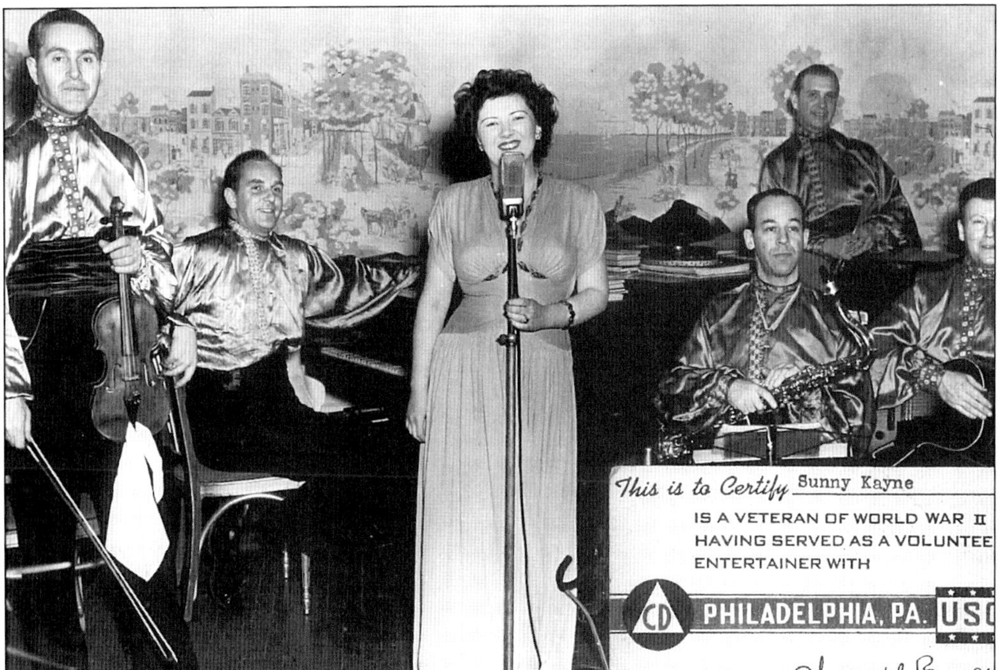


**Sunny Korostuff Rosenstein.** Sarah Korostuff grew up at 737 Jackson Street with a love for old Yiddish music inspired by her tante (aunt) Becky who wrote parodies for many Yiddish songs. Sarah taught Hebrew school at JEC #2 Marshall & Porter, where she kept the interest of the children through constant Jewish melodies. Sarah adopted her show business name as Sunnie Kayne when she performed in Atlantic City during WW II. Sunnie performed many times at USO functions around the country and with the Abe Neff orchestra pictured above. (Courtesy of Sunnie Korostuff Rosenstein.)

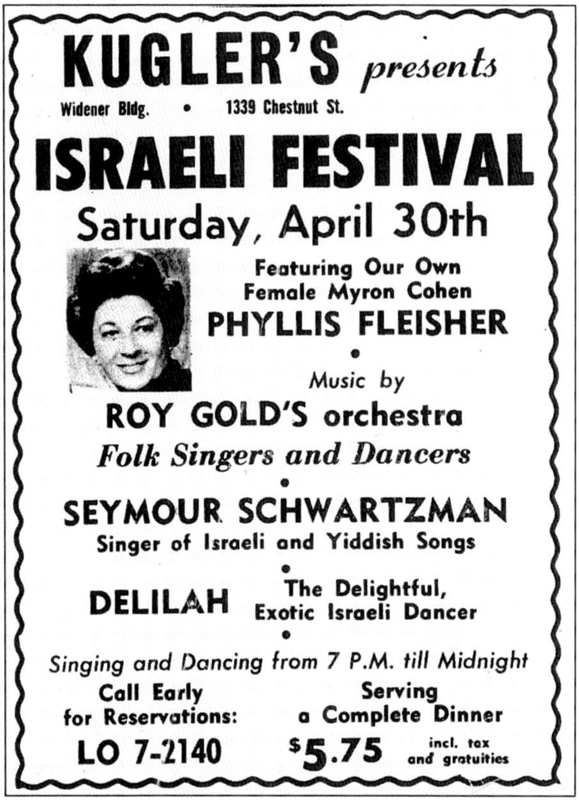


**PHYLLIS FLEISHER.** Phyliss Fleisher grew up near Seventh and Ritner Streets and always had a smile on her face in the 1930s. That friendly smile led to a career of making other people forget their troubles, if only for an evening of fun. Leon Brown, a professional journalist with the *Philadelphia Exponent*, wrote, "this lady is funny" and called her "a female Myron Cohen." Phyllis met with many Hollywood stars, but she remained a mentch, a person with respect for others due to her philosophy, "I'm not better than anybody, I'm different!" (Courtesy of Phyllis Fleisher.)

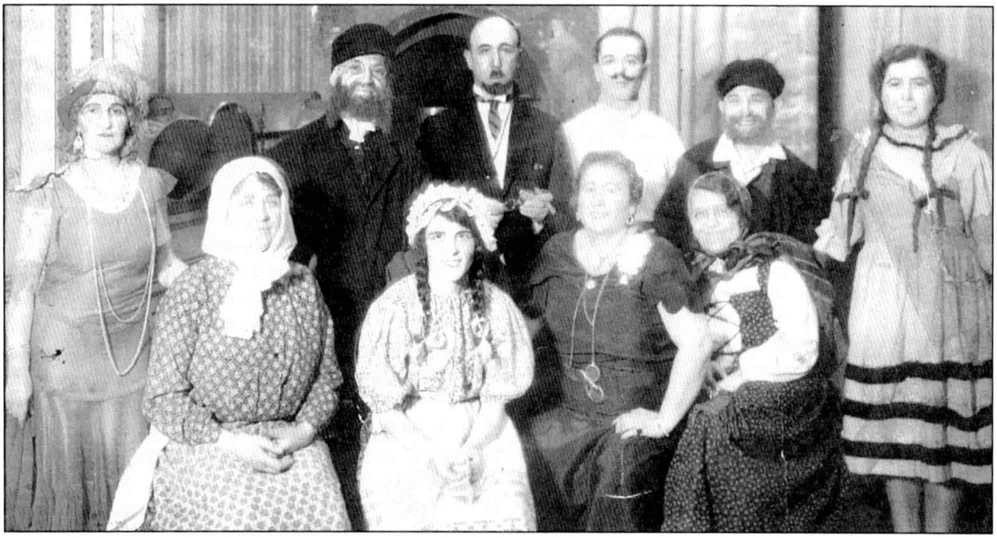

**THE PROFESSIONAL CIRCLE.** Entertainment had been the key to survival for the Jews over the centuries. The arrival of thousands of East European Jews to South Philadelphia in the early 20th century provided an instant audience. The Professional Circle, a troupe of ladies and men who labored as physicians, dentists, and pharmacists during the day, entertained the masses at night. The amateur actors wrote, produced, and staged their own productions in Yiddish. The productions were held at the Lincoln Theater at Broad and Lombard Streets until the new YMHA was built at Broad and Pine Streets in 1924. (Courtesy of Hillard Sorokin.)

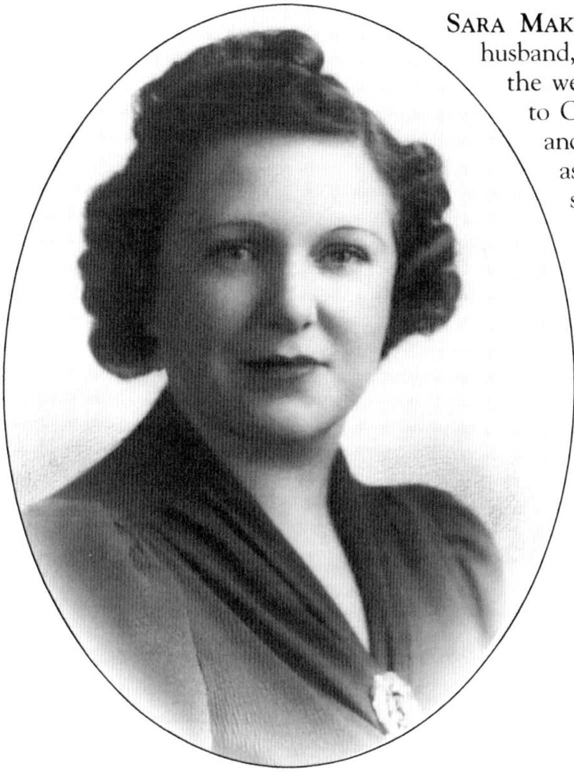

**SARA MAKLER.** Sara Youngelson Makler and her husband, Joe, lived at 1818 S. 24th Street on the west side of Broad Street. They belonged to Congregation Shaare Shomayim at 23rd and Wharton Street where Joe served as the men's club president, and Sara served as the sisterhood president. Sara entertained the ladies with her stories from the old country told in English and she won the Albert A. Light trophy, as Philadelphia's Champion of Jewish Wit, held at the YMHA at Broad and Pine Streets, in 1950. (Courtesy of Lorraine Makler Wagner.)

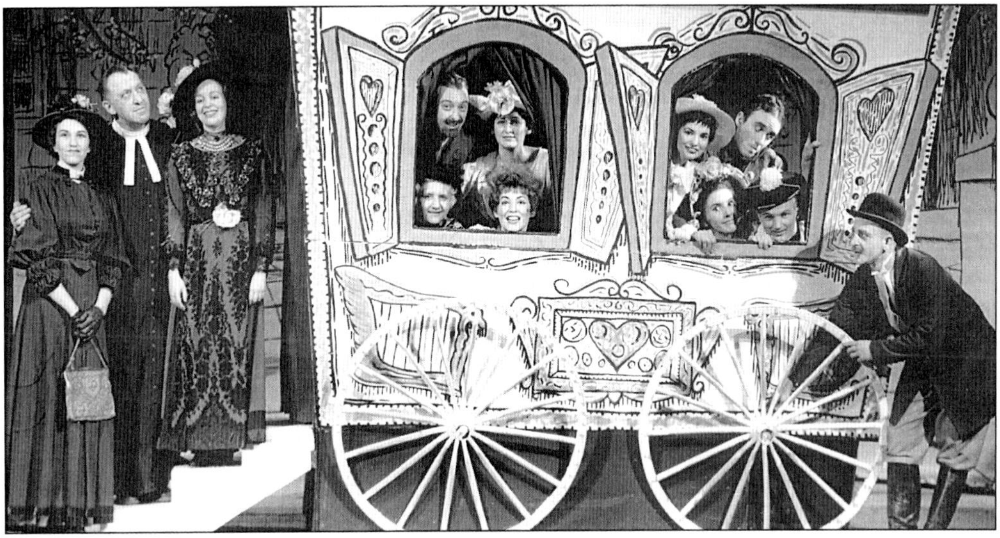

**THE NEIGHBORHOOD PLAYERS ACTORS GROUP.** Several groups of Jewish men and women performed small skits in the side streets of South Philadelphia for self-entertainment. The Neighborhood Settlement Center at Fifth and Bainbridge gave rise to productions in both Yiddish and English in the early 1900s. The Neighborhood Players once included Sonny Halpern, Chuck Romm, Doris Jacobson, Herb Cohen, Milton Moss, Milton Jason, and Rudy Bond. The picture above is a scene from Clerambard, a 1960 production starring Barbara Moskow, Ted Fertik, Jaon Kauders, Mickey Zacher, Lenore Propper, and Jay Hill. (Courtesy of Mickey Zacher and her brother Al Erlick.)

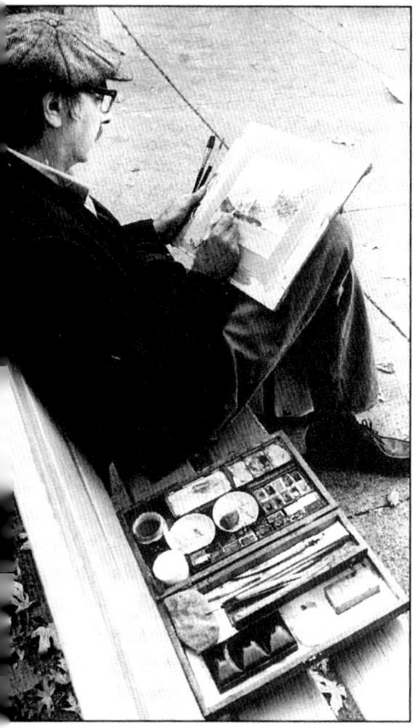 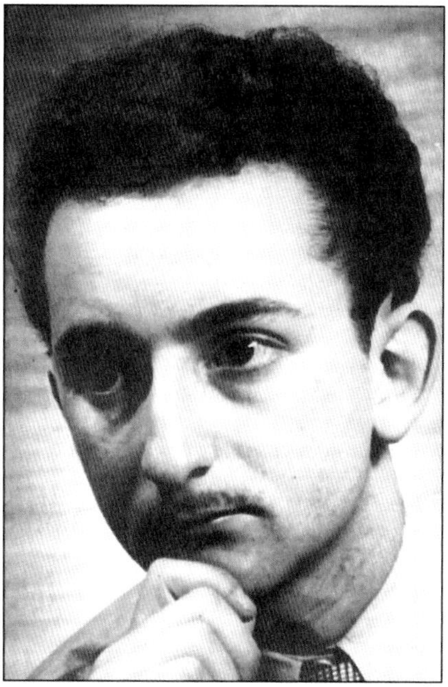 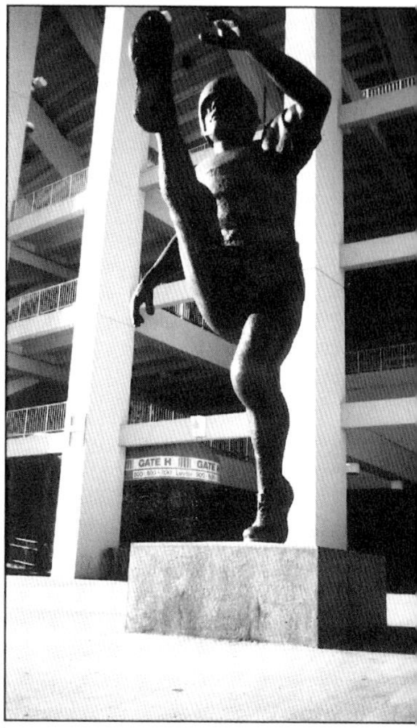

*Left:* **SEYMOUR REMENICK.** Seymour Remenick, a romantic-realism artist, was inspired as a child through his surroundings. He studied at the Fleisher Graphic Sketch Club, the Tyler School of Fine Art, and the Pennsylvania Academy of Fine Art. (Courtesy of Ed Bernstein, *Pat Little-Phila Journal.*) *Center:* **HAROLD MESIBOV.** Harold Mesibov, born at the Mt. Sinai Hospital, and his brother Hugh attended the Graphic Sketch Club in the 1930s. Harold is an abstract expressionist and Hugh, a Barnes Foundation graduate, is world-renown. (Courtesy of Harold Mesibov.) *Right:* **JOE BROWN.** Joseph Brown, a world-class sculptor from 23rd and Wharton, created the gigantic sports figures that surround Vet Stadium in South Philadelphia. They represent Joseph's philosophy on the exercising of real-life success and failure. (Courtesy of Allen Meyers.)

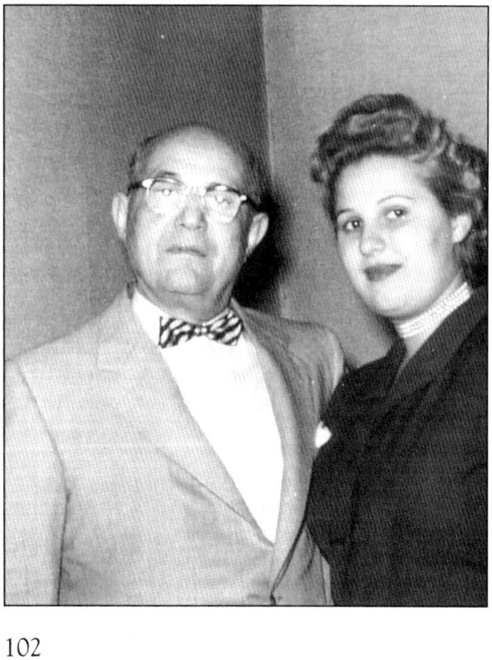

**JACOB SCHMIDT.** Jacob Schmidt, an Old World iron smith from Russia, handcrafted many wrought iron masterpieces when he was employed by Sam Yellin, and when he had his own shop at 2320 S. Tenth Street from 1910 until 1945. (Courtesy of Robin Fern Adelman.)

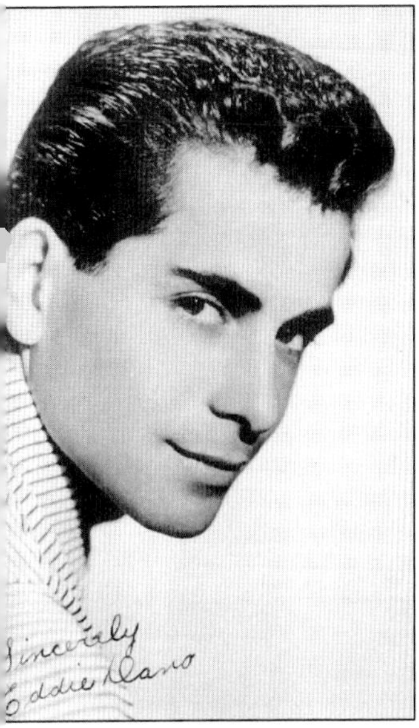

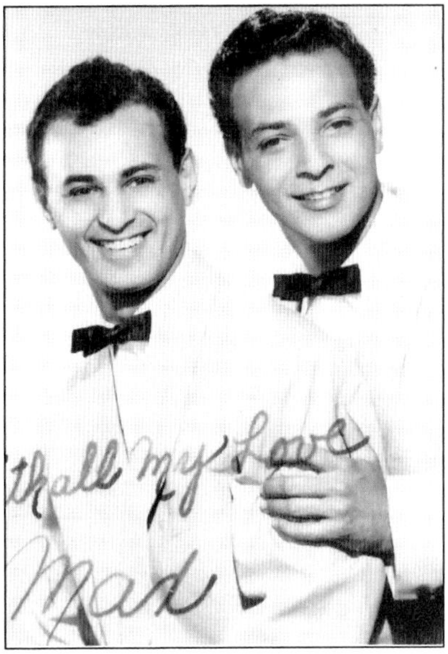

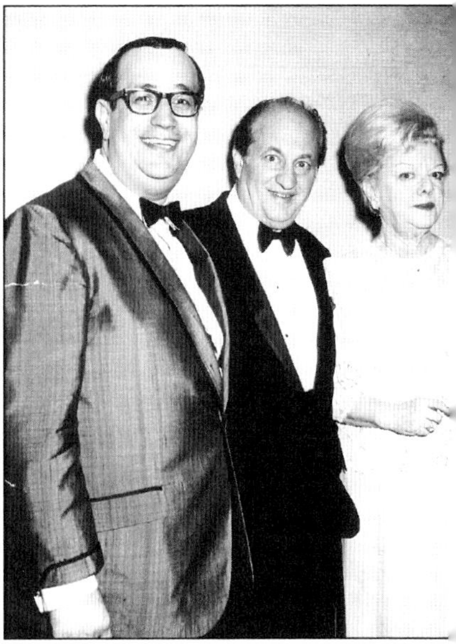

*Left:* **ED DANOWITZ.** Ed Dano (witz), from 432 Watkins Street, idolized Eddie Fisher, and was recognized by Hollywood promoter Larry Cohen, in 1955. Ed Dano worked for CBS as a teenage singer, best known for his hit, "My Last Night in Rome." (Courtesy of Ed Dano.) *Center:* **MAX AND EDDIE DAVIS.** Hollywood could have been in South Philadelphia! Max and Eddie Davis performed a song and dance duo similar to Dean Martin and Jerry Lewis, and they rehearsed in a house at 528 Fernon Street, in the 1950s. (Courtesy of Rose Davis.) *Right:* **LARRY FINE.** South Philadelphia, Home of the Stars, toted by Krass Brothers clothiers is based on fact. Larry Fine, pictured above, one of the Three Stooges, lived at Fourth and South Streets with Norman Fell, whose family owned the Bass Dairy Restaurant. (Courtesy of Bobby Block.)

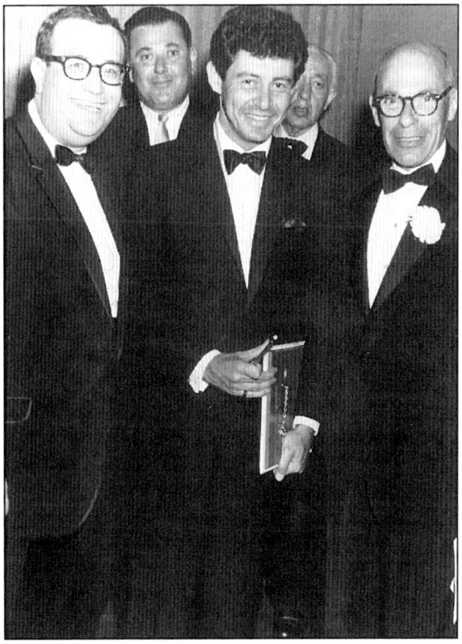

**EDDIE FISHER.** Eddie Fisher once sang throughout South Philadelphia as a huckster, and in the Eighth and Porter Street Shul (Kol Nidre) under Cantor Nate Grossman. Other stars included Joey Bishop, David Brenner, and Jack Klugman from the area. (Courtesy of Bobby Block.)

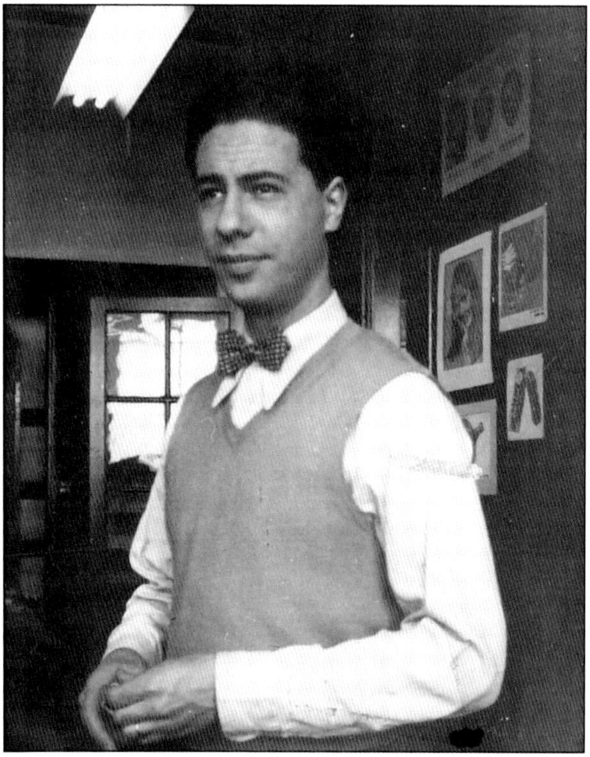

**ED BODEN.** Ed Boden, son of a South Seventh Street shoe merchant, went to the Fleisher Graphic Sketch Club at Seventh and Catherine Streets to study graphic arts. After graduating from Southern High in 1937, Ed attended the first post-graduate class at Bok Vocational High School at Eighth and Mifflin. Upon his return from service in WW II, Ed taught at Bok Vocational with the distinction as the first student to join the teaching staff in the graphic arts department. (Courtesy of Ed Boden.)

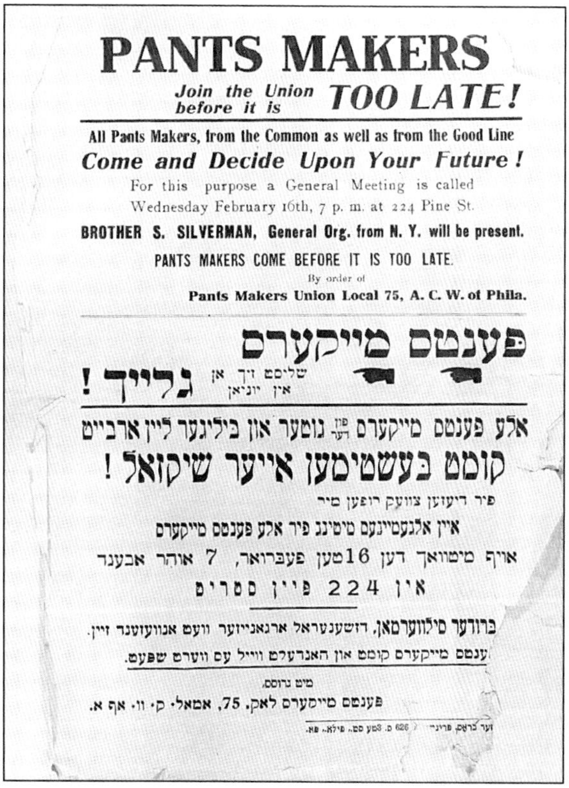


**UNIONS.** South Philadelphia became a hotbed of union organizing in the early 1900s. The Workman's Circle, or Arbeter Ring, acted as an umbrella organization to unite many workers with one voice. The amalgamated clothing workers union joined other groups including, the Hebrew Waiters, the musicians, the Jewish Baker, the Baker Drivers, Bathhouses Worker, Matzoh Bakers, the Cantors, the News Carriers, the Shocktim (Ritual Chicken slaughters), and the Jewish Wallpaper Hangers Union to demand fair pay, work conditions, and benefits in the workplace. (Courtesy of the Philadelphia Jewish Archives Center at the Balch Institute.)

# *Ten*

# FAMILY TIME

## RELATIVES, FRIENDS, AND FAMILIES CELEBRATE LIFE CYCLE EVENTS IN THEIR HOMES AND IN COMMUNITY INSTITUTIONS

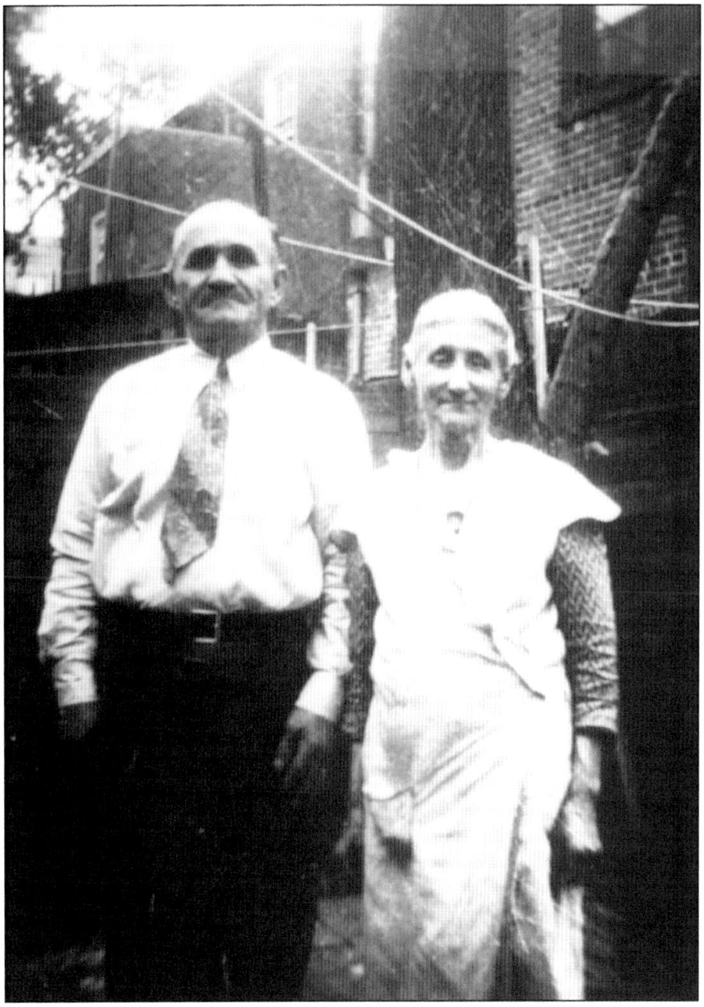

**NATHAN AND ROSE STURMAN.** Nathan and Rose of 512 Dickinson Street proudly pose in their own backyard. The parents of Maurice, Ben, Jack, and Bessie lived in South Philadelphia all their lives after they arrived from Russia in the early 1910s. An East European tradition to put down roots was passed onto the children, and Ben took pride in living in his parents home until his death in 1996, even as the neighborhood changed (Courtesy of Jack Sturman.)

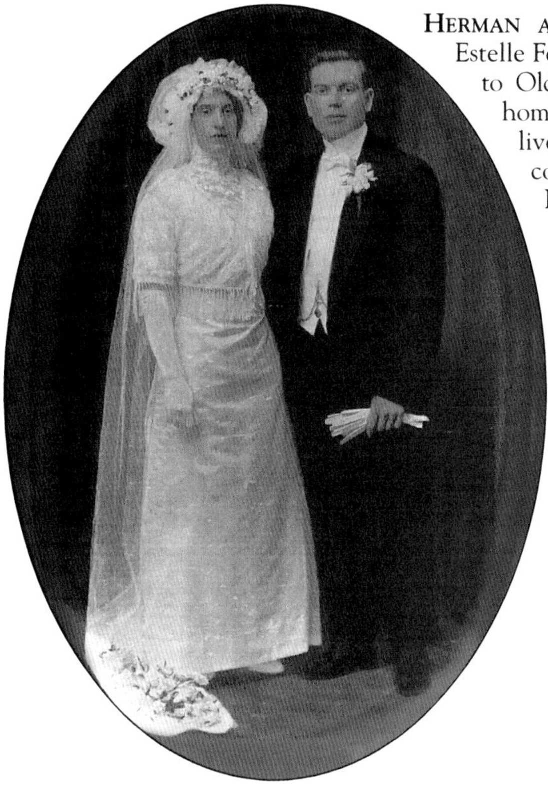

**HERMAN AND ESTELLE FEINSTEIN.** Herman and Estelle Feinstein were married in 1912, according to Old World traditions, right in the bride's home at Third and Spruce Streets. The couple lived at 514 Wharton Street, around the corner from the family-run Victory Soda Bottling Works, which in the 1920s had 14 trucks in operation. The company logo atop the beverage cap included an American flag with the word victory written on top, until the government told them to remove the writing on the flag. (Courtesy of Fred Feinstein.)

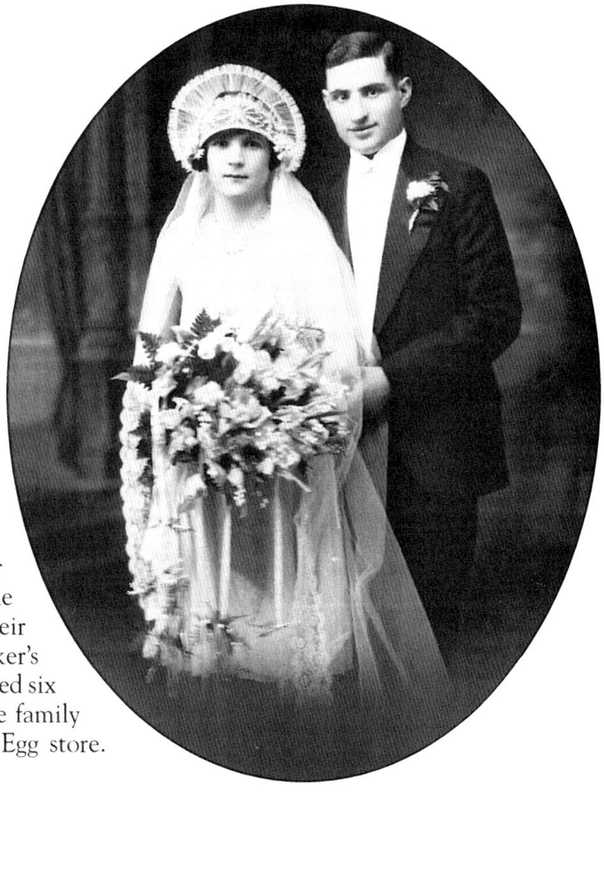

**RUBIN AND RAE LEVIN.** Rubin and Rae Levin were married on February 28, 1926, in the bride's house near Third and Catherine Streets. The couple so humbly accepted their wedding portrait as a present from Baker's Union Local #201, where Rubin worked six days a week. Meanwhile, Rae ran the family business, the White Rose Butter & Egg store. (Courtesy of Lee Levin.)

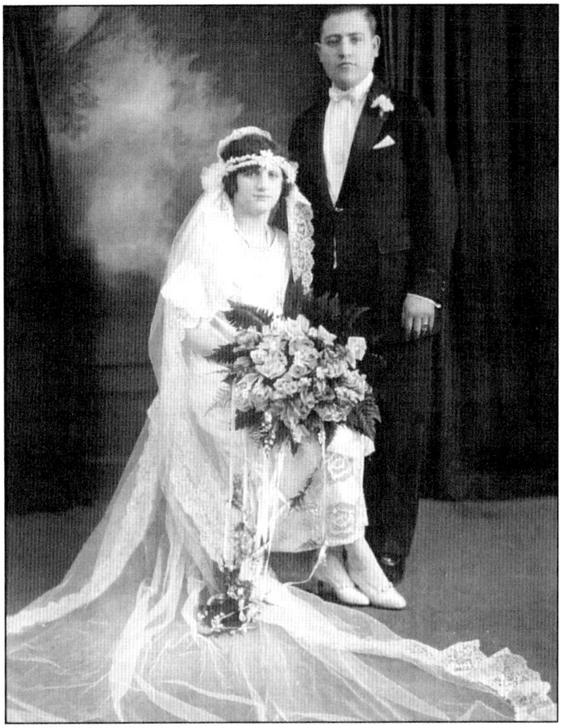

**HERMAN AND GUSSIE TAYLOR.** Herman and Gussie Taylor met as a couple in South Philadelphia in the 1920s. The large wedding took place at Stanton Hall, at the foot of Moyamensing and Snyder Avenues. The couple lived first at Fifth and McKean and later across the street from the Kremintzer Rebbe at 1903 E. Moyamensing, near Moishe's Delicatessen. (Courtesy of Jerome and Phil Taylor.)

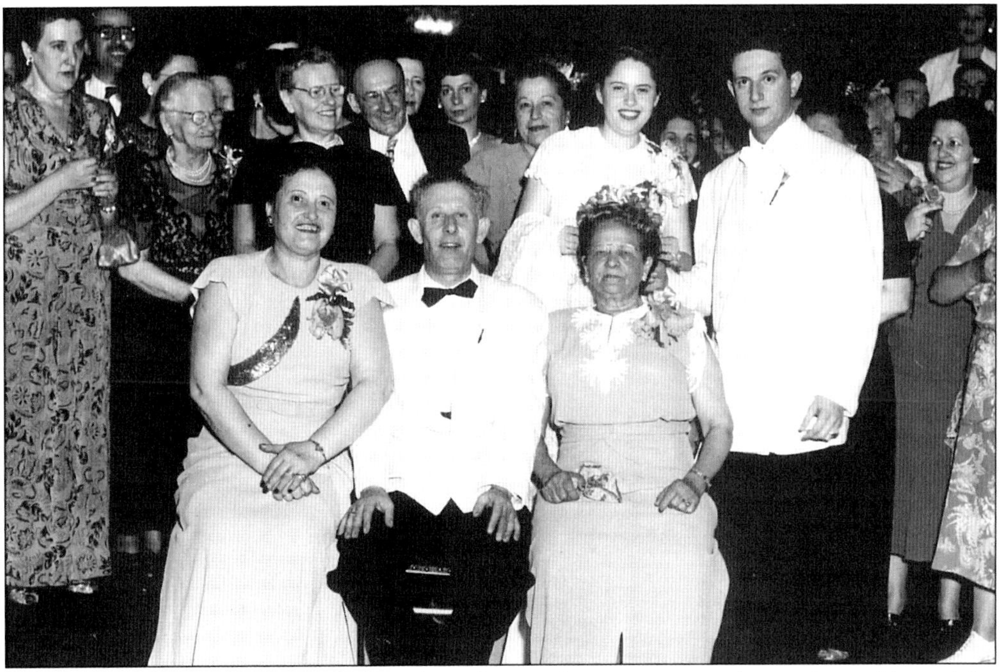

**THE CROWNING CEREMONY.** The Jewish tradition of crowning a mother at the wedding of the last child to get married is an old custom brought to America. Bud Liedman and Jean Stein were married on June 20, 1948. Seated left to right are the following: Sylvia Stein, Jack Stein, the Kosher Butcher from 2550 S. Seventh Street, and Mary Liedman, receiving the crown from Jean with the whole mispocha (family) looking on in great relief! (Courtesy of Bud Liedman.)

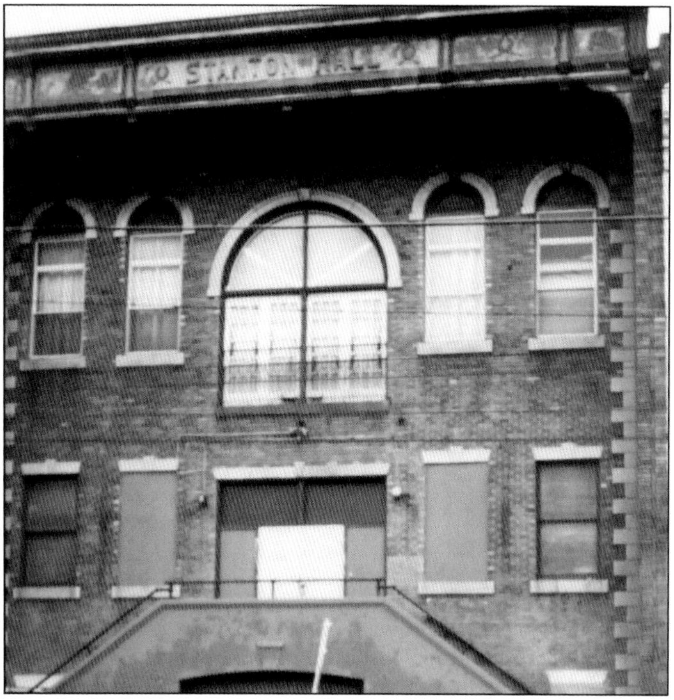

**STANTON HALL.** The largest hall in South Philadelphia below Washington Avenue was Stanton Hall, developed and built by real estate developer Jacob Babis, in the late 1920s. Social halls like bakeries, synagogues, bathhouses, and old age homes multiplied as the Jewish population migrated farther downtown in South Philadelphia. In addition, weddings, bar mitzvahs, sweet 16 parties, High Holiday services, and Hebrew Sunday school were held at the facility that could seat more than 750 people. (Courtesy of the Allen Meyers Jewish History Collection.)

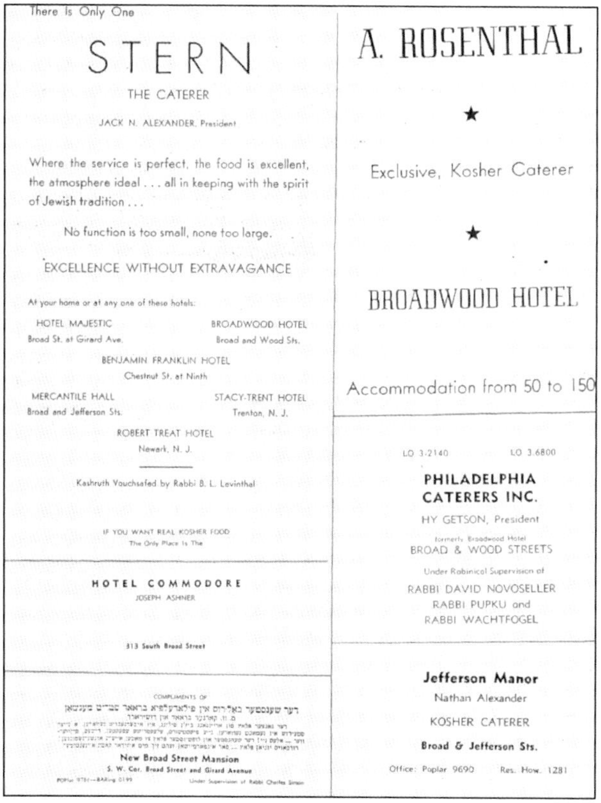

There Is Only One

STERN

THE CATERER

JACK N. ALEXANDER, President

Where the service is perfect, the food is excellent, the atmosphere ideal . . . all in keeping with the spirit of Jewish tradition . . .

No function is too small, none too large.

EXCELLENCE WITHOUT EXTRAVAGANCE

At your home or at any one of these hotels:

HOTEL MAJESTIC
Broad St. at Girard Ave.

BROADWOOD HOTEL
Broad and Wood Sts.

BENJAMIN FRANKLIN HOTEL
Chestnut St. at Ninth

MERCANTILE HALL
Broad and Jefferson Sts.

STACY-TRENT HOTEL
Trenton, N. J.

ROBERT TREAT HOTEL
Newark, N. J.

Kashruth Vouchsafed by Rabbi B. L. Levinthal

IF YOU WANT REAL KOSHER FOOD
The Only Place Is The

HOTEL COMMODORE
JOSEPH ASHNER

313 South Broad Street

COMPLIMENTS OF

דער שענסטער באל־רום אין פילאדעלפיא בראד סטריט מענשאן
ס. וו. קארנער בראד און דזשירארד

New Broad Street Mansion
S. W. Cor. Broad Street and Girard Avenue

POPlar 9751—BARing 0199 Under Supervision of Rabbi Charles Simon

A. ROSENTHAL

★

Exclusive, Kosher Caterer

★

BROADWOOD HOTEL

Accommodation from 50 to 150

LO 3-2140 LO 3-6800

PHILADELPHIA CATERERS INC.

HY GETSON, President

formerly Broadwood Hotel
BROAD & WOOD STREETS

Under Rabinical Supervision of

RABBI DAVID NOVOSELLER
RABBI PUPKU and
RABBI WACHTFOGEL

Jefferson Manor

Nathan Alexander

KOSHER CATERER

Broad & Jefferson Sts.

Office: Poplar 9690 Res. How. 1281

**CATERERS.** South Philadelphia Jews expected and received caterers that followed the Kashruth laws. Chief Rabbi L. Levinthal supervised several well-known caterers, including Stern the Caterer that traveled to different hotels to ensure Kosher accommodations for its clientele. The Philadelphia Jewish community supported 31 Kosher Caterers throughout the 1950s. (Courtesy Allen Meyers Jewish History Collection.)

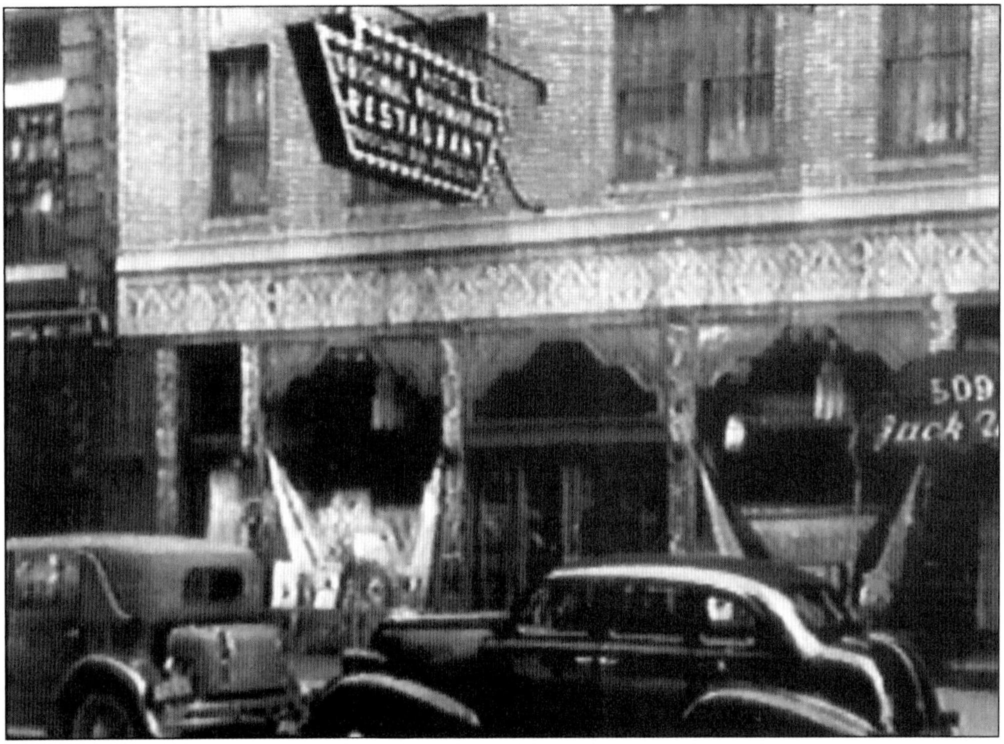


**UHR'S RESTAURANT.** Jack Uhr came from Romania in the early 1900s and he established an institution that lasted a lifetime for him and his boys, Bernie and Mort. Uhr's Real Romanian Restaurant, located above Fifth and South Streets, became a landmark with its three rooms for private affairs and main dining room that catered to three hundred people every night for dinner from kreplach to knishes. (Courtesy of Bernie Uhr.)

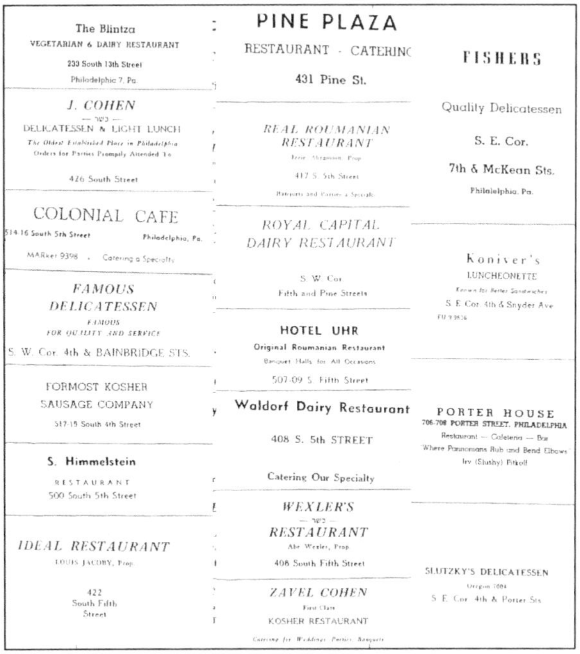

The Blintza
VEGETARIAN & DAIRY RESTAURANT
233 South 13th Street
Philadelphia 7, Pa.

J. COHEN
— כשר —
DELICATESSEN & LIGHT LUNCH
The Oldest Established Place in Philadelphia
Orders for Parties Promptly Attended To
426 South Street

COLONIAL CAFE
514-16 South 5th Street Philadelphia, Pa.
MARket 9398 . Catering a Specialty

FAMOUS DELICATESSEN
FAMOUS
FOR QUALITY AND SERVICE
S. W. Cor. 4th & BAINBRIDGE STS.

FORMOST KOSHER SAUSAGE COMPANY
517-19 South 4th Street

S. Himmelstein
RESTAURANT
500 South 5th Street

IDEAL RESTAURANT
LOUIS JACOBY, Prop.
422 South Fifth Street

PINE PLAZA
RESTAURANT - CATERING
431 Pine St.

REAL ROUMANIAN RESTAURANT
Izzie Abramson, Prop.
417 S. 5th Street
Banquets and Parties a Specialty

ROYAL CAPITAL DAIRY RESTAURANT
S. W. Cor.
Fifth and Pine Streets

HOTEL UHR
Original Roumanian Restaurant
Banquet Halls for All Occasions
507-09 S. Fifth Street

Waldorf Dairy Restaurant
408 S. 5th STREET
Catering Our Specialty

WEXLER'S
— כשר —
RESTAURANT
Abe Wexler, Prop.
408 South Fifth Street

ZAVEL COHEN
First Class
KOSHER RESTAURANT
Catering for Weddings, Parties, Banquets

FISHERS
Quality Delicatessen
S. E. Cor.
7th & McKean Sts.
Philadelphia, Pa.

Koniver's
LUNCHEONETTE
Known for Better Sandwiches
S. E. Cor. 4th & Snyder Ave

PORTER HOUSE
706-708 PORTER STREET, PHILADELPHIA
Restaurant — Cafeteria — Bar
"Where Pannonians Rub and Bend Elbows"
Irv (Slushy) Pitkoff

SLUTZKY'S DELICATESSEN
Oregon 7004
S. E. Cor. 4th & Porter Sts.

**KOSHER RESTAURANTS.** South Philadelphia was the home of the Kosher Restaurant during its heyday from 1920 to 1960, with more than 50 establishments that maintained the Kashruth laws. Many restaurants had middle-aged men who made a good living, and some belonged to the Hebrew waiters union. Some restaurants were dairy or meat only, while others maintained two separate menus. Foremost Kosher Sausage Company made the kosher meat provisions for many establishments in the heart of the immigrant section at Fourth and South. (Courtesy of the Allen Meyers Jewish History Collection.)

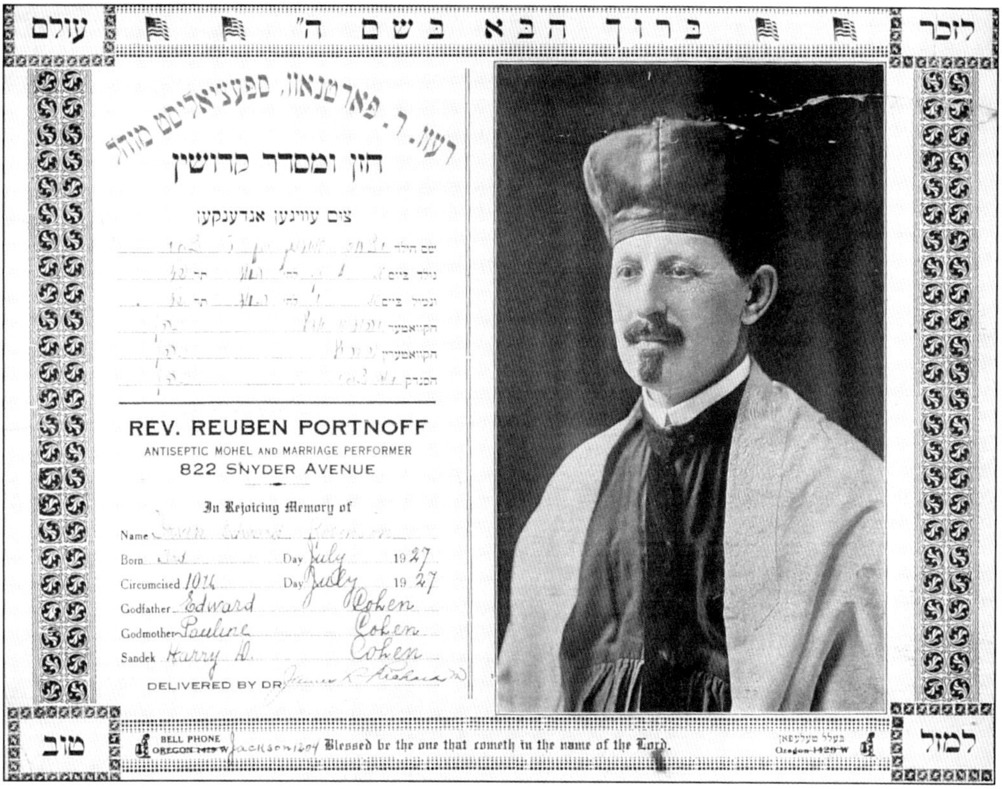
לזכר ברוך הבא בשם ה" עולם

הזן ומסדר קדושין

צום עוויגען אנדענקען

REV. REUBEN PORTNOFF

ANTISEPTIC MOHEL AND MARRIAGE PERFORMER

822 SNYDER AVENUE

In Rejoicing Memory of

Name

Born Day July 1927

Circumcised 10th Day July 1927

Godfather Edward Cohen

Godmother Pauline Cohen

Sandek Harry H. Cohen

DELIVERED BY DR.

למזל טוב

BELL PHONE OREGON 1419 W Jackson 1204 Blessed be the one that cometh in the name of the Lord.

Oregon 1429 W

**MOHELS.** Life-cycle events for Jewish people included the celebration of a son, with a Bris (circumcision). The celebration in the home of the proud parents automatically commenced on the eighth day of life according to Biblical law. For Edward Robinson, the ceremony was performed by Mohel Rev. Reuben Portnoff on July 10, 1927. The simcha (joyous occasion) demanded a day off from work! South Philadelphia, with a Jewish population of 125,000, kept several dozen Mohels busy throughout the 1930s. (Courtesy of Captain Edward Robinson.)

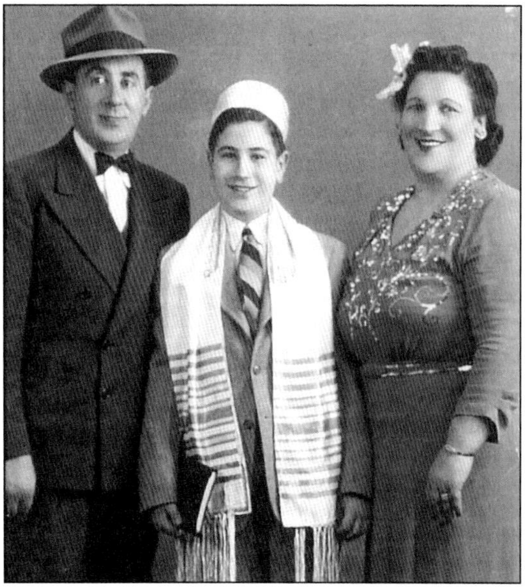

**BAR MITZVAH.** The bar mitzvah (son of the commandments) boy in South Philadelphia was an institution all by himself. Preparation for that special moment in time took years of studying and planning. Hebrew school training lasted five or six years four times a week after school, and then a young man could take his rightful place in the synagogue. Bobby Block, the bar mitzvah boy, stands tall with his parents at his side. (Courtesy of Bobby Block.)

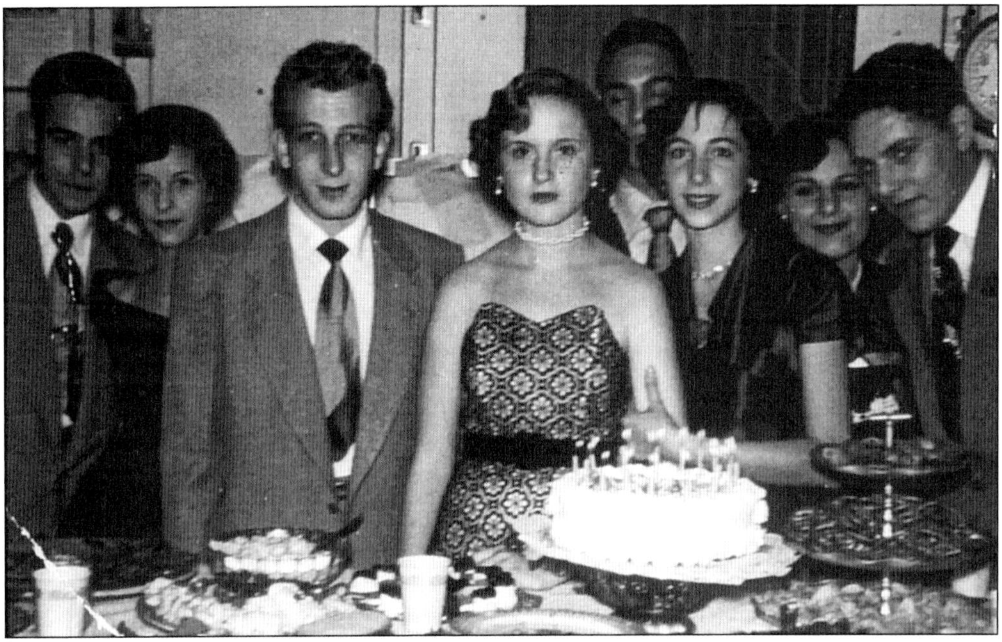

**SWEET 16 PARTY.** The South Philadelphia Jews became assimilated in their own community and celebrated American traditions. A party filled with presents for the girl who turned 16 was most sought after, especially by Betty Kaplan, whose Uncle Harry Betoff sponsored the life cycle event right in the Abe Kaplan Kosher Meat Market at 1612 S. Seventh Street. (Courtesy of Betty Kaplan Lerner.)

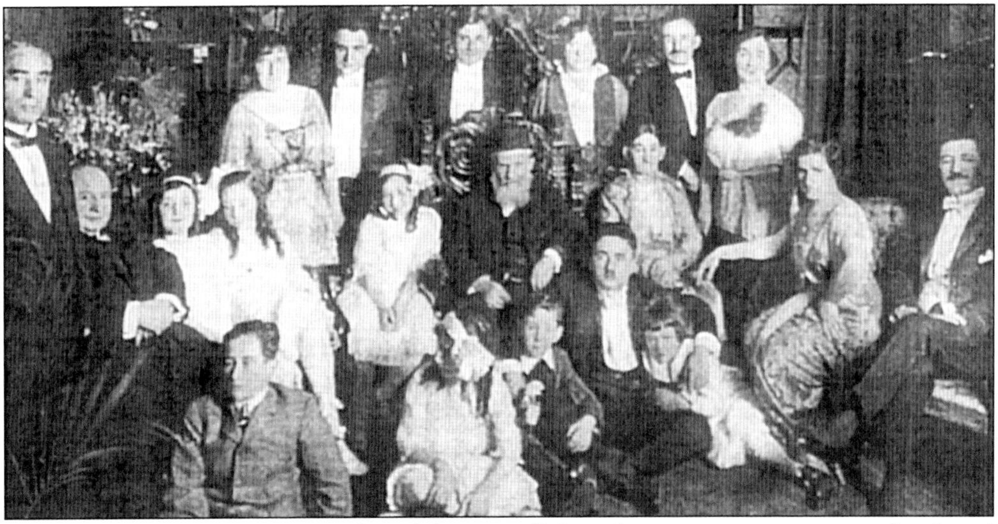

**50TH WEDDING CELEBRATION.** The celebration of life-cycle events is a testament to family and friends that binds large groups into extended families. Disruption of this natural process with the dispersal of Jews from their homeland in the Pale of Settlement made wedding anniversaries even more meaningful here in America. Michael and Mindell of Silverman from Vilna owned Silverman and Son's Department Store at Sixth and South Streets. They celebrated their Jubilee wedding anniversary of 50 years in their home at 507 Pine Street. The Silverman, Koffler, and Gartman families sponsored this simcha in 1908. (Courtesy of Rosalie Goldstein.)

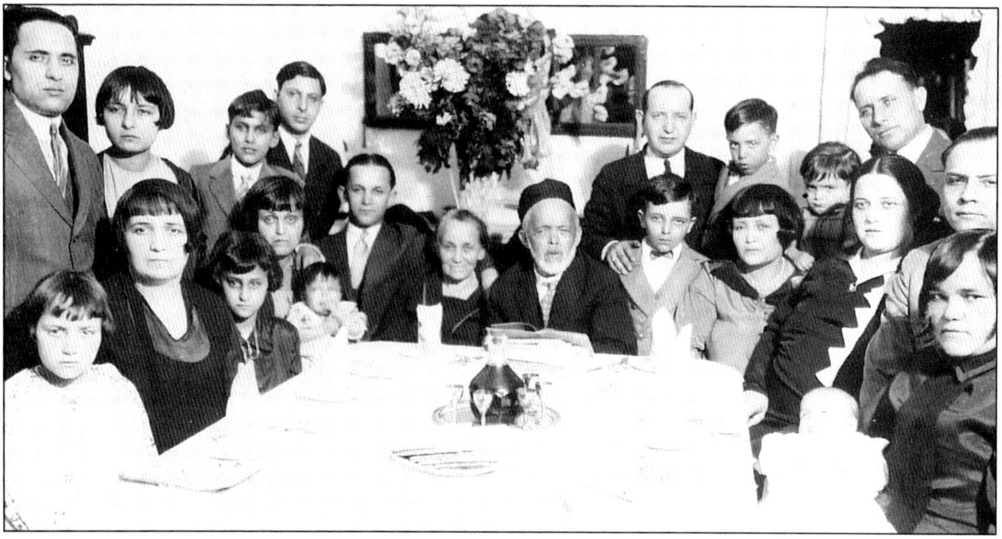

**FAMILY SEDER.** Family gatherings especially at Yontav (holidays) allowed whole extended families to see one another and enjoy each others company. The Passover Seder in South Philadelphia occupied a very special time in the home of Itzchok and Freda Moliver who lived next to the B'nai Moishe Synagogue at 1705 S. Fifth Street. The Solomon Gorewitz, William Benoff, Isadore Rodansky, and Ben Burkat families walked from different sections of South Philadelphia, including Third and Porter, to attend the first Seder according to tradition in the wife's family household. (Courtesy of Edith Gorewitz Weinstein.)

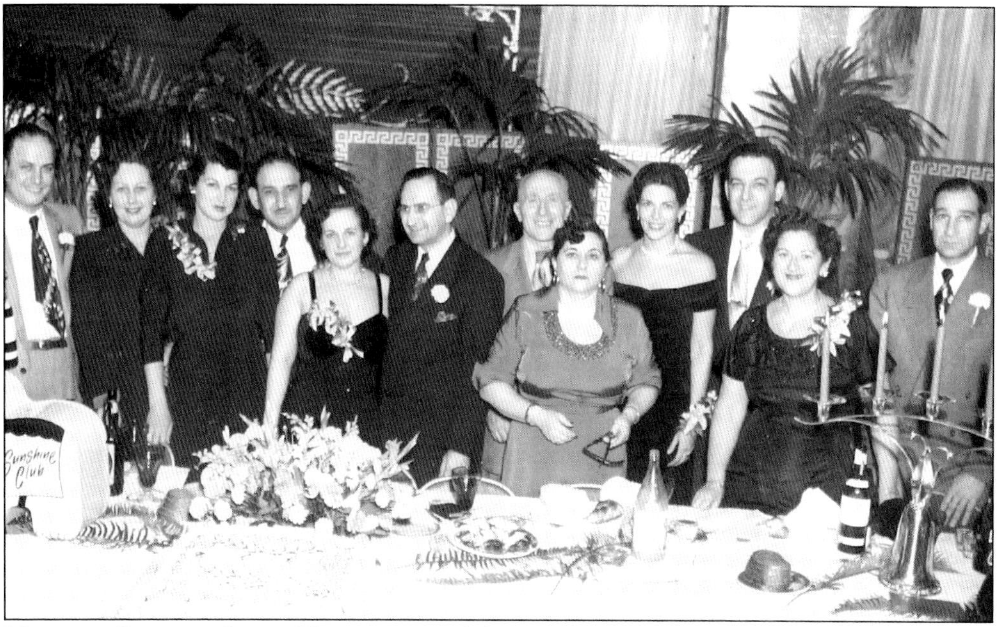


**MARRITZ COUSINS CLUB.** The creation of the Cousins Club defined the American-Jewish family as one unit. Social affairs binded the Meritz, Marrits, and Marritz Cousins Club into a cohesive group separated by migration to newer neighborhoods after WW II. The annual and sometimes monthly affairs were held at Uhr's Restaurant for all to Kibbitz (talk) about their adjustments to neighborhoods such as Oxford Circle, Mt. Airy, and Overbrook Park while they broke bread in their old neighborhood downtown. (Courtesy of Lois Sernoff.)

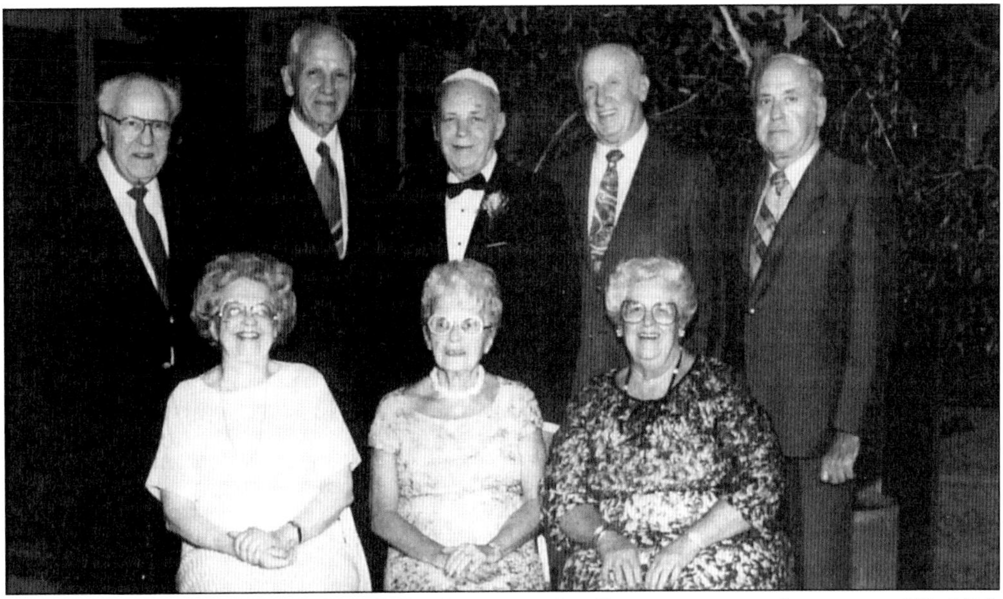

**THE PEARSON FAMILY.** Large Jewish families existed in Russia to ensure the saying of Kaddish (prayer for the deceased) due to the high mortality rate. In America, that tradition continued in the early 20th century based on a desire to build a strong sense of family. The nine children in the Pearson family lived with their parents, Lena and William, at 340 Queen Street. William supported Harry, Albert, Jack, Dave, Lou, Monte, Sylvia, Rose, and Anne by working as a supervisor for Freidman's Matzoh Bakery at Seventh and Bainbridge Streets. (Courtesy of Monte Pearson.)

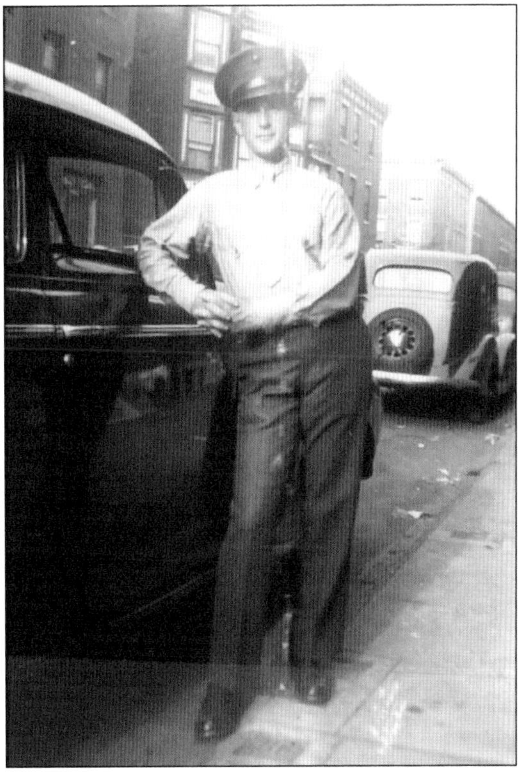

**BEN STURMAN.** The proud and the few South Philadelphia Jewish boys who joined the U.S. Marines signed up at Draft Board #58 on Snyder Avenue. Ben Sturman (right) from Dickinson Street, informed his parents that the men in his platoon enjoyed the Passover survival kit of Matzoh, assorted nuts, and hard candy, in 1942. Mike Feldman from Feldman's Malt Shop at Fourth and Snyder made the ultimate sacrifice when Pearl Harbor was attacked on December 7, 1941. Irv Borowsky's father proudly displayed five blue stars on a felt drapery in his front window at Third and Moyamensing Avenue to indicate he had five sons in the service. (Courtesy of Jack Sturman.)

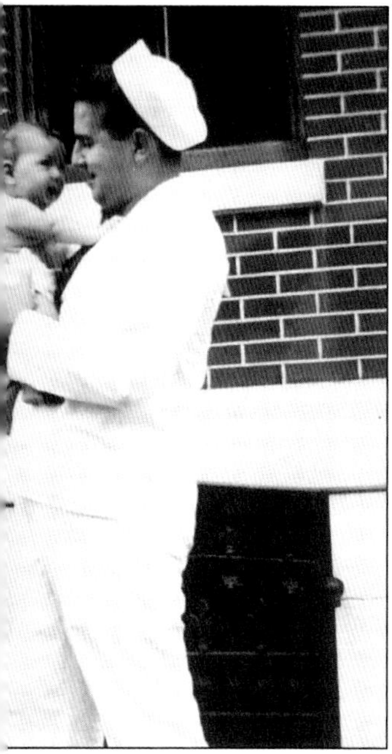
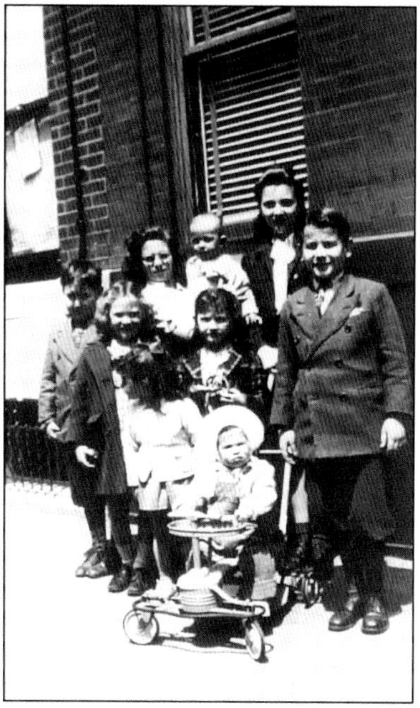
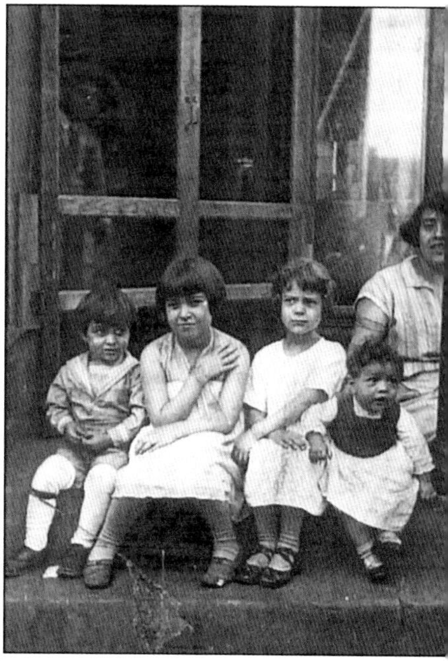

*Left:* **SAILOR.** Precious moments were shared by Kalman Balsham who held his daughter Bobbie in front of 2600 S. Alder Street during 1943, while on leave from the U.S. Navy. (Courtesy of Norman Leibovitz.) *Center:* **THE WINTON STREET CHILDREN.** Winton Street, home of the Winton Tigers baseball team, was quiet on the High Holidays. Morris and Howard Grossman, Sylvia Stern, and Eli Debs pose with their new shoes at 427 Winton Street. *Right:* **FISHMAN'S CANDY STORE.** Fishman's Candy Store at American and Porter, with its familiar corner pole, became the perfect setting for Bella, Sylvia, Sol and his mom, Rose, as they pose for a family portrait, in 1925.

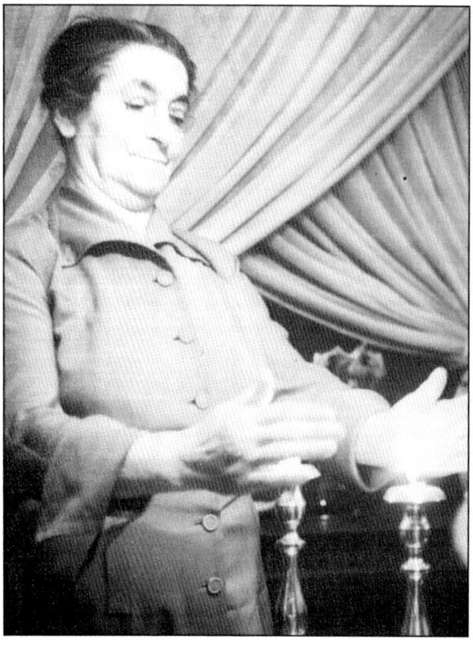

**DORA ROBINSON CANTEEN MANAGER.** Dora Robinson, a devoted mother and wife, ran the Canteen at the YMHA on Broad and Pine Streets. The service men and women received a meal, a hot shower, and had their uniform pressed by hand. (Courtesy of Captain Edward Robinson.)

# *Eleven*

# NEIGHBORHOOD SYNAGOGUES

## THE CORNER SYNAGOGUES, HOUSE STREIBLES, AND MUSHROOM SHULS, ALONG WITH THE CANTORS AND RABBIS

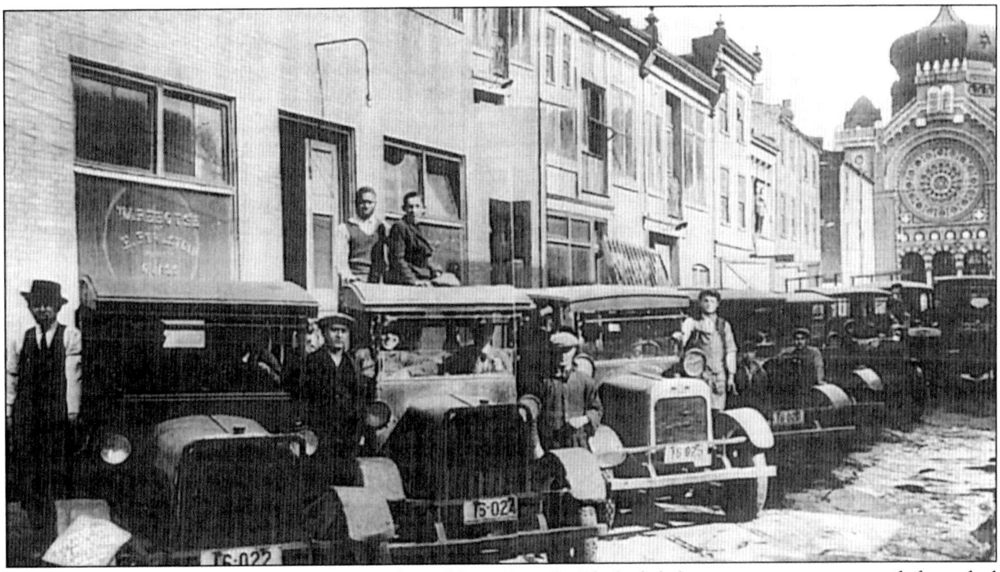

**B'NAI ABRAHAM.** B'nai Abraham, the oldest South Philadelphia congregation and founded in 1882, served as the official synagogue for Chief Rabbi B.L. Levinthal when he arrived in Philadelphia in 1891. The large Russian synagogue at 521 Lombard Street had an onion dome similar to Russian palaces. The dome topped the building and metaphorically represented the Crown of Israel. Harris Perilstein was a member, and his glass company was situated on Randolph Street leading up to the synagogue. Today, the onion dome no longer exists and the synagogue enjoys a rebirth with the help of the Lubavitch. (Courtesy of Robert Perilstein.)

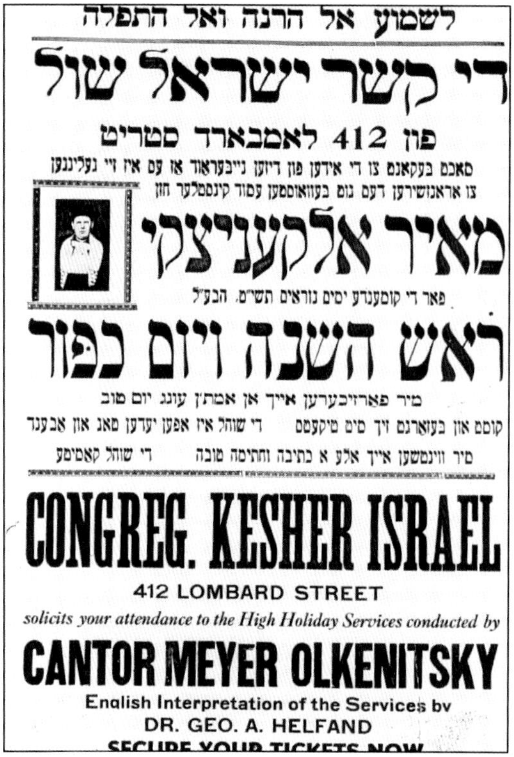


**CANTOR MEYER OLKENITSKY.** The Kesher Israel Synagogue at 412 Lombard Street on an annual basis engaged the Cantor for its High Holiday services. The Cantor's union listed available positions, and the men auditioned before synagogue boards in August. Mr. S. Romm booked and sent religious leaders to synagogues to serve as the Chazzan (Cantors). The best voice landed the most prestigious jobs in South Philadelphia's synagogues. (Courtesy of Michael Yaron and Abe Mersky.)

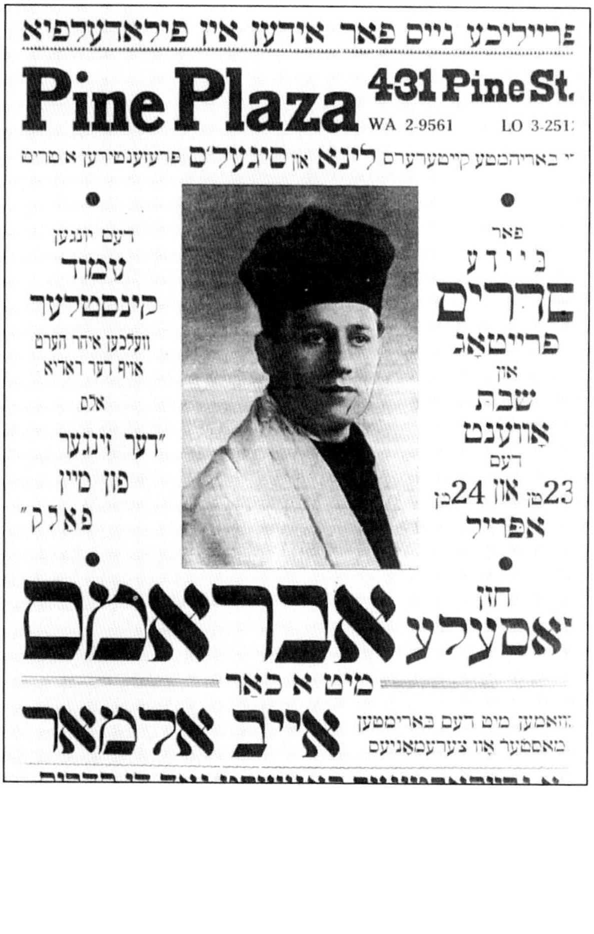


**CANTOR JOSEPH ABRAMSON.** South Philadelphia's large Jewish population created more than 155 synagogues to provide a dignified place of worship. The overflow of the masses for High Holiday services, which ushered in a new year, created the demand for a Mushroom Shul, a building such as a movie theater, social hall, or empty store sprouted up only for the High Holidays. Cantor Joseph Abramson (of blessed memory), the father of Leonard Abramson, led the Kosher Butcher Association in Philadelphia. (Courtesy of the Allen Meyers Jewish History Collection.)

**HEBREW BOOK STORE.** The ultra-religious men who observed the Sabbath made a living by slaughtering meat or chicken according to Jewish Law. Some men conducted a cheder (a private Hebrew school) in their small quarters or became the shamus (caretaker for a synagogue) to ensure that they did not have to work on the Sabbath. This led to the creation of private streibles (synagogues in houses). Rev. Israel Rovinsky and the Grand Rabbi Twersky both opened their places of prayer to the public, but they owned the synagogue, in the 1920s. (Courtesy of the Allen Meyers Jewish History Collection.)

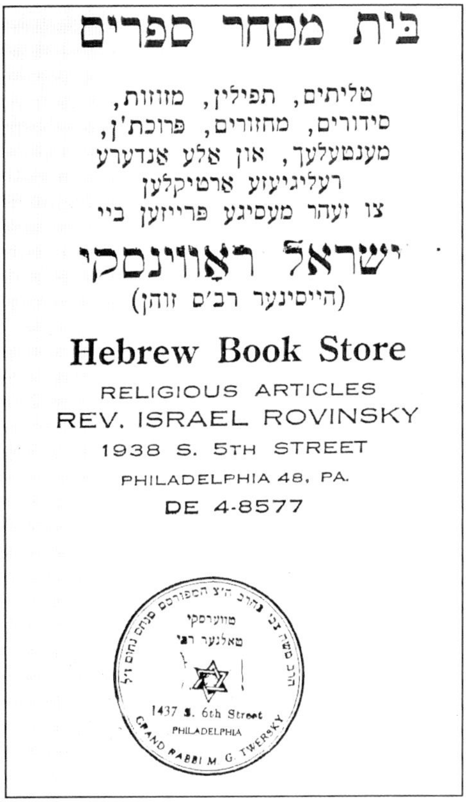


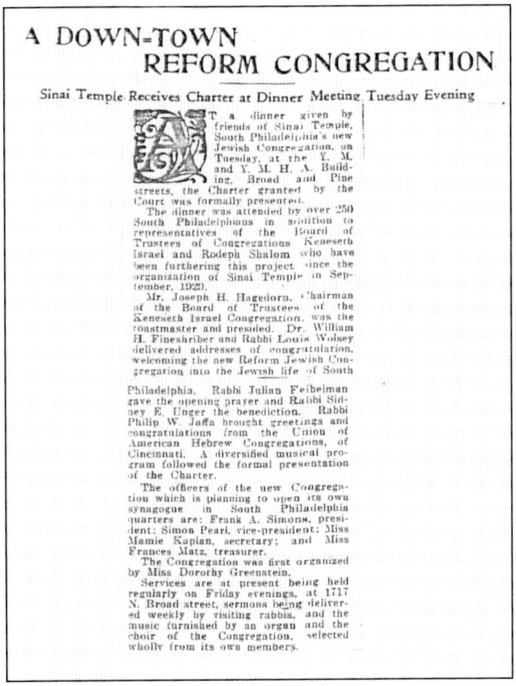

## A DOWN-TOWN REFORM CONGREGATION

### Sinai Temple Receives Charter at Dinner Meeting Tuesday Evening

AT a dinner given by friends of Sinai Temple, South Philadelphia's new Jewish Congregation, on Tuesday, at the Y. M. and Y. M. H. A. Building, Broad and Pine streets, the Charter granted by the Court was formally presented.

The dinner was attended by over 250 South Philadelphians in addition to representatives of the Board of Trustees of Congregations Keneseth Israel and Rodeph Shalom who have been furthering this project since the organization of Sinai Temple in September, 1929.

Mr. Joseph H. Hagedorn, Chairman of the Board of Trustees of the Keneseth Israel Congregation, was the toastmaster and presided. Dr. William H. Fineshriber and Rabbi Louis Wolsey delivered addresses of congratulation, welcoming the new Reform Jewish Congregation into the Jewish life of South Philadelphia. Rabbi Julian Feibelman gave the opening prayer and Rabbi Sidney E. Unger the benediction. Rabbi Philip W. Jaffa brought greetings and congratulations from the Union of American Hebrew Congregations, of Cincinnati. A diversified musical program followed the formal presentation of the Charter.

The officers of the new Congregation which is planning to open its own synagogue in South Philadelphia quarters are: Frank A. Simons, president; Simon Pearl, vice-president; Miss Mamie Kaplan, secretary; and Miss Frances Matz, treasurer.

The Congregation was first organized by Miss Dorothy Greenstein.

Services are at present being held regularly on Friday evenings, at 1717 N. Broad street, sermons being delivered weekly by visiting rabbis, and the music furnished by an organ and the choir of the Congregation, selected wholly from its own members.

**REFORM CONGREGATION.** In a sea of many orthodox congregations, a reform congregation ventured to set up a liberal format for prayer and worship in South Philadelphia. Sinai Temple opened its doors to the public at 1908 S. Sixth to advance the principles of Reform Judaism, in 1929. Reform congregations Rodeph Sholom and Keneseth Israel gave seed money to start Sinai Temple. The new congregation folded with the outset of the Great Depression and remained the one and only reform congregation to form in South Philadelphia. (Courtesy of the Philadelphia Jewish Archives Center at the Balch Institute.)

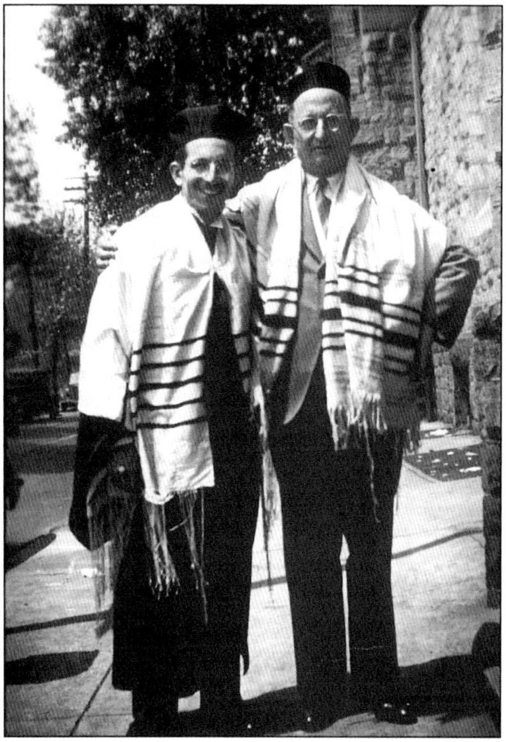

**RABBI AARON DECTER.** Jewish migration to the west side of Broad Street below Spruce Street limited itself to two distinctive neighborhoods. Two business districts, 17th and South and Point Breeze Avenue near 23rd and Wharton Streets, served as centers of Jewish life complete with a synagogue and Hebrew School. Pictured to the left is Rabbi Aaron Decter and Sam Dash, a delicatessen owner and congregation member of Shaare Shomayim at 23rd and Wharton Street, in 1950. Beth Jacob served the business merchants at 1706 South Street. (Courtesy of Lorraine Makler Wagner.)

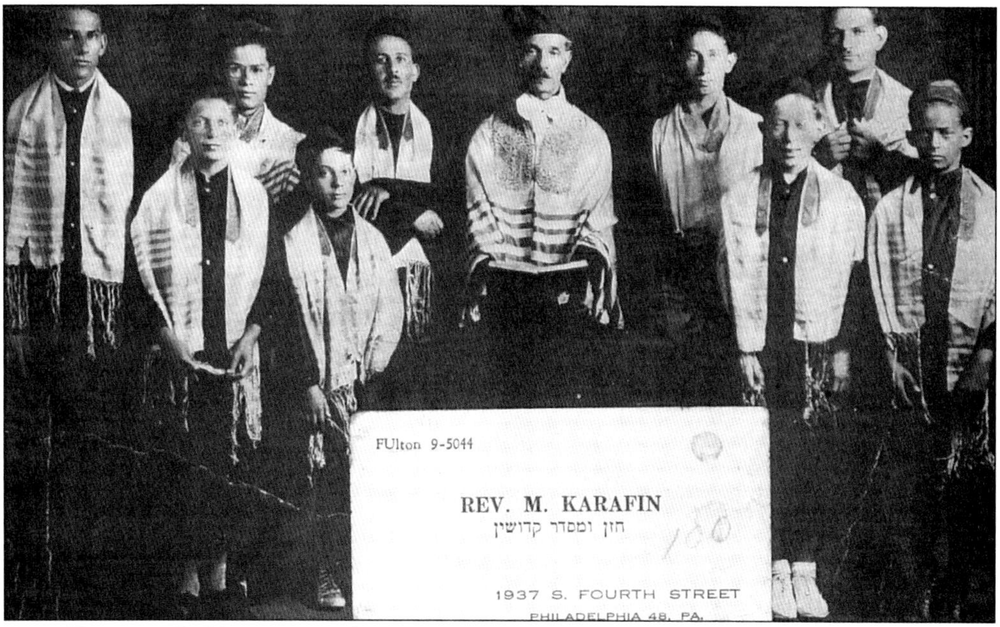


**REV. KARAFIN.** Rabbi Max Karafin came to America from Odessa, Russia, and settled at 309 Cantrell Street, in the1920s. Baila Karafin, the rabbi's wife, helped Congregation Shivtei Yeshurun at Fourth and Emily Street survive the Depression when she formed a ladies relief fund for needy members. Rabbi Karafin is pictured above with the all-male choir. The men wore white sneakers because wearing leather on the Holidays is forbidden, according to Jewish law. (Courtesy of Linda Karafin Needleman.)

**THE ROSE WINDOW AND ARK OF B'NAI MOISHE.** B'nai Moishe, at Fifth and Watkins, founded in 1904, hosted a large congregation of more than two hundred men. The synagogue, with its large main floor, had two large balconies on both sides of the building located on the second floor. The carved animals, in the Trump L'oei style, represented a fake realism that surrounded the ark in many South Philadelphia synagogues. This was usually the work of Itzok the Schnitzer, a wood carver, according to Carousel historian Murray Zimilies from New York State. (Courtesy of Allen Meyers.)

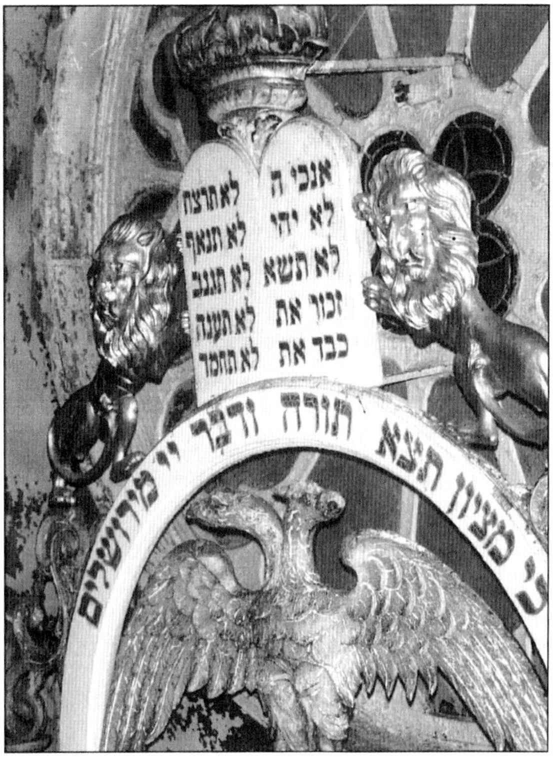


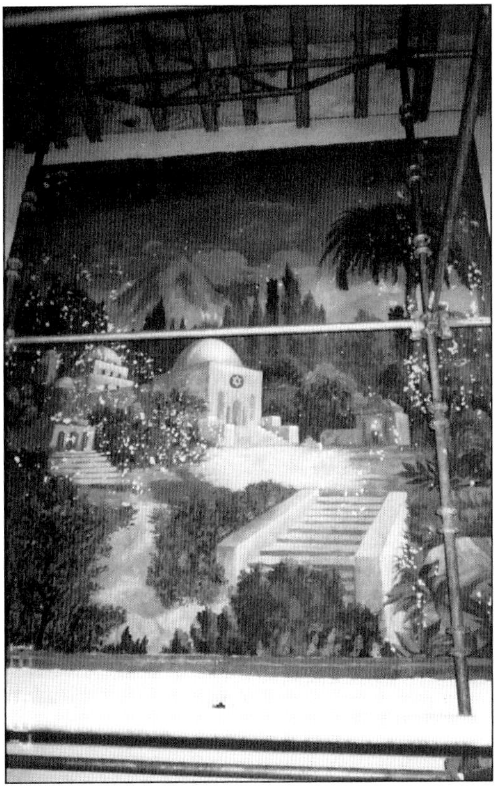

**MORRIS BALK.** Morris Balk came to America from Russia to escape the pogroms, in 1904. Morris became South Philadelphia's Jewish Michael Angelo. Many synagogues featured Mr. Balk's works, which he developed around holy sites in Jerusalem, the Jewish months of the year painted on the ceilings, and his own migration out of Russia. The trademark of his work included a violin hanging from a tree overlooking a river, and his marbleized painted columns made to look real were preserved during renovation of the Kesher Israel synagogue in 1998. (Courtesy of Michael Yaron at Kesher Israel.)

Adath Israel Nusach Sfard .............224 Christian ( 1902 )
Adath Jeshurun Talmud Torah 1918 .....2113 S. 6th / Cantrell (1918 )
Adath Sholom ...........................607 Ritner ( 1950 )
Agudas Achim.............................1921 S. 6th / Mercy ( 1908 )
Agudas Achim Anshe Neziner ...........771 S. 2nd / Fitzwater ( 1889 )
Ahavas Achim Anshe Vitebsk..........1929 S. 6th/ Mercy ( 1918 )
Agudas Achim Roumanian..........512 S. 3rd ( 1886 )
Ahavas Chesed Anshe Shavil..........322 Bainbridge ( 1887 )
Ahavas Israel.....................322 Bainbridge ( 1919 )
Ahavas Zion ..........................815 S. 4th ( 1901 )
Aitz Chaim..........................7th & Dickinson ( 1930 )
Anshe Birz....................6th & South ( 1889 )
Anshe Brahen V' Choimetch ..........505 Catherine ( 1903 )
Anshe Emeth .......................1537 S. 7th / Dickinson ( 1927 )
Anshe Hisan..........................1717 S. 8th / Moore ( 1915 )'
Anshe Zhitomer Nusach Sfard.......620 Minister ( 1892 )
Atereth Israel.......................1638 S. 6th / Morris ( 1906 )
Austrian Galizan.....................507 Tasker ( 1910 )
Austrain Hungarian Raim Ahuvim.....343 Monroe ( 1892 )
Bessarbier Talmud Torah Cong............1627 S. 6th / Mountain ( 1912 )
Beth David..........................328 Catherine ( 1899 )
Beth Elohim............................510 S 5th ( 1879 )
Beth Ha Keneseth Rabbi Eichler ......417 Monroe ( 1900 )
Beth Ha Keneseth Rabbi Hersel..........417 Monroe ( 1924 )
Beth Ha Keneseth Ben Markowitz..........5th & Moore ( 1927 )
Beth Ha Keneseth Rabbi Sofronski...3rd & Mc Kean ( 1923 )
Beth Hamedrash Anshe Kaneav.........1924 s. 6th / Mercy ( 1908 )
Beth Hamedrash Hagodol ......SW cor 4th & Wharton ( 1907 )
Beth Hamedrash Hagodol Nusach Askenze......426 Spruce ( 1911 )
Beth Israel.........................................417 Pine ( 1901 )
Beth Jacob Anshe Dadmoor.............SW cor 6th / Wolf ( 1927 )
Beth Jacob Anshe Lubavitz............414 Christian ( 1897 )
Beth Judah ........................232 Lombard ( 1905 )
Beth Samuel..........................Ritner & Marshall ( 1922 )
Beth Solomon - Monstreicher Shul......2300 S. 6th / Wolf ( 1948 )
Beth Zion................................NE cor Phillip & Porter ( 1937 )
Bialick Cong..................2455 S. Phillip ( 1933 )
Bialostotski Minyan.............1410 S. 5th ( 1914 )
B'nai Abraham Anshe Russe........521 Lombard ( 1882 )
B'nai David.......................913 S. 5th ( 1894 )
B'nai Israel.............................922 S. 4th ( 1901 )
B'nai Israel...............................1214 3rd ( 1914 )
B'nai Israel Anshe Poland............324 Fitzwater ( 1905 )
B'nai Jacob.........................725 Lombard ( 1883 )
B'nai Moishe Anshe Sfard.............1711 S. 5th ( 1904 )
B'nai Moses Montifiore Anshe Poland.......342 Queen ( 1887 )
B'nai Reuben Anshe Sfard.................629 S. 6th / Kater ( 1883 )
B'nai Zion.............................532 Pine ( 1901 )
Bukier Cong........................1527 S. 6th / Cross ( 1919 )
Chevra Ahavas Achim Anshe Sfard..........320 Christian ( 1909 )
Chevra B'nai Joseph .....................525 Bainbridge ( 1892 )
Chevra Chesed Shel Emeth............515 S. 9th ( 1890 )
Chevra Heisner...................1729 S. 6th / Mifflin ( 1920 )
Chevra Kadisha Cong...............414 Christian ( 1910 )
Chevra Kadisha Independent Cong..........809 S. 5th ( 1895 )

A-Z LISTING OF SOUTH PHILADELPHIA SYNAGOGUES. This list was excerpted from, In the Presence of His Shelter, *South Philadelphia Synagogues 1880-1960*, by Allen Meyers-1996, an unpublished work. The creation of a detailed list of synagogues in South Philadelphia took many years of dedicated research work and communication with hundreds of people who observed religious rituals on a daily basis. The 142 synagogues listed, represent 30 percent (466) of all the synagogues that ever existed in Philadelphia during its peak in the late 1930s.

A-Z LISTING OF SOUTH PHILADELPHIA SYNAGOGUES. Hundreds of immigrants served as leaders of the South Philadelphia Synagogues, which included rabbis, cantors, and lay people. The quantity and quality of these individuals led to a strong Jewish community. The full list of synagogues is dedicated to Rabbi Yehuda Shestack (of Blessed memory) who conducted the day to day operation of Shar Israel at Fourth and Porter and Shaare Eli at Eighth and Porter Streets from the late 1910s until the early 1920s.

**Gomel Cheses Shel Emes..................319 Catherine ( 1895 )**
**Independent Fastover Cong................1826 S. 6th / Sigel ( 1907 )**
**Jewish Roumanian Cong.................518 Spruce ( 1926 )**
**Joseph Asbell Cong...........................511 Mifflin ( 1926 )**
**Kehilas Adas Israel....................843 S. 3rd ( 1905 )**
**Kehiloth Israel.............................234 Bainbridge ( 1912 )**
**Kehiloth Kodesh Sdai Loben..............2024 S. 5th / Mercy ( 1913 )**
**Kesher Israel............................412 Lombard ( 1893 )**
**Kesher Torah Anshe Wohliner.........324 Catherine ( 1894 )**
**Kesher Torah Anshe Lubliner ...........610 S. 3rd ( 1923 )**
**Keneseth Beth Zion......................1514 S. 6th ( 1918 )**
**Keser Torah.........................335 Christain ( 1919 )**
**Kieve Tserkasser Bulgarian Cong.......1815 S. 6th ( 1930 )**
**Kra- Kauer ................................4th & South ( 1876 )**
**Kra- Kauer - Beth Elohim...........417 Pine ( 1889 )**
**Kreminitizer Synagogue...................1908 E. Moyamensing ( 1930 )**
**Lenas Ha Zedek....................542 Queen ( 1891 )**
**Magide Thillium.............2027 S. 6th / Mercy ( 1913 )**
**Mishkan Israel..........................5th & Dickinson ( 1929 )**
**Mogen Abraham.............1709 S. 4th / Morris ( 1913 )**
**Ohavas Achim Oestricher.........1525 S. 5th / Greenwich ( 1930 )**
**Ohev Itzchok.......................2440 S. 9th / Porter ( 1913 )**
**Ohev Sholom.........................7th & South ( 1884 )**
**Ohr Achim...............................1517 S. 5th ( 1938 )**
**Or Chodosh Agudas Achim.........512 S. 3rd ( 1894 )**
**Otik Mohliver....................922 S. 4th ( 1899 )**
**Poale Zedek..........................322 Bainbridge ( 1896 )**
**Poale Zedek - Sharith Israel..................1011 S. 5th ( 1900 )**
**Podovlier Gubernia Lodge Cong.........1514 S. 6th ( 1919 )**
**Poneviezher Lodge Cong.............4th & Reed ( 1919 )**
**Poras Joseph........................754 S. 3rd ( 1905 )**
**Prushvier - Shershow Cong.............542 Queen ( 1897 )**
**Raim Ahuvim Anshe Kolker .........1929 S 5th / Dudley ( 1925 )**
**Rudivller Lubliner Lodge Cong...........410 Christian ( 1919 )**
**Rodeph Tzedek Anshe Szager................788 S. 2nd ( 1887 )**
**Samuel Rosenwald Lodge Cong.........1655 S. 6th ( 1919 )**
**Sinai Temple Reform Cong...................1908 S. 6th ( 1929 )**
**Shaare Eliyhu.................................8th & Morris ( 1919 )**
**Shaare Torah ............................728 W. Moyamensing ( 1911 )**
**Shaare Shomayim....................23rd & Wharton ( 1912 )**
**Shaare Zedek.............................922 S. 4th ( 1892 )**
**Shari Eli....................................SW cor 8th & Porter ( 1919 )**
**Shari Zedek Anshe Reisicher..................3rd & Manton ( 1902 )**
**Shar Israel Cong..........................2509 S. 4th / Porter ( 1916 )**
**Shar Israel Young People's Cong...........342 Porter ( 1947 )**
**Sharith Israel.............................4th & Gaskill ( 1894 )**
**Shearith Israel Talmud Torah Cong.......2132 S. 6th ( 1911 )**
**Shivtei Yeshurun ........................2014 S. 4th / Emily ( 1909 )**
**Shivtei Yeshurun............................4th & Lombard ( 1898 )**
**Shivtei Yeshurun Anshe Phila...............322 Bainbridge ( 1892 )**
**Shomre Emunas Anshe Kelm.............1302 S. 4th / Wharton ( 1890 )**
**Shomre Emuno Anshe Kelm................718 S. 5th ( 1907 )**
**Shomre Shabbas .............................922 S. 3rd ( 1894 )**
**Shomre Shabbas................................410 Christian ( 1894 )**
**Shomre Shabbas ....................................232 Lombard ( 1907 )**

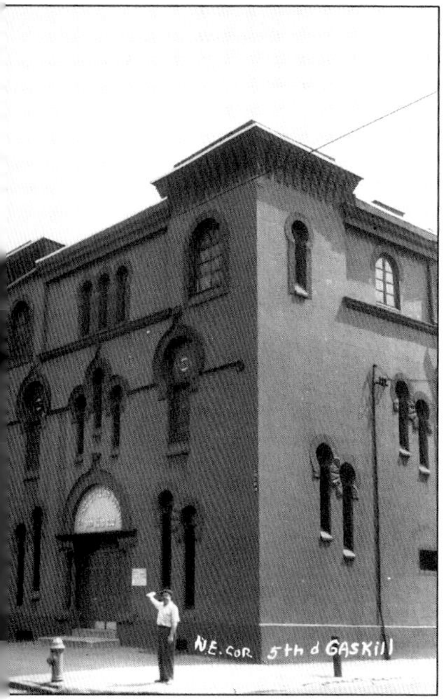


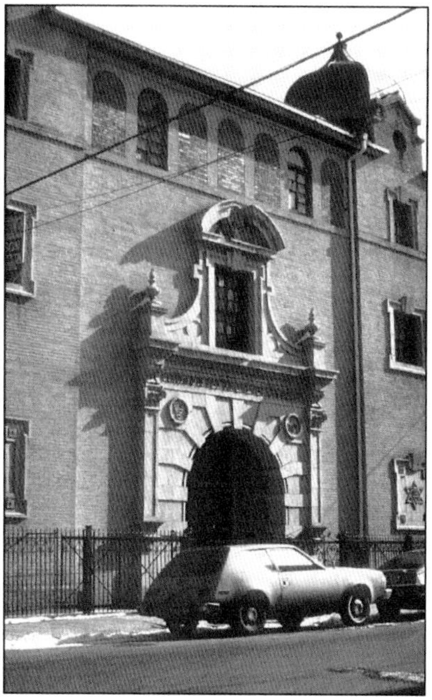

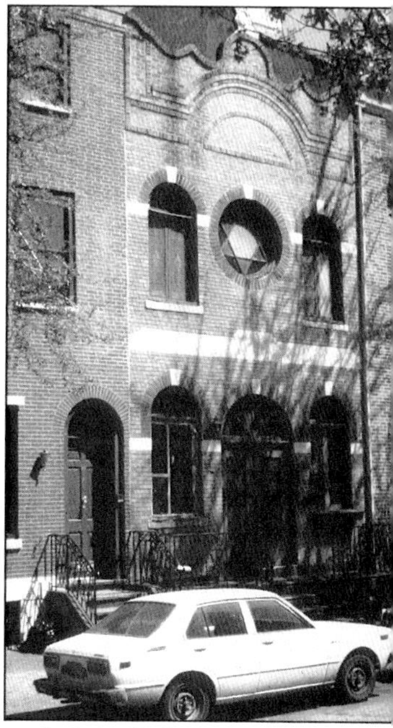

*Left:* **THE HUNGARIAN SHUL.** Emes Israel Rodeph Sholom Hungaria, at 515 Gaskill Street, was formed in 1887 and led by Rabbi Simon Englander for 50 years. The synagogue closed and was demolished in 1967. (Courtesy of Philadelphia City Archives.) *Center:* **B'NAI REUBEN.** B'nai Reuben, at 629 S. Sixth Street, was formed in 1883 by Reuben Kanefsky, a Russian Jew. Harry Publicker, the giant whiskey manufacturer, supported the synagogue. The synagogue closed in 1968. (Courtesy of Allen Meyers.) *Right:* **THE VILNA SHUL.** The Vilna Synagogue, at 509 Pine Street, formed in 1904 and served the Lithuanian community led by Rabbi Joseph Snapir. The synagogue functions today under the Lubavitch movement. (Courtesy of Allen Meyers.)

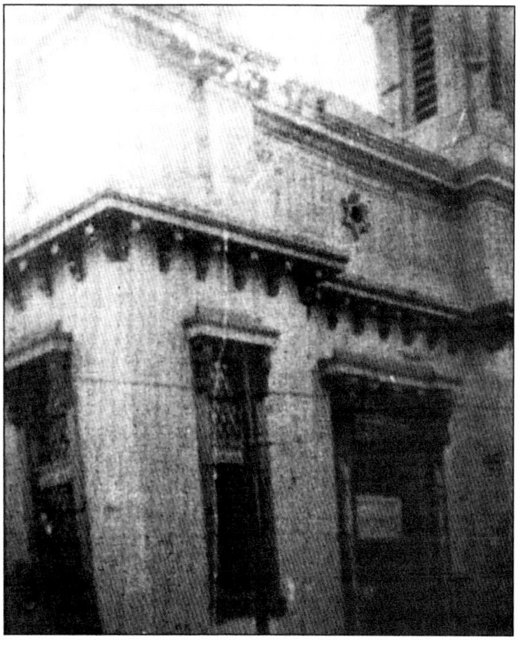

**THE ROMANIAN SHUL.** Also known as Chodosh Agudas Achim, at 426 Spruce Street, it formed in 1892 and served the Romanian community when it bought an old church for use as a shul. Today, the building serves Society Hill Synagogue. (Courtesy of Bob Yeager, Philadelphia Historic Preservation Corporation.)

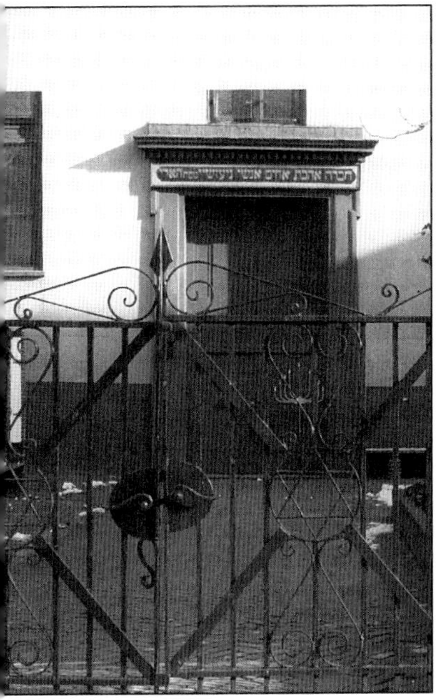
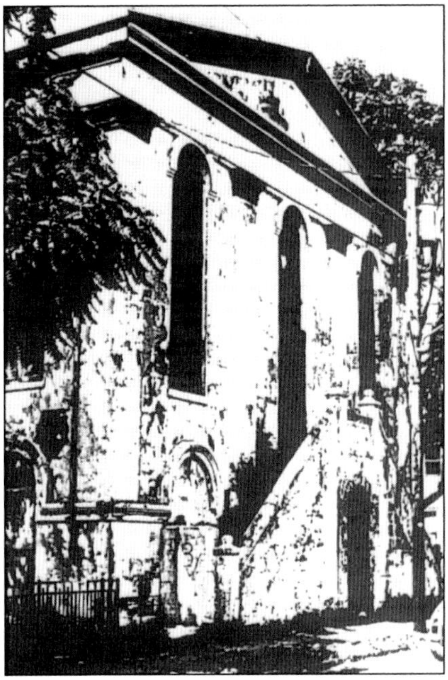
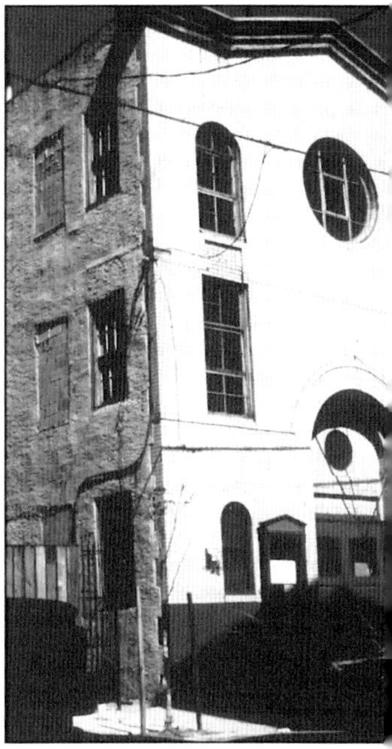

*Left:* **THE NEIZENER SHUL.** The Neziner Synagogue, at 772 S. Second Street, formed in 1889 by a group of men from the town of Nazin, 70 miles northeast of Kiev, and observed Nusach Ha-Ari, an Hasidic. The synagogue closed in 1984. (Courtesy of Allen Meyers.) *Center:* **REISISTER SHUL.** The Shari Zedek Anshe Reisicher Synagogue, Third and Manton, was originally a church formed in 1902. The synagogue closed in 1974, and the ark was preserved by the New York Jewish Museum. (Courtesy of Julian Preister.) *Right:* **THE POLISH SHUL.** B'nai Israel Anshe Poland formed in 1905 as an orthodox congregation that served the Polish community. The long-standing shamus Rev. Israel Levy and Dr. Harry Orlitsky ran the shul. (Courtesy of Allen Meyers.)

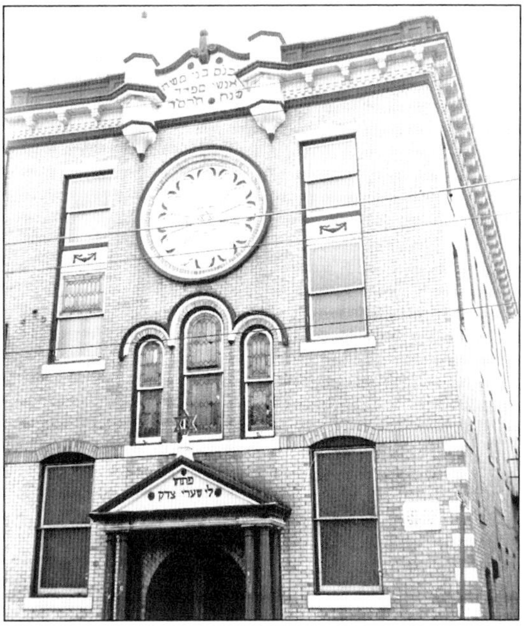

**B'NAI MOISHE.** B'nai Moishe Anshe Sfard formed in 1904, at Fifth and Watkins Streets, as an Austro-Hungarian Synagogue, led by Rabbi Joseph Grossman. The shul closed in 1981. (Courtesy of Allen Meyers.)

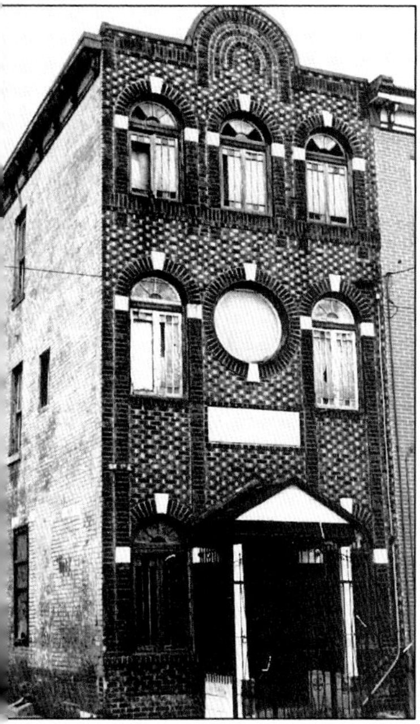

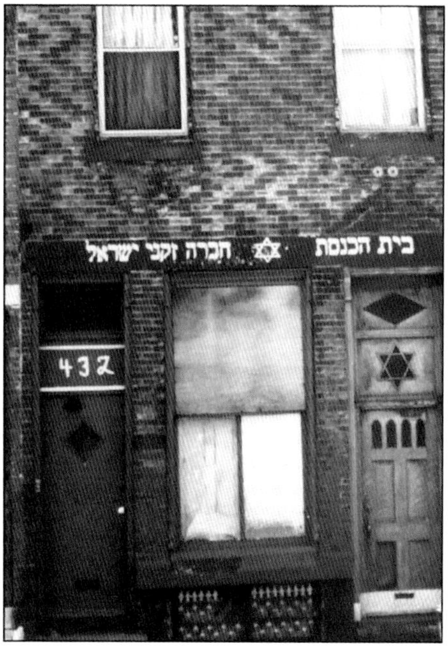


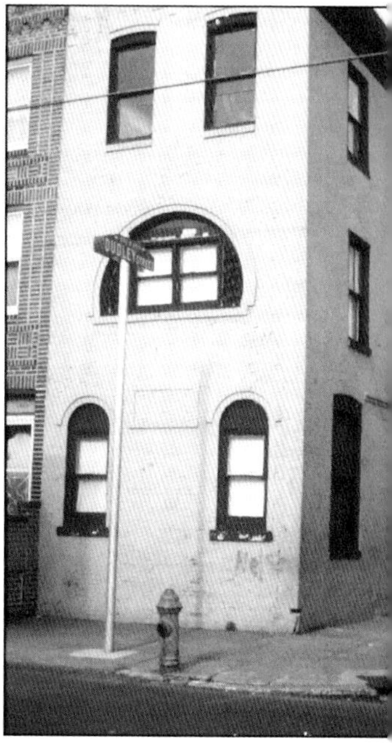

*Left:* **MAGIDE THILLUM.** Magide Thillum, at 2027 S. Sixth Street, formed in 1913. Rabbi Hyman Shestack led the shul. The translation of the Hebrew name is the reciting of psalms in the Bible. The shul closed in 1965. (Courtesy of Allen Meyers.) *Center:* **ZIKNE ISRAEL.** Zikne Israel, 432 Dickinson Street, formed more than 12 blocks farther north and attracted people similar to six other congregations. The Budnick family cared for the synagogue until it closed in 1979. (Courtesy of Allen Meyers.) *Right:* **CHEVRA MISHKAN ISRAEL.** Chevra Mishkan Israel, at Sixth and Dudley Streets, formed in 1904. The corner house synagogue provided enough space for 150 people to worship. The building crumbled to the ground 15 years after it closed, in 1985. (Courtesy of Allen Meyers.)

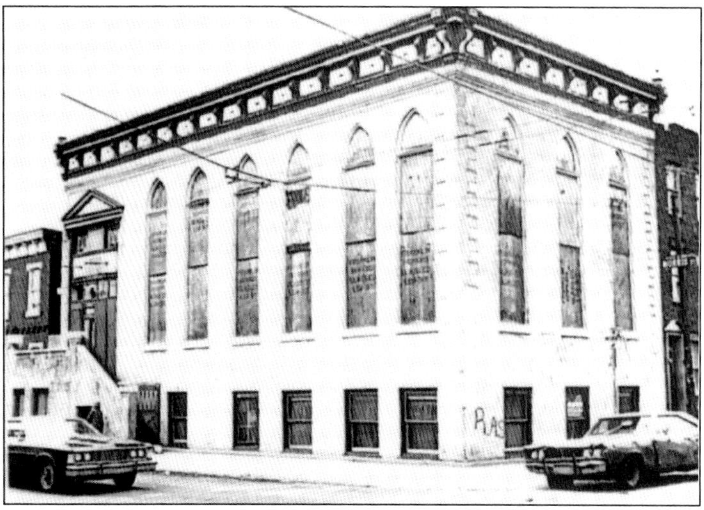

**ATERETH ISRAEL.** Atereth Israel Anshe Brahin Va Cholmetch at Sixth and Morris Streets, formed in 1906. Ben Gurion marched past the shul in 1918, according to Morris Bennett. The shul closed in 1978. (Courtesy of Allen Meyers.)

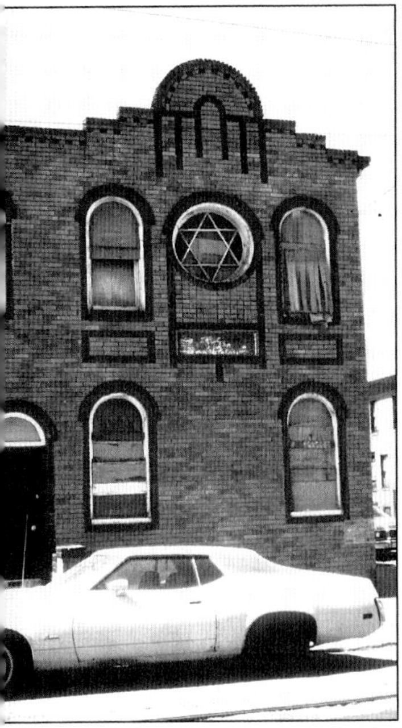 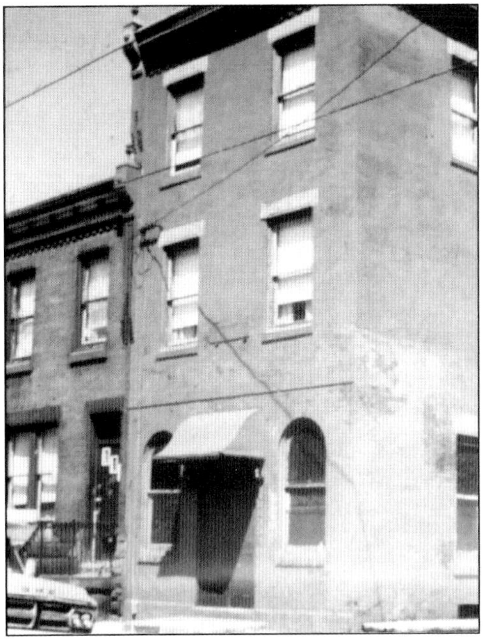 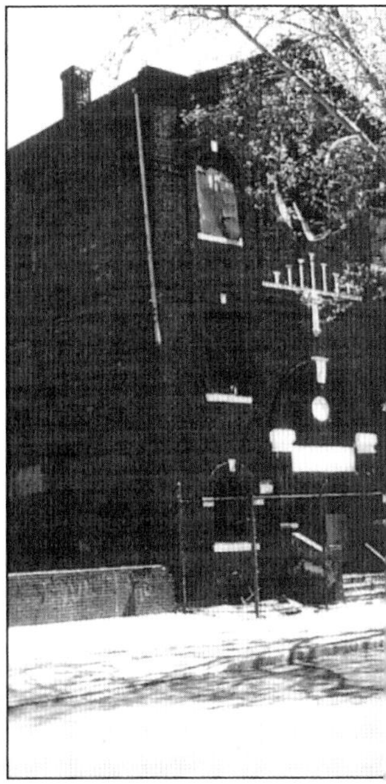

Left: **BETH JACOB.** Beth Jacob, at Sixth and Wolf, formed in 1927. The synagogue changed hands four times, and the famous Monastreicher Rabbi Rabinowitz sold it to Rabbi Meyer Isaacson in 1952. The synagogue closed in 1973. (Courtesy of Allen Meyers.) *Center:* **ADATH YESHURUN TALMUD TORAH.** Adath Jeshurun Talmud Torah, at 2113 S. Sixth Street, formed in 1918. Rabbi Moses secured funds in 1931 and had bricks with people's names attached to the synagogue's facade. The shul closed in 1962. (Courtesy of Allen Meyers.) *Right:* **SHAR ISRAEL.** Shar Israel, at Fourth and Porter Streets, formed in 1916. The new synagogue developed in the Porter Street Corridor between Front and Eighth Street. The synagogue closed in 1980, and its assets were sent to Israel. (Courtesy of Allen Meyers.)

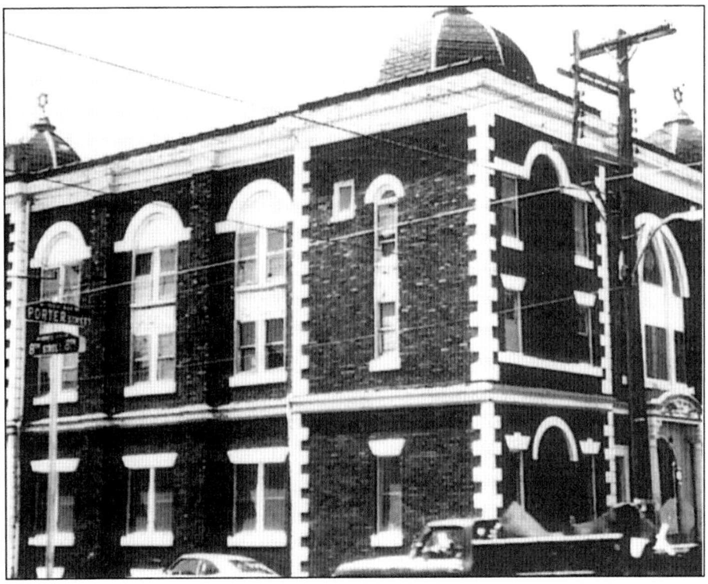

**SHAARE ELI.** Shaare Eli, at Eighth and Porters, formed in 1917. The Eighth and Porter Shul served as the leading downtown synagogue, with a blind cantor in the 1930s. The shul closed in 1982 and was demolished, according to its will. (Courtesy of Allen Meyers.)

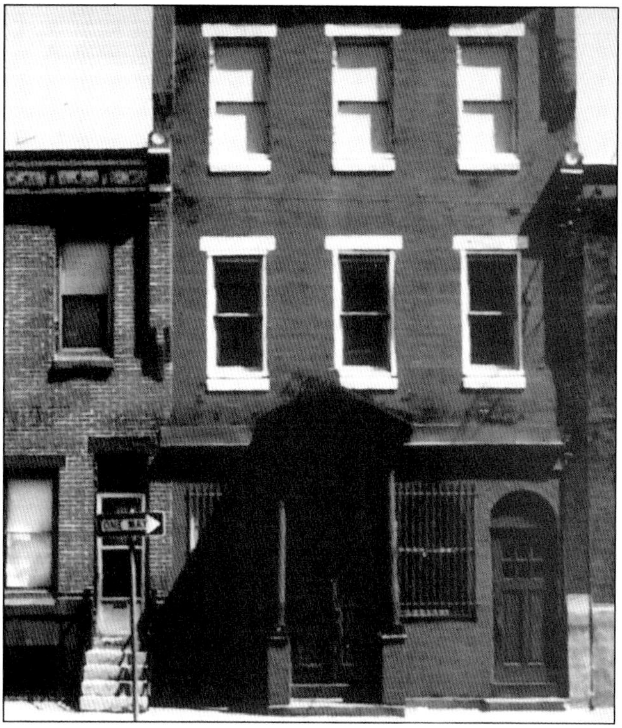

**SHIVTEI YESHURUN.** Shivtie Yeshurun, at 2015 S. Fourth, formed in 1876 as the third Sephardic synagogue in Philadelphia. In 1909, the congregation moved to its present location. The synagogue absorbed the members of six other synagogues that closed around them from 1970 to 1983. Today, Alvin Heller, a lay person, leads the only orthodox congregation in South Philadelphia below Lombard Street. (Courtesy of Allen Meyers.)

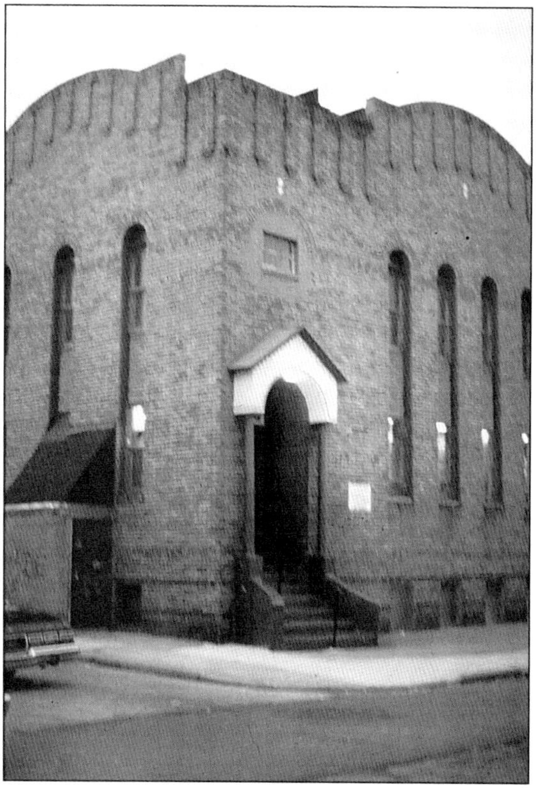

**ADATH SHOLOM.** Adath Sholom, at 607 Ritner at Marshall Street, formed in 1950. Two groups of young people merged to form a conservative congregation and assumed the orthodox shul Beth Samuel after its members passed away. Samuel Cander, a lifelong resident of South Philadelphia, along with a cadre of dedicated men and women, maintains this Old World synagogue. (Courtesy of Allen Meyers.)

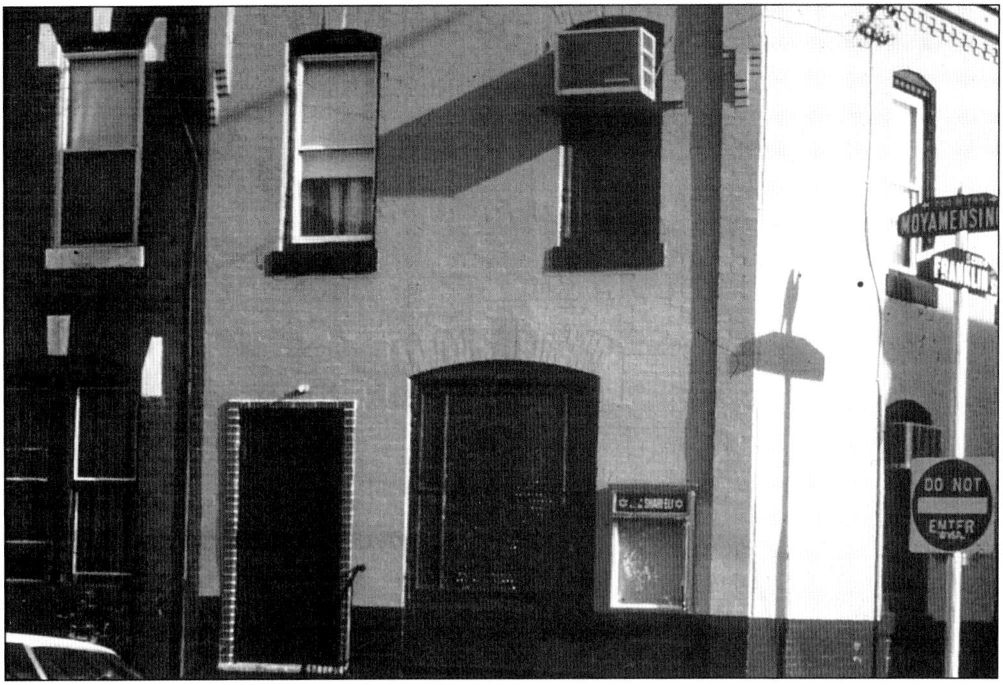


**YOUNG PEOPLE'S SHARI ELI.** Young People's Congregation Shari Eli, at 728 W. Moyamensing Avenue, formed in 1948. The second generation broke away from Shari Eli and formed a conservative synagogue after W WII under the guidance of Kelman Israel and assumed the orthodox Shaare Torah shul. Today YPC Shari Eli is one of three synagogues that exists in South Philadelphia below McKean Street. (Courtesy of Allen Meyers.)

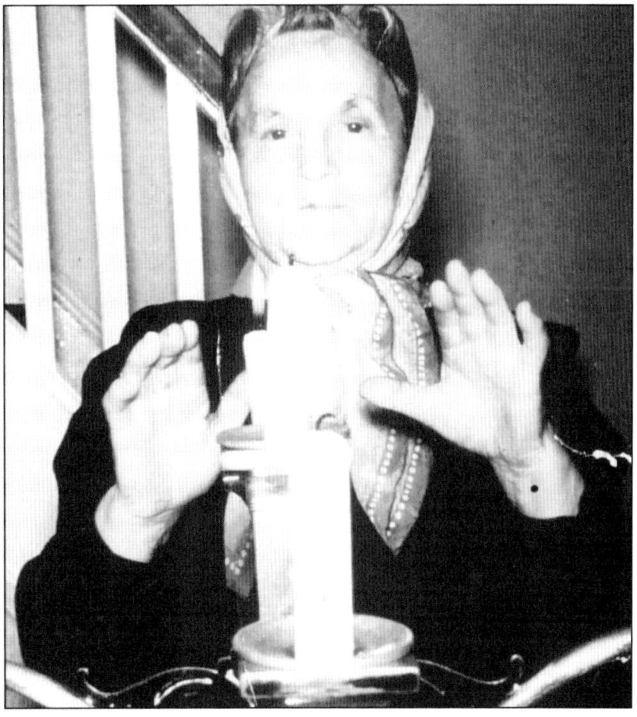

**ROSE LEVITSKY.** Rose Levitsky Freedman, the wife of Samuel Freedman, was a life-long resident Bentsh Licht (lights the candles and recites the blessings to usher in the Sabbath). She is pictured to the right in her home at 2533 S. Marshall Street in the 1970s. The small row home served as the sanctuary in South Philadelphia where the Jewish East European immigrants built a family and conducted their daily lives throughout the 20th century. (Courtesy of Lois Sernoff.)